关于价格和货币流通状况的历史

A History of Prices, and of the State of the Circulation

（英）托马斯·图克（Thomas Tooke）
（英）威廉·纽马奇（William Newmarch）著

中国财富出版社

图书在版编目(CIP)数据

关于价格和货币流通状况的历史．第三卷 = A History of Prices, and of the State of the Circulation Volume 3:英文 /(英)托马斯·图克(Thomas Tooke),(英)威廉·纽马奇(William Newmarch)著．—北京:中国财富出版社,2019.12

ISBN 978-7-5047-7106-3

Ⅰ.①关…　Ⅱ.①托…　②威…　Ⅲ.①经济史—英国—1793-1856—英文
Ⅳ.①F156.194.1

中国版本图书馆 CIP 数据核字(2019)第 270159 号

策划编辑	郑晓雯	**责任编辑**	张冬梅　郑晓雯		
责任印制	尚立业	**责任校对**	杨小静	**责任发行**	白　昕

出版发行　中国财富出版社

社　　址　北京市丰台区南四环西路 188 号 5 区 20 楼　　**邮政编码**　100070

电　　话　010-52227588 转 2098(发行部)　010-52227588 转 321(总编室)
010-52227588 转 100(读者服务部)　010-52227588 转 305(质检部)

网　　址　http://www.cfpress.com.cn

经　　销　新华书店

印　　刷　北京九州迅驰传媒文化有限公司

书　　号　ISBN 978-7-5047-7106-3/F·3132

开　　本	710mm×1000mm　1/16	**版　　次**	2020 年 8 月第 1 版
印　　张	18.75	**印　　次**	2020 年 8 月第 1 次印刷
字　　数	261 千字	**定　　价**	118.00 元

CONTENTS

INTRODUCTION

The experience of the two years that have elapsed since the period to which the Work of which this is a continuation was brought down, namely, to the close of 1837, embraces events of considerable interest in relation to the agriculture, the manufactures, and the commerce of this country, and is strikingly illustrative of the circumstances on which variations in prices, in the rate of interest, and in the state of trade and of credit depend. A sketch, therefore, of the prominent features of the markets for produce, and of the money market, or, in other words, of the state of prices, and of the circulation, cannot but be useful, if only as a record of events in a continuous form, and in the order and connection of their occurrence, and of facts which, however important or essential to a right conclusion on the points under discussion, are apt either to escape recollection, or, if remembered, to present themselves in a confused heap, from which reasoners, on one side or the other, feel themselves at liberty to select such as suit their purpose, with the aid only of such transposition as renders particular events apparently the effect or consequence of those which in reality occurred subsequently, and vice versa. In truth, statements of historical facts, professing to be illustrative of particular conclusions on questions relating to prices and the circulation, unless guarded by a careful reference to dates and an explanation of attendant circumstances, may be made subservient to the most distorted views. It is my purpose in the present, as it was in the former part of this Work, to lay before the reader the most prominent of the facts relating to the state of prices and of the circulation in the period under consideration, with a careful reference to dates, and with such explanation of attendant circumstances as may enable him, if he differs from me in my conclusion, to ascertain the precise ground of difference, and to point out, consequently, the source of error in the reasoning which led to that conclusion. The order which it is proposed to pursue in this examination and explanation, as in the former part of this work, is, to pass in review, —

1. The state of prices of corn, and the circumstances connected with them.

2. The state of prices of produce other than corn.

3. The state of the circulation.

And as there are two topics which more than any other, party politics excepted, engross the attention of the public, namely, the Corn Laws and our Banking institutions, I propose to bestow some remarks upon each of them. Accordingly, some of the main points connected with the working of the corn laws will immediately follow the account which will be given of the state of the corn trade in the two last years; and a review of our banking institutions, but chiefly of the management of the Bank of England, with observations upon the defects of the existing system, and of the proposed remedies, will form the concluding part of the present work.

CHAPTER Ⅰ
ON THE CORN TRADE IN 1838 AND 1839

SECTION 1 *Cursory review of the seasons and crops of 1836 and 1837*

In order to the more clear appreciation of the state of the corn trade in the two last years, it may be necessary to revert briefly to a few of the leading features of it in the period immediately preceding, which have been adverted to in the former part of this work.

The four consecutive seasons from 1832 to 1835 were singularly propitious to the growth of wheat, which crop, besides being on an extended scale, and in an improved state of cultivation, probably produced more per acre, taking the kingdom throughout, than was ever before known. Among the favourable circumstances which distinguished those seasons, may be mentioned that of a prevalence, during the summer and autumnal months, of a sufficient proportion of dry weather to admit, with few and insignificant exceptions, of the whole of the harvests in the northern, as well as in the southern division, being secured in good order and with little, if any, waste. The spring crops, on the lighter soils especially, suffered from the drought of the summers, and the pastures were a good deal burnt. But the winters were singularly mild and open, with little frost, and hardly any snow, and the spring seasons genial and forward; so that, although the stocks of provender were rather short, the consumption as winter food, for cattle and sheep, was also on a reduced scale. Still the prices of spring corn and pulse ranged above their usual proportion to wheat, and the price of barley especially approached, in an unprecedented degree, to that of wheat. The effect of this disproportionate cheapness of wheat was, in the first place, greatly to increase the relative consumption of it, or rather to apply it to consumption of an unusual description, namely, to the feeding of cattle, sheep, and pigs, besides malting for beer, and distillation; and in the next place to induce, after the harvest of 1835, when wheat reached its lowest point of depression, a diminution of the breadth of land sown with this description of grain, and a substitution of barley and oats in cases where the lands were suitable, and where the leases admitted of such substitution, or where the landlords consented to a deviation from the accustomed and stipulated rotation of crops.

It is probable that the higher range of the price of wheat in 1836 and 1837 had a tendency to restore the ordinary relative proportions of sowing in the autumn of 1837, although, perhaps, not fully to the former extent.

Previously to entering upon the description of the season of 1838, and of the harvest of that year, I will briefly advert to some particulars respecting the crops of 1836 and 1837; which, when referring to them formerly, I noticed only cursorily; because my means of appreciating the degree of their productiveness were then still imperfect, although, as far as related to the explanation of the state of markets, the general estimate which I made of them seems to have been borne out by the event.

The spring of 1836, as I have before had occasion to observe, although following a winter of no marked severity (not quite so free, however, from frost as the preceding four winters), was very cold and dry, and all vegetation was very backward, compared with the preceding spring seasons. The wheat on the ground presented an unpromising appearance.① And this circumstance, among others, had the effect of raising the markets from their previous extreme depression. But so fallacious are the means of judging of the eventual produce from appearances in the spring, that the crops on some of the very lands of which it was confidently reported, even as late as the first week in June, that they were not likely to yield half the usual produce per acre, did, in point of fact (the weather from that time proving to be most propitious), turn out to be abundant beyond any precedent. This description applies to the south, and south-eastern, and midland districts of the kingdom. And if in all the other districts, the wheat crops had equalled these, and had been equally well got in, the general produce per acre in 1836 would perhaps have equalled even that of 1834. But in some of the other parts of the kingdom, viz., in the district from Gloucestershire to the Humber, the drought of the spring and part of the summer had proved too great for the soil, and in those the crops, although well secured, did not equal those of 1834. In the more northern division of the island, the season was, upon the whole, unfavourable; but more especially in the summer and autumn of 1836, being wet, cold, and in every sense of the word, inclement. In Scotland, the wetness and inclemency of the season, during the whole

① See evidence of Messrs Ellman, Sturge, Sandars, Ruding, and Cramp, before the Committee of the House of Commons on agricultural distress, in 1836.

progress of the harvest of 1836, from its commencement to its close in December of that year, almost equalled in description that of the season of 1816. In consequence of these drawbacks, there is reason to believe that, taking the kingdom generally, the produce per acre was below that of the average of the three preceding years, besides a diminution of the breadth of land sown with wheat. But still the stock remaining at the harvest of 1837 (although considerably reduced, compared with the stock at the harvest of 1836), was, according to all the most generally received computations, equal to several weeks' consumption beyond the time when the new crop appeared in the markets.

SECTION 2 *Character of the season in 1838. prices and estimated produce of wheat*

The harvest of 1837 was the last in a series of six successive seasons in which the produce of the wheat had fully sufficed for the consumption of the kingdom, without any aid from foreign supply, beyond two comparatively insignificant quantities, entered for home consumption, viz., in 1832, and again in September, 1837. With reference to the admission of this last-mentioned quantity, I had occasion, in the former part of this work, to make the following remark: — "It is to be observed that this admission of foreign wheat did not occur till a great part of the harvest had been secured; it was not, therefore, wanted, unless in as far as the yield of the last crop may be found insufficient to meet the demands upon it till next harvest." This was written at the close of 1837, when opinions were still a good deal unsettled as to the productiveness of the wheat crop of that year; there having been no reports of districts presenting such abundance of arable produce as in some of the immediately preceding seasons, but neither were there any instances mentioned of marked deficiency. It was only as approaches were made to the ensuing harvest that general experience, on threshing out, tended to prove that the crop throughout had not been equal in produce to the least productive of the five preceding seasons. This comparative deficiency of yield per acre, while perhaps the breadth of cultivation had not been restored to that from which it had been reduced at the close of 1835, at the same time that an unusual rate of consumption had absorbed the super-abundance of former seasons, brought the old stock that met the harvest of 1838 (which, however, was a late one) into a smaller compass than had been known for several years past. But, low as the stock of old wheat was at the harvest of 1838, yet, considering that harvest was later, by at least a fortnight, than usual, and that no foreign corn was entered for home consumption till the middle of September, the evidence was complete that there had been sufficient fully to meet the consumption. And if the season of 1838, from its outset to the ordinary time of harvest, had been propitious, there would in all probability have been no rise, perhaps even a fall, of prices, as long as the prospects were favourable; the further course of prices being determined by what might be estimated as the result of that harvest.

But the winter, which till the second week of January, 1838, had been open and mild, then suddenly assumed a character of extraordinary rigour. The frost began on the 6th January, and on the 20th became extremely severe; Fahrenheit's thermometer indicating in the neighbourhood of London so low a degree as 5 below zero. A considerable severity of cold continued, with only occasional and short intermissions, through the greater part of February; and the whole of the spring season following was cold, raw, and backward. The extreme severity of the frost in January gave rise to apprehension of injury to the wheats in the ground, more especially as there was no covering of snow to protect the plant. These apprehensions were proved by the event to be but too well founded. *Still, notwithstanding that the Bank of England and the country circulation were increasing, and the money market was in so easy a state, or in other words, such were the facilities of borrowing money at a very low rate of interest, as to afford the utmost scope to speculation, if the tendency to it had existed*, the advance of prices was slow, and hardly commensurate with the unfavourable appearances and reports. Thus the average prices of wheat, which in each of the months of December and January had been about 53*s*., advanced in February to 55*s*. 3*d*., and in March to 56*s*. 6*d*.; still, however, being lower than they had been in February and March, 1837, when, as may be yet in recollection, the money market was in a state of extreme restriction, and credit was very much deranged.

The wheat plant is fortunately a very hardy one; and there have been seasons when, in consequence of severe frosts in winter, there were reports of serious injury to the growing crops, which, however, by subsequent more genial weather, recovered from the injurious effects. In some instances, such was said to be the case with the wheats which had suffered from the frosts of January, 1838; while, in other instances, they never recovered at all, or only partially. There were at the same time districts in which, from difference of soil and exposure, little or no injury had been sustained; and, as may be seen by reference to contemporary reports, there was no confident anticipation of decided deficiency of produce. The spring, as usual, and I rather think as is invariably the case after winters of great severity of frost, was ungenial, and there were frosts in May, which gave rise to renewed apprehensions, and to a consequent further, but still moderate, advance of price. As the season advanced, the weather continued its character of unpropitiousness; there were cold rains, and in northerly exposures, frosts, at the critical period of the blooming. There was here, doubtless, sufficient ground for a further rise of price, and additional grounds were afforded, both by the increasing certainty of a great reduction of stock, and by the prospect of the harvest being much later than usual, and thus entailing an extra call upon the existing low stock. So little, however, was there of the spirit of speculation at that time in the corn market, that while free wheat was advancing very slowly, there was absolutely a retrograde movement in the prices of bonded wheat in the early part of the summer of 1838. The prevalence of caution in the corn market at that time is the more especially to be remarked, because the rise of the prices of free wheat, reluctant and hardly adequate as it was to the prospect of scarcity, while bonded wheat, upon which speculation usually turns, had been retrograding, was actually, in some of the publications of the period, ascribed to the influence of the bank circulation, which appeared by the returns just then published to have been enlarged.

The weather in July, although deficient in the proportion of bright sun and high temperature that had characterised the month in the preceding years, which have been described as sunny seasons, was not considered unfavourable to the growing crops, and the markets, in consequence, were for the most part stationary during the greater part of that month, at about 68*s*. Towards the close of July, as the lateness of the harvest became a matter of certainty, and the low state of the stock was now manifest, while fears at the same time were becoming prevalent of a general deficiency of the wheat crops, a decided advance took place; the average price, which in the week ending July 20th, 1838, was 68*s.* 2*d.*, reached in the week ending August 24th, 77*s.* And although the markets declined from that time for some weeks, the aggregate averages by which the duty is regulated attained, by the 13th September, to 73*s.*, reducing the duty to 1*s.*; at which rate the whole quantity then in bond, about 1,500,000 quarters, was entered for home consumption.

After the third week in August, the markets experienced a temporary decline of upwards of 15*s.* per quarter: the average of the week ending 21st September having fallen to 61*s.* 10*d.*; and the duty rose in October to 22*s.* 8*d.* This decline of prices is easily accounted for. The large admission on a sudden of so large a quantity of foreign wheat and flour, some of which had been long in bond, and held by persons whose patience and power of holding were nearly exhausted, naturally caused an immediate pressure of sellers. The home crops of wheat within the whole, or nearly the whole, of the southern division of the kingdom, namely, south of the Severn on one side, and of the Thames on the other, had been secured, if not in the best condition, without any material injury in the harvesting: for the weather during August, although unsettled, was not in the southern and home districts attended with heavy or continued rains. And the deficiency, on the threshing of the quantities earliest brought to market, had been found to be rather within than beyond the previous reports. Those, moreover, of the farmers whose crops had been secured in tolerable order, and were not so deficient as they had apprehended, were naturally anxious to realise prices so much higher than they had for some years past been accustomed to. These considerations are sufficient to explain the temporary reaction of the markets in September. But the weather in the latter part of August, and through a great part of September, was very rainy, more especially in the northern division of the kingdom, where the crops being more backward, were exposed to greater injury from the inclemency of the season during the height of their harvest. Besides the injury in the harvesting, the crops of wheat in the midland and northern districts were ascertained to be deficient from previous injury in a greater degree than had been found to be the case in the southern. These circumstances occasioned a rally of the markets, which renewed their tendency upwards, and continued it through the remainder of the year; the weekly average reaching 78*s*. 4*d*. by the end of December, and attaining its greatest height, viz. 81*s*. 6*d*. , in the second week of January, 1839.

That the wheat crop of the harvest of 1838 was greatly deficient has been placed beyond all doubt by very sufficient proof. The several surveys which were instituted, the information derived from farmers of the comparative produce per acre from particular fields and districts, and the absorption of an unprecedented foreign supply, which, large as were the quantities suddenly admitted to home consumption at the lowest duty, went into consumption nearly as fast as they could be delivered, all tended to realise and surpass the worst forebodings to which the unfavourable appearances of the plant, and the unpropitious character of the weather had given rise. It proved to be the most deficient crop of any since 1816. The degree of deficiency, owing to the want of statistical returns, does not admit of being ascertained, or even estimated, with any near approach to accuracy; and the difficulty which usually attends all endeavours to obtain any clear result of the produce of the kingdom was greater in the case of 1838; because the inequality of the produce, according to the soil, and the exposure, and the climate, existed in a most extraordinary degree. In some parts of the southern division of the kingdom, the produce was stated to be not more than one tenth deficient, compared with the three preceding years; while in the western, and midland, and northern, there were considerable districts in which the deficiency was reported to be more than one half.

According to the best materials for conjecture that I have been able to collect, taking the whole island, it is thought not to be an exaggerated estimate to set down the aggregate deficiency at one fourth, including of course the difference of yield in flour. And if the comparison were made with the three years 1832-1833-1834, it would probably not be less than one third, inasmuch as, independently of the arable produce of 1837 not having been equal to that of former years, there is no doubt that the breadth sown with wheat after the harvest of 1835 was diminished; such diminution having been probably not less than one twentieth, and not more than one tenth—more nearly, however, the former than the latter.

As every part of the ground for estimate of the supply is vague, so likewise is that for an estimate of the rate of consumption. The average consumption of wheat as food for man, and consequently excluding the extra consumption of it for cattle and other purposes, in 1834-1835, has been variously estimated by some as high as 8 bushels per head of the population, while by others it has been thought to be more nearly 6 bushels. This last, which appears to me the most reasonable computation, would, for the present estimated population of Britain, (being, if the ratio of increase has continued since 1831, about 18 millions of souls,) at 6 bushels each, be 13, 500, 000 quarters, which, with the quantity requisite for seed, would make the aggregate produce required for consumption as food and seed about 15, 000, 000 of quarters, rather perhaps more than less. The produce of 1835-1836-1837 having been, by the excess of the two former seasons, against a bare average in 1837, probably an aggregate average of 16, 000, 000 of quarters, the deficiency of 1838, if taken in comparison with those three years, and estimated as one fourth less, would be 4 millions of quarters, and if taken with reference to the mere necessary consumption, would leave a deficiency of somewhat about 3 millions of quarters, as the minimum to be made up by foreign supply.

This view seems to be borne out in some degree by subsequent facts, as will be seen by the farther course of the corn markets in 1839. In the mean time, I would only remark upon the enormous variation between seasons in point of productiveness, as instanced in the harvests of 1834 and 1838.

There is reason to believe, from the surveys at the time, from concurrent testimony of farmers, and from the large quantities of the wheat of 1834 which were in the markets during the two or three following years, notwithstanding the extra consumption, (not only as may be supposed by the population being in the fullest employ at good wages, but for cattle-feeding and other unusual purposes,) that the produce of that crop was more nearly a third than a quarter, that is, more nearly 5 millions than between 3 and 4 millions of quarters, above an ordinary crop. The difference, therefore, between the crops of 1834 and 1838 must have been something like 7 to 8 millions of quarters.

SECTION 3 *Character of the season of 1839. prices and estimated produce of wheat*

The weather in January, 1839, and in the remaining winter months, was not characterised by anything like the severity of the corresponding season in 1838. This was so far fortunate, because whatever may be thought of the effects of severe winters on the crops in the ground (and I believe that they are generally injurious), there can be no doubt that they have the effect of increasing the consumption of dry food, if only as provender for cattle; and thus directly or indirectly affecting the price of wheat. But the spring of 1839 was equally backward; and in May, more especially about the middle of that month, the weather was extremely inclement for the season: snow fell, even in the neighbourhood of London, and several nights were marked with an extraordinary degree of frost. This character of the season led to some apprehension that injury might be sustained from it by the wheat crops.

Partly from this cause, and partly from the increasing impression of the low state of the stocks of wheat in the country, which rendered the prospect of the growing crops a matter of peculiar interest, the markets generally exhibited a considerable degree of firmness. But although the weather in June was unsettled and cold, and by no means favourable to the blooming process, yet as the season advanced, and no opinion decidedly adverse to the crops admitted of being formed, while at the same time, as harvest approached, it became manifest that the stock on hand, with the liberated foreign supply, would prove adequate to the consumption, the average price declined; the Gazette average being for the week ending July 5th, 67*s*. 10*d*.; a fall of 13*s*. 8*d*. per quarter from the weekly average in January preceding; and the duty on the six weeks' average was 16*s*. 8*d*. Immediately previous to this rise of the duty, all the wheat then in bond was entered for consumption. The whole quantity entered, from September, 1838, to July 5th, 1839, was about 3,300,000 quarters.

Reports then became prevalent that as the wheats were ripening they exhibited appearances of injury from previous weather; therefore, although the first fortnight of July was not unfavourable to the progress of the crops, the markets were slightly advancing. But the latter part of July and the whole of August were attended with very unsettled, and upon the whole, unpropitious weather. Frequent rains occurred, sometimes heavy, and accompanied mostly by a low temperature, which, although it counteracted in a considerable degree the tendency to sprouting, yet retarded the ripening and otherwise injured the condition and the yield. Under these circumstances, the markets advanced: the weekly average ending August 16th reached 72*s*. 3*d*. , and the aggregate average of the six weeks ending September 6th was 71*s*. 8*d*. ; making the duty 6*s*. 8*d*. At this rate the duty continued till October 4th, when it rose to 10*s*. 8*d*. Immediately previous to this rise of the duty, the whole of the wheat and flour then in bond, about 800, 000 quarters, was entered for home consumption.

The average prices fell after this time; but only to 67*s*. and 66*s*. , so as to make the duty vibrating from 18*s*. 8*d*. to 20*s*. 8*d*. during the remainder of 1889. This recession, however, of the averages, and the consequently high and prohibitory duty, has not been the effect of a more favourable estimate of the crop than had, at the time of harvest, prevailed, when the average price rallied to 71*s*. 8*d*. The fall of the average has been principally in consequence of the extreme inferiority of the condition of the wheats of the last crop; so that, while in fact there is an increased want of good dry foreign wheat to make that of our own growth fit for being made into wholesome and palatable bread, it is excluded by the operation of our most impolitic and absurd law.

Of the general produce of the wheat crop of 1839, the estimate of the best informed persons with whom I have communicated on the subject is, that in the southern district it is, although somewhat heavier in straw, inferior in number of grains and in weight to last year, while in the midland it is heavier in straw and with more ears, but lighter than last year, making the aggregate of the two districts as nearly as may be equal; but its general condition this year is inferior. In the northern division of this island, and more especially in Scotland, the crop is better, both in bulk and in yield, than last year; but, on the other hand, in Ireland it is worse; and apprehensions have been expressed by persons well informed as to the corn trade of that part of the kingdom, that instead of a clear import, as of late years, *from thence*, we may receive about 200, 000 to 300, 000 quarters of their very inferior produce, while an *import into Ireland* of 300, 000 to 500, 000 quarters of foreign may be required.

In the estimate of the produce of the wheat crop of 1839 is to be included whatever may be considered as an adequate allowance for an increased breadth sown in the autumn of 1838—restoring probably the proportions between wheat and barley and oats, as they existed previous to the autumn of 1835. What this increased breadth for the crop of 1839 has been is matter of considerable uncertainty; but on the same grounds as applied to the converse in 1835, I have reason to believe that the difference would be from one twentieth to one tenth; and an allowance of about one million of quarters would probably not be wide of the mark.

Estimating, as it appears to me there are fair grounds for doing, the crop of 1839 at about the same arable produce as that of 1838, (on the supposition that the better crops in the north of Britain may be set against the much worse crops in Ireland,) with an addition of about one million of quarters for increased number of acres, there would, according to the computation which I have made in the case of 1838, be a deficiency, as regards the mere crop of 1839, of about 2 millions of quarters from the quantity necessary for consumption till the harvest of 1840. But it should seem, according to the general impression, that there was rather more wheat in the farmers' hands at the harvest of 1839 than there had been in 1838; and there has also been a portion, not less, probably, than 1,500,000 quarters, of the foreign supply admitted to entry, applicable in aid of our own growth, between the last and the ensuing harvest.[①]

These computations of quantity are only conjectural; and I offer them not as possessing the slightest authority, but merely as giving a more definite and tangible form to the impression which I would convey of my own conclusions, from a comparison of the different accounts I have met with, than could be derived from mere general expressions regarding comparative produce.

According to this view, if there were nothing in the character of the seedtime, and of the further progress of the season to give ground for apprehensions as regards the next harvest, and more especially, if that should prove to be an early one, it would be perfectly within fair calculation, that the existing stock might be eked out without the addition of any further foreign supply than such as might, from the apprehension of the holders of a still higher duty, be entered at about the present rate, which would be otherwise prohibitory. But the extraordinary wetness of the last autumn and of part of the winter, which has occasioned a vast breadth of the wheat lands to remain unsown till an unusually late period; the greater precariousness, therefore, of the crop, and the more importance, consequently, attaching to any appearances of backwardness or inclemency of the spring, may be expected to operate powerfully on opinion; thus

① For the total quantity of wheat and wheat flour entered for home consumption, from July 5th 1838, to January 5th 1840, see Appendix.

causing what would be called speculation, (which, if there should happen to be any enlargement of the circulation or reduction of the rate of interest, would be said to be caused by the Bank or the Currency,) and such a consequent fall of the duty as might admit a considerable further foreign supply. This, however, is all in the regions of conjectural anticipation; my present purpose being to give the best record and explanation in my power of prices and the causes of them in these two years, which will be memorable in the corn trade.

SECTION 4 *Relative prices of wheat and barley*

In the account which, in treating of the prices of agricultural produce, I had occasion to give of the state of the corn markets during the fall in the value of wheat after the abundant crops of that grain in the four successively favourable seasons ending in 1835, it was observed that the *relatively* high prices of barley and oats, and of other descriptions of grain and of pulse, had operated in causing a greatly increased consumption of wheat, as a substitute for these on the one hand, and on the other hand a considerable diminution of the breadth of land sown with wheat in the autumn and winter of 1835-1836. The land so withdrawn from the cultivation of wheat was appropriated to the growth of barley and other corn and grain, which were comparatively high. It was in consequence partly of the notoriety of the extra consumption of wheat while there was a diminished cultivation of it, as was stated by several of the witnesses before the agricultural committees of the Lords and Commons in the spring of 1836, that the price of wheat advanced: and the combined effect of the seasons and of the varying extent of consumption and cultivation, as between wheat and barley, was naturally to alter their relative prices. The average prices were for the year —

					s.	d.
1835	–	Wheat	–	–	39	4
		Barley	–	–	29	11
		Oats	–	–	22	0
1838	–	Wheat	–	–	64	7
		Barley	–	–	31	5
		Oats	–	–	22	5

In consequence of this great alteration of the relative prices, the case, as regards consumption and cultivation, has been reversed. There is no doubt that in the course of last year a great deal of barley, which would otherwise have been used for malting and distilling, was manufactured into flour, entering largely into consumption as bread, at the same time that in the autumn and winter of 1838-1839 there was, if not earlier, a restoration of the full proportion of wheat under cultivation, that had formerly been withdrawn, and possibly a further quantity of land appropriated to wheat, at the expense of other grain or pulse.

Having passed in review the chief variations in the prices of corn, principally those of wheat, with a description of the seasons as affecting the home growth, and with an account of the quantities of foreign wheat entered for home consumption during the same interval, I shall proceed to examine the degree of influence to be ascribed to the corn laws. How far variations in the value of the currency have been connected with the prices of corn in that interval, in the relation of cause and effect, has been incidentally noticed in the preceding chapter, and will be further considered when the state of the circulation comes to be examined in the concluding part of this Work.

SECTION 5 *Influence of the corn laws on prices*

It would be foreign to the immediate purpose of this work to enter into an examination of the general question of the policy of the corn laws; and even if it were necessary to form a part of the present inquiry, I should despair of being able to add arguments that could be deemed to be new, or to add any force to those which have been in the recent discussions, both in and out of parliament, urged so incontrovertibly, in my opinion, against those laws, on grounds of justice and of an enlightened and enlarged view of the public interests. But inasmuch as the corn laws have, during the last two years, formed a very striking feature in the corn trade, it cannot be considered as irrelevant to an inquiry into the circumstances affecting the markets for agricultural produce, to enter into the question how far the operation of the present scale of duty on the importation of foreign corn has exercised, and is calculated to exercise, an important influence on prices?

After the disastrous experience of the signal failure of the corn law of 1815 in securing any one of the objects proposed by the promoters and supporters of it, and after the necessity had arisen for several relaxations of it by partial admissions under orders in councils in 1825 and 1826, and under a special act in 1827, the law of 1828, which has ever since continued in force, was passed. Among other of the professed objects of this, as of the former law, were, —

First—The securing to the farmer a constantly remunerating price (the estimate of which was now reduced to 8*s*. instead of 10*s*. the bushel); and more especially, —

Second—To prevent, by the ingenious device of what is called the sliding scale, any considerable degree of fluctuation in the price of corn.

How far the first of these purposes was attained may be judged of from the circumstance that, in 1830, 1833, and 1836, there were complaints and lamentations of agricultural distress, loud enough to call forth special notice in the speeches from the throne on the meeting of parliament in each of those years. And that there was good cause for complaints and lamentations on the part of the farmers may readily be admitted, when it is seen that, instead of 64*s*. or even 60*s*., which they were taught to expect by their landlords, who had been instrumental in obtaining the law, (and who had regulated their rents accordingly, as a great concession from 80*s*., which had before been their standard) they found that they were obliged, after a feverish state of high but rapidly fluctuating prices between 1828 and 1831, to submit to a nearly progressive decline, protracted through five successive seasons, of no less than 50 per cent, in the price of wheat; viz., from 75*s*. in February, 1831, to 36*s*. in January, 1836.

Of the precise nature of the distress complained of by the agriculturists in the session of parliament following the harvest of 1829, I have elsewhere given an account. Of the complaints in 1833, the grounds are stated at great length in the Report of a Committee of the House of Commons, appointed in the spring of 1838, with the evidence on which it professed to be founded; while, of the still louder complaints in 1836, the evidence taken by the committees of both Lords and Commons, although unaccompanied by reports from those committees, furnish still more ample details. The witnesses having been such as were brought forward almost exclusively by the landed interest to prove their case, must be considered as constituting a body of evidence which furnishes irrefragable proof of a degree of losses and suffering among the farmers which could hardly be exceeded if all the forebodings of the friends of the corn laws, on the supposition of a free trade, were to be realised to their fullest extent.

The description thus given, on the authority of committees of the Lords and Commons, of the total failure of the first of these objects, namely, that of securing to the grower a steady remunerating price, involves the supposition of what was the fact, — a very great decline of price compared with that rate during a considerable interval of the period under consideration. But it affords no adequate idea of the degree in which another and, in the declared opinion of some of the promoters of the bill of 1828, the more important object of the measure, has signally failed of its purpose.

Of the great evils attending fluctuations in price, and of the importance, consequently, of securing as much steadiness as possible, the committee of the House of Commons on agriculture, in 1833, have expressed themselves in the following terms: —

"Fluctuations of price, whether they arise from alteration in the value of money or from changes of the corn laws, cannot fail to produce evils in every branch of rural economy, which, independently of these disturbing causes, must ever remain exposed to grievous vicissitudes from the uncertainty of seasons. These artificial fluctuations, however, only aggravate the natural evil: they render the income of the landlord precarious, the fixed rent of the farmer a hazardous speculation, and the wages of the labourer an uncertain remuneration."

"Steadiness of price, which is conducive to settled habits, and forms the basis of all fixed engagements, is the primary object never again to be overlooked."

The Report then proceeds to add, — "And your committee cannot fail to remark, that there has been, coincident with the present system of corn laws, a steadiness in the price of corn of which there has been rarely, if ever, an experience in any former period of equal duration; and as, during the same period, there has been a very considerable difference in seasons, and in the actual amount of corn produced, it is but just to ascribe to the present system a great degree of that steadiness of price which has unquestionably prevailed."

It is not easy to conceive reasoning more illogical, and proceeding on a more imperfect analogy, and drawing a general conclusion from a narrower induction and more incorrect assumption of facts, than is contained in the above passage.

The committee, in corroboration of their position as to the steadiness of the prices of wheat in the five years immediately following the enactment of the present law, refer to a table which they insert, dividing the whole time between 1797 and 1833 into terms of five years each. — "Figures," they then add, "establish the assertion, resting on the concurrent testimony of the most experienced witnesses, that the price of wheat for the last five years, under the present corn law, has been more steady than for any other period of five years since 1797, beyond which time no official returns of accuracy can be produced."

The reason stated in the concluding part of this passage, for confining the comparative table to a period not antecedent to 1797, namely, that no official returns of accuracy can be produced beyond that time, is insufficient.

The returns of the Windsor market, upon which the Eton tables are constructed, supply quotations sufficiently accurate for the purpose. I have noticed in the foregoing part of this work, the striking proofs adduced by C. Smith, the author of the well-known Corn tracts published in the middle of the last century, of the degree in which those Windsor prices are to be relied upon. And from these it would appear that there are several instances of a steadiness of price much beyond that of the period here in question. But if it were otherwise, the fact would not be of great value, since, during the whole period, we have been under an artificial system, the machinery of which, objectionable, as it doubtless may be considered, was less so as regarded liability to causing fluctuation of prices than that of the existing system; and might, in some points of view, be looked upon as mitigating, instead of aggravating, the tendency to such fluctuation.

Allowing, then, (for the point is not worth disputing for the present purpose, although much stress is laid upon it by the committee), that there exist no returns of accuracy anterior to 1797; the committee had still to make out reasonable grounds of analogy, not only as to vicissitudes of the seasons, but as to the state of external politics, and of internal restriction, not to mention what the committee, with most exemplary inconsistency, notice as a great cause of variation in prices; namely, alterations in the state of the currency, which could bring any one of the periods of five years from 1797 to 1828 within the same category as that of 1828 to 1832. In these last five years was there any thing like the scarcity from the seasons of 1799-1800, when foreign supplies were subject to war freights; but which was succeeded immediately by the abundant crops and peace charges of importation of 1802? Or, again, the deficient crops from

1808 to 1812, during one part of which period a foreign supply was obtained, but subject to freights and insurances, amounting to between 40*s*. and 50*s*. per quarter, and during the two latter years of which, we could obtain no foreign supply whatever, succeeded by greatly increased home growth, and large importations at reduced charges from 1813 to 1815? With regard again to the period following 1815, were the committee not aware of the existence of a corn law which prohibited importation up to 80*s*., and which *insured* a great range of fluctuation? — not to mention the effects of the desolating character of the season of 1816 throughout Europe, which has since had no parallel. How then was it possible that a majority of the committee should have concurred in a report which set up such a monstrous attempt at analogy as a ground for acquiescing in the conclusion which it was proposed to establish?①

It is stated in the Report, that the assertion of steadiness rested on the concurrent testimony of the most experienced witnesses. The first of the witnesses, and certainly one of the most experienced that were examined on this point, was Mr. Jacob, who delivered into the committee "an account showing the highest and lowest prices of wheat in each of the last 20 years (1813 to 1832), and the rate of fluctuation taken in periods of three years." And his examination, with reference to this account, was as follows: —

"Admitting that the fluctuation has not been so great in the latter as in the former periods, do you conceive that is solely attributable to the state of the law? —I am not sure, two things happening together are not

① If the committee had simply stated that the corn law of 1828 had produced less fluctuation, and was less likely to produce it than the law of 1815, there would have been no ground for denying the assertion.

necessarily cause and effect.

"Is it not the case that the seasons since 1828 have been all deficient, and pretty nearly equally so? —No; the year 1828 was certainly deficient; the year 1829 was deficient about its average; the year 1830 about the same; the year 1831 the same; 1832 would have been deficient, but that the harvest happened one month earlier than usual.

"You are aware that just previous to the harvest of 1831, there was a very large admission of foreign corn into the market? —Yes.

"Supposing the harvest of 1830, instead of being deficient, had been an abundant harvest, would not a large admission of foreign corn into the market just before have interfered with the character of steadiness you have given to the latter period, in a degree which would have been important? —Yes, I think it would to a great degree."

I have introduced this extract from the evidence for the purpose of showing from the questions that there were members of the committee who were aware of the real explanation of the comparative steadiness of the prices in the period in question. The steadiness may be distinctly accounted for by a very great and, as far as by means of observation and research have extended, a very unusual similarity in the seasons (which is admitted by Mr. Jacob, in his answer to the question on that point, although he begins with a negative), and in the actual amount of corn produced in 1828, 1829, 1830, and 1831.

If, therefore, the committee had, with reference to the tendency of the law of 1828 to cause fluctuations, stated the facts, and drawn the conclusion correctly, they might simply have given the converse of their propositions thus: —

"There have been several equal periods anterior to 1797 exhibiting a greater degree of steadiness than that which occurred in the five years 1828 to 1832. And as the circumstances from 1797 to 1828 bear no analogy to those of the five years alluded to; as moreover, during these five years, there has been a much less difference in seasons and in the actual amount of corn produced than in any equal term of five years since 1797, there is no ground whatever for ascribing to the present system any part of that steadiness which apparently prevailed in the five years 1828 to 1832."

But notwithstanding the comparative steadiness of the annual averages, there was a very great degree of unsteadiness in the variations within the several years, from 1828 to 1832, and of inconvenience to farmers, dealers, and merchants, from the time and manner in which the foreign supplies were admitted. They came in by jerks in large quantities at once, not according to the immediate wants for consumption, but according to the perpetually varying duty, and according to the opinion among the importers of the probability of a rise or a fall of the averages. I could state, in detail and upon the unquestionable authority of intelligent farmers and dealers, how sudden and unexpected was occasionally the change, and how much they were perplexed, by the disturbing causes hence arising, how to act, those of them at least who were not under the influence of undeviating routine, —in sending their supplies to market. But such details would be tedious, and so far superfluous, inasmuch as to most readers it must be obvious that supplies of such magnitude coming into the market in so irregular a manner could not fail of being most perplexing to the farmers who depended upon those same markets; and that, in point of fact, the fluctuations, although not very marked in actual quotation, were much more perplexing and distressing than they could have been in an unrestrained state of the corn trade.

It might seem that too large a portion of this inquiry has been allotted to the discussion of the point which has thus been dismissed; but the fact of that apparent equableness or absence of fluctuation in the period alluded to, is a most important feature in the table of prices, especially if the yearly averages only are taken; and although I noticed and explained it in the former part of this work, I did so in a more brief and cursory manner than I should have done if the corn laws had then been a subject of any public interest; and I have been induced thus again to enter upon the explanation more at large, because that particular instance of steadiness of price has been chosen as one of the strong places, if not the strongest, which has been taken up in defence of the corn laws.

The state of prices, from the harvest of 1832 to the present time, has been a sad stumbling block in the way of the advocates of the corn laws, who contend for the beneficial operation of the present system. The experience of this interval, instead of furnishing them, as in the case of 1828 to 1832, with a prima facie case for praise of the law as insuring steadiness of price, has reduced them to more humble but still untenable grounds of defence. These are, —

1. That the fluctuations, although undeniably great and very distressing, are not more so than some that have occurred in the experience of former times.

2. That the corn law has worked well, inasmuch as when the market was exceedingly depressed the home grower was secured against a foreign supply, and when prices rose to the rate which indicated deficiency of our home growth, a foreign supply of unprecedented extent has been admitted at a very low duty.

3. That all agricultural produce is necessarily liable to fluctuations of

price, from vicissitudes of the seasons, and other causes, independently of the corn laws, and that several other articles of raw produce, although not under restriction, have fluctuated more than corn.

These pleas in favour of the corn laws, although, perhaps, more properly in mitigation of the obvious objections to their operation, than in support of an opinion of their beneficial effects, admit of the following answers: —

1. There is no experience of an unrestricted trade in corn in the last two centuries, so as to admit of comparison between the recent fluctuations and those in any former equal period, and thus to form grounds of inference as to what would, under circumstances in other respects similar, have been the fluctuations in a perfectly unrestricted state of the trade. But both from analogy and from a reference to the working of the law, it is perfectly clear that the fluctuations could not have been greater, would most probably have been on a smaller scale, and would most certainly not have been attended with such disturbance in the direction of commercial capital and credit.

2. With regard to the assertion of the corn law having worked well, it remains for the advocates of the measure to reconcile this assertion with the facts; viz., that under its operation the farmer had to sustain a progressive fall in the price, through no less than five successive years, from 75*s.* till it got down to 36*s.* for the imperial, or 34*s.* 11*d.* for the Winchester quarter; a continuance and degree of declining markets, accompanied by great distress and loud complaints on the part of the farmer, being a state of things which it is not easy to conceive admitted of aggravation by a perfectly free trade in corn; while, on the other hand, upon the occurrence of the first season following, of marked deficiency, the public was prevented from obtaining relief by the admission, for consumption, of any

foreign wheat to make up for the deficiency, until (the weekly average having reached 77*s*. in August) the aggregate averages of the six weeks had attained in September 73*s*. 2*d*., when, suddenly, in the single week 1,513,113 quarters of wheat and wheat-meal were liberated at the low duty of one shilling the quarter.

This sudden admission of so enormous a quantity of foreign corn had the effect, notwithstanding the ascertained deficiency of our own growth, of depressing the markets, insomuch that the average price, which, on the 24th of August had been 77*s*., declined within the following four weeks to 61*s*. 10*d*.; so that, whereas the previous rise to 77*s*., which had been grievously felt in the price of bread by the working classes, and was for the benefit only of the wealthier farmers who had been enabled to hold their stocks of the crop of 1837 to the last; the subsequent fall was to the detriment of the numerous class of small farmers, who having, by that time, got in their crops in all the division of the island south of the Humber, were threshing out and, as usual, bringing the earliest supplies to market.

At the same time a great deal of the commercial capital was diverted from its usual channels, for the purpose of supplying funds, immediately available, for transmission to every corner of the globe from whence corn, however unsuitable it might be in point of quality, could be obtained. And independently of the inconvenience inevitably attendant upon the diversion of so large an amount of capital from its ordinary direction, is the evil of disturbance of the circulation by the great drain of bullion entailed by so sudden and extensive a transmission of funds abroad.

On the occasion, too, of a prospect of the opening of our ports at the low duty, such is the suddenness and extent of demand for shipping, that not only are vessels very unsuitable for corn cargoes engaged, but a deficiency of tonnage is experienced, to the inconvenience of other branches of trade. The shipowners, indeed, are gainers by the great rise of freights, and of the value of shipping on such occasions; and the shipping interest is, at such periods, necessarily in a flourishing condition, as at present. But the mischievous working of the system is again felt in this very interest; for no sooner are the ports again shut, than there is a sudden cessation of all such extra demand for shipping; vessels are built under the influence of the casual demand and high freights: hence, by the subsequent competition, the rate of freights is reduced temporarily below even its ordinary level; and the shipowners, who, like the landed interests, consider themselves entitled to apply to the legislature on occasions of any considerable decline from a previous adventitious rise in the value of their property, become loud in their complaints of a decay of British shipping, and pray for additional protection, as was the case between 1819 and 1822, and again in 1832 and 1833.

It is perfectly true that the prices of corn are liable to great fluctuations from the vicissitudes of the seasons, and from other causes independent of the restrictions on importation; it is likewise true, that several other articles of raw produce, on the importation of which there are no restrictions, have experienced fluctuations as great as those which have occurred in the prices of corn; but it is difficult to understand how these undeniable propositions bear upon the question of the influence of the corn laws.

They convey no answer to the charge against those laws, as operating in aggravation of the tendency from other causes to fluctuation of the prices of corn; and, if in some few instances, other articles of raw produce have varied more than corn, there would be very little hesitation on the part of persons possessed of competent mercantile experience to give it as their opinion, in every individual instance, that restrictions on importation, analogous to those which apply to corn, would add to whatever might be the causes of variation inherent in and peculiar to such article.

I am glad to be enabled to refer, in support of my view of the mischievous working of the machinery of the corn laws, and of the inevitably great fluctuation which they entail, to a very clear and able exposition of the mode of their operation by a writer who, while from mercantile knowledge he is practically acquainted with the subject, is at the same time largely interested, as a landed proprietor, in the prosperity of agriculture, and evinces by the tone and temper with which his argument is conducted, a strong bias in favour of protection for the landed interest.

"If the present shifting scale of duty was intended to protect the farmer, keep the prices of corn steady, insure a supply to the consumer at a moderate price, and benefit the revenue whenever an imposition was required, it has signally failed. During the continuance of the corn laws the farmers have suffered the severest privations. The variations in price have been extreme, and when a supply of foreign corn has been required for the consumption of the country, it has not reached the consumer except at a very high price, whilst but little advantage has accrued to the revenue. Instead of the descending scale of duty promoting a supply in proportion to the rise in the price, experience has demonstrated the contrary. The risks which persons must incur by bringing corn from abroad are inevitably great; for should it afterwards appear that the home supply was sufficient for the wants of the country, and no advance of price consequently took place sufficient to compensate the importer, his loss would be considerable. Whenever, therefore, a demand for foreign corn takes place, his gain must bear some proportion to the risk he has incurred. It is evident that the fall in the duty operates as a *bounty* in favour of the speculator, tempting him to keep his corn out of the market as long as possible. For this object, whenever circumstances indicate that a foreign supply will be required, and an advance in the market takes place, the speculators, without any other combination than that arising from self-interest, withhold making sales, notwithstanding the rise of price may afford them a fair profit on their corn. Their gain is calculated not only on the advance in the price of the corn, but also on the fall in the scale of the duty, and as the duty falls in a greater ratio than the price of the corn rises, the duty operates as a bounty to withhold sales until it reaches its *highest protecting point*, when the *duty is also at the lowest*. It is by this means that the revenue received from grain admitted for home consumption is inconsiderable, for corn is seldom taken out of bond until the lowest rate of duty is attained. Then, again, should there be a large supply of corn taken out of bond and entered for home consumption, the average *price is sure to fall*, and *the duty to rise*, for the speculator, having made his profit by the reduction of the duty, is less concerned about selling a few shillings per quarter higher or lower. His profit is secured by the operation of the duty, as may be seen by the following description. Let it be supposed an opinion prevailed that a supply of foreign corn would be required for the consumption of the country, and that with this impression a purchase of corn had been made on the Continent deliverable in London at 40*s*. per quarter, and that it arrives here when the average price is at 66*s*. per quarter. The duty on wheat at 66*s*. being 20*s*. 8*d*. , a moderate profit might be made by selling the corn, duty paid at that price. But the impression that the supply will be required induces the speculator to hold back in the confidence, that, should the averages reach 70*s*., he not only would gain 4*s*. by the rise in the market, but 10*s*. more by the diminution in the duty, making an increase of profit of 14*s*. Should the averages reach 71*s*., *he gains another profit of* 4*s*. *in the duty* with only an increase of 1*s*. in the price, making an addition of 5*s*., or an increase of profit of 19*s*. Should the averages advance to 72*s*., *another gain of* 5*s*. *is secured*, being a rise of 1*s*. in price, and a diminution of 4*s*. in duty, making his profits 24*s*. When the averages are at 73*s*., the extreme limit is attained, the duty being only 1*s*. per quarter; so that if an importation were made that might be sold at or about 66*s*., paying a duty of 20*s*. 8*d*., by withholding the supply until the extreme limit of 73*s*. be reached, a *gain* of 7*s*. not only would be made by the *rise* in the averages, but also a *profit* of 19*s*. 8*d*. by the *reduction* of the duty, making a *total increased profit of* 26*s*. 8*d*. Can we wonder that in seasons of apprehended dearth the price of corn reaches the utmost limit provided by the Act, when the tendency of the fluctuating scale is, not to promote, but to withhold the supply, not to keep corn from fluctuation, but to offer a *bounty* for raising it to that extreme point when the merely nominal duty is imposed? And, again, can the depression in the market occasion surprise? The corn importer, having succeeded in getting his corn admitted at a low duty, has no longer any object in keeping back the supply, and presses it forward for sale, which, *reducing* the price, *raises* the duty. Thus, by the operation of the double action of a rise in price and diminution in the duty, he protects himself from the admission of any corn on the same advantageous terms that he has secured for himself. If a state of things such as above described be conceived occurring just before harvest time, an accumulated quantity of foreign corn being admitted for home consumption, you may easily suppose that the price will be affected by the supply thrown into the market, to the great injury of the British grower, who, in fact, would have to contend with a mass of foreign corn *duty free*, instead of having that fair protection which a better system would undoubtedly afford." — (*Reflections on the Operation of the Present Scale of Duty on Foreign Corn.* By David Salomons, Esq.)

But the charge against the corn law, under the head of causing fluctuations, is not only that it has aggravated, and is calculated to aggravate, whatever might otherwise be the tendency to variations of price, but that, circumstanced as this country has been and is, with an increasing population, and with an extent and degree of cultivation barely keeping pace with the rate of consumption, such a range of fluctuation as we have witnessed within these few years, namely, a fall to less than half, and again, a rise to more than double, that is, a fall of upwards of 50 per cent, and a rise of upwards of 100 per cent, is *necessarily incident* to the existing system of restriction on importation. This view of the extent of the fluctuation, inevitable under the present system, is founded on experience of the past, corroborated as the inference from that experience is by reasoning, *à priori*, upon the probable consequences to be deduced from the operation of a scale of duties so constructed. In three memorable instances since 1812, when prices had been raised by deficiency from the seasons combined with restrictions on importation, the recoil upon the restoration of abundance from the combined effect of favourable seasons, extended and improved cultivation, and an excess of importation after the cessation of the scarcity, has been attended with a fall of prices to less than one half.

The high prices in 1812 were not, indeed, the effect of *legislative* restriction on importation, but the obstruction to foreign supplies from political causes, operated exactly in the same way. In less than four years from that time, the price of wheat fell to one third of what it had been; namely, from 156*s*. to 52*s*. 6*d*. And so large was the surplus, according to all computation, at the harvest of 1816, that if the season had turned out propitious (instead of being, as it was, signally adverse in this country, and still more so on the continent of Europe), there can be little doubt but that the fall would not have stopped short of 36*s*.

The subsequent rise was unquestionably aggravated by the circumstance that, as it was very doubtful, till late in the autumn of 1810, whether the ports would open by a rise of the average of six weeks to 80*s*., there was hardly any importation in that year; whereas, in the two following years, 1817 and 1818, when the urgency of the want was over, there were imported upwards of three millions of quarters of wheat and wheat-flour. Of this large supply, a good deal arrived late in 1818 and remained as a surplus, which, with extended cultivation and abundant crops to the close of 1822, reduced the price to less than one third of what it had been in the spring of 1817, namely, from 117*s*. to 38*s*. The large stock which existed from the surplus of the three preceding years prevented such a rise as the indifferent crops of 1823 and 1824 must otherwise have caused; and if it had not been for the partial admissions of foreign corn by special acts in 1825-1826-1827, and the alteration of the law in 1828, it is beyond question, that upon the occurrence of so decidedly deficient a crop as that of 1828, the price must have risen above 80*s*., and the fluctuations through the three following years of deficiency would have been more abrupt than those which occurred under the altered law.

The alteration of the law was an improvement, and 73*s*. being then the rate at which the low duty attached, the averages at three several times reached that rate, in 1828, 1830, and 1831; such rise, although beyond the immediate occasion, being the necessary condition of an adequate foreign supply. As usual, however, and as it almost inevitably happens on such occasions, the impulse to importation being given, the foreign supplies continued to come in after the deficiency had ceased to be felt, and a great part of those supplies was entered for consumption at a gradually increasing duty, till the rate of it became prohibitory. And, as we have seen, this surplus of foreign corn, combined with our own extended cultivation and abundant harvests, brought prices, at the close of 1835, down to less than one half of what they had been in the spring of 1831. When again, more recently, in the early part of 1838, it became manifest that the deficiency of our own growth, combined with the exhaustion of the surplus of former harvests, would require a large foreign supply, no entry for home consumption was made, or was, indeed, likely to be made till the six weeks average reached 73*s*. , being a doubling of the price since the close of 1835.

How soon there may be a return of more favourable seasons, it is impossible to say; but it requires no peculiar gift of prophecy to venture to predict that, upon a recurrence, if such there should be, of seasons of *arable* produce equal to those between 1831 and 1836, we shall again see the price of wheat, at, or below 36*s*. There will then, with our still growing population, be a repetition of the circumstances analogous to those we have witnessed, of increased consumption, a disturbance of the usual proportions of grain sown, a consequent gradual reduction to exhaustion of surplus, till a season of moderate deficiency should render a foreign supply necessary, when, as a condition of receiving an adequate quantity, the *price must* rise to, at least, 73*s*.

It appears, therefore, inevitable, that on the supposition of seasons of abundance alternating with intervals of only moderate deficiency, the minimum of the range of fluctuation must be between 73*s*. and 36*s*. Should there, however, be a desolating season like that of 1816, inflicting scarcity approaching to famine throughout Europe; and still more if two seasons in succession like 1794 and 1795, and again 1799 and 1800 should occur, there is no saying to what a height the price might not rise; and in proportion to the excessive elevation under such extraordinary circumstances, would be the chances of eventual extreme depression. Against inconveniences and sufferings resulting from vicissitudes of the season in this extreme degree, there is no foresight of the legislature or the government that can adequately provide: but a system like that of our present corn laws is calculated to aggravate in a peculiar degree the evil of such visitations. It operates to this effect in a two-fold way: the one, by its tendency to cause an exhaustion of our home stock before any resort is made to a foreign supply; the other, by confining the radius, from which our supply is habitually drawn in ordinary seasons, to multiply the chances of occasional deficiency from the prevalence of unseasonable weather.

No one can be more alive than I am to the circumstance, that within certain degrees of longitude and latitude, extending over the central parts of the continent of Europe, there is, in the majority of seasons, a prevalence of weather of the same general character of propitiousness or unpropitiousness to the growth and gathering of the corn crops, as prevails in this country. But this circumstance, instead of being an argument, as by some persons it has been set up to be, against a free trade in corn, is the strongest ground in favour of it. An extension of the radius of our habitual supply to the north and south-east of Europe, to parts of Asia bordering on the Black Sea and the Mediterranean, to Egypt, and above all to the United States of America, would greatly mitigate the effects of visitations of peculiar inclemency of weather prevailing simultaneously in this country, and within a certain range on the continent of Europe.

In ascribing to the present system the necessary effect of a range of fluctuation of the price of wheat between 73*s*. and 36*s*. , I am assuming that the improvements in agriculture, and the extension of cultivation, which it is said to be a main object of the existing restrictions on importation to promote, continue in the same ratio to the progressive increase of the population as they have done within the last twenty years. If the rate of production should outrun that of the population, there may be periods of depression below the above minimum. If, on the contrary, and according to the more probable supposition, the increased rate of production should not keep pace with that of the population, the low duty price of 73*s*. would be more frequently reached and exceeded, and the subsequent subsidence might not be to so low a rate. The range between the highest and lowest might be diminished, but the variations would be more frequent and more abrupt.

A great deal of superfluous ingenuity was displayed by some of the supporters of the existing restrictions, in showing that in some instances during the last ten years, the variations between two or three consecutive years had been very small, —instancing those from the close of 1832 to the close of 1835. Now it must be quite obvious, that as the decline of prices was progressive, and as at the former date there had already been a great fall, there was so much less room for a further fall.

Therefore, how the fact proved any thing for the argument which went to the whole range of variation between 1831 and 1839, it is not easy to conceive.

There is this further consideration when viewing the enormous fluctuation from 73*s*. of progressive fall during four years and a half to 36*s*., and of the oscillating rise in the four years and a half following to 81*s*., that, instead of about 56*s*., which would be the average result of these figures, the home grower can hardly have averaged a price of 50*s*. for the whole of their crops of wheat during that interval. The reasons for this opinion are these.

As one of the effects of miscalculation, the liability to which is greatly increased by the addition to all the other elements of uncertainty of speculation upon the rapidly shifting duty, the quantity of corn which was admitted in March, 1831, at the low duty, and in the following months during the remainder of the year at progressively increasing rates of duty, amounted to no less a quantity than 1,661,673 quarters, —a quantity which, by the event, proved to be beyond the occasion, inasmuch as it appeared that a larger surplus existed at the harvest of 1831 than had been expected. And if it had not been that the harvest of 1831 was, in the south-eastern districts, deficient in acreable produce, the fall of prices would have been much more rapid; but, as it was, the price fell to 60*s*. by October of that year. And it must be evident that the bulk of the foreign wheat, upwards of 1,600,000 quarters, must have shared, with the home growers, the benefit of the sales at the comparatively high prices, 73*s*. to 60*s*. Now the averages of the six years following, when there was no foreign wheat, or no proportion worth mentioning in the market, were, —

		s.	d.
1832	–	58	8
1833	–	52	11
1834	–	46	2
1835	–	39	4
1836	–	48	6
1837	–	55	10
	6)	301	5
		50	3

But if it be considered that by far the largest quantities sold were in the three years of the lowest prices, viz. —

		s.	d.
1834	–	46	2
1835	–	39	4
1836	–	48	6
	3)	134	0
		44	8

The average of which was 44*s.* 8*d.* ; and that during that period, although, as usual, upon the occurrence of low prices, there were loud complaints of agricultural distress, the country never exhibited a greater extent nor higher degree of cultivation; it is perfectly fair to presume that at a price of about 45*s.* there would be no reason to apprehend that much, if any, land would be thrown out of cultivation; and by land being thrown out of cultivation must be understood, as it is held out *in terrorem*, that the land would be suffered to run waste. If indeed, while wheat was on an average of three years under 45*s.* , barley and other grain were higher in proportion, there would be a tendency, when leases, and the land, and the habits of the farmers were not opposed, to sow more largely of barley, or other grain which paid better, in lieu of wheat. Such was the case at the close of 1835;

and this, with less droughty seasons, accounts for the larger crops and the lower relative prices of barley in 1836-1837.

In the evidence taken by the agricultural committees in 1836, the leading questions were clearly intended to elicit answers which should go to prove that cultivation was undergoing diminution or deterioration; but it was only in isolated cases and under peculiar circumstances, that cultivation could be shown to have either been deteriorated or diminished. Those peculiar circumstances seem to have applied chiefly to some parts of Buckinghamshire and Yorkshire. With reference to the latter, one of the witnesses, Mr. C. Howard, stated that some of the poor strong soils of Howdenshire had gone out of cultivation; not, however, in consequence of the low prices of 1832 to 1836, but in consequence of the wet seasons (notwithstanding the high prices) of 1829-1830-1831.[①] It would appear, indeed, generally, that the greatest sufferers among the farmers were those who occupied the poor heavy soils, to which those wet seasons were peculiarly destructive; and it was to this circumstance that was mainly owing the reference in the King's speech of 1830 to the distressed state of agriculture. The Duke of Wellington, indeed, expressly explained the nature of the distress, which was attributable to the wet seasons and to the extra expenses attendant thereon. But the general fact is, in proof, by results beyond controversy, that the agricultural productions of the kingdom were never, as far as the seasons permitted, on a larger scale than in 1836 and 1837, notwithstanding the alleged discouragement of the low prices of 1834-1835.

Although, however, there is every reason, founded on the experience of that period, and on other grounds which it is not here the place to enter

① Agricultural Report of the Committee of the House of Commons, 1836. Questions 5346 to 5348.

upon, that at a range of prices of about 45*s.* for wheat there would be no just cause for apprehending any diminution of the breadth of arable land, unless the land were to become, as I believe it will with the growth of population become, applicable to more valuable productions than corn; it would form no valid reason for perpetuating on the country the infliction of the corn laws. At the same time, if it could be fairly shown, that the growing lands of this country, constituting any considerable proportion of those destined for the supply of food for the community, could not be continued under cultivation, except at prices much higher than those of the foreign grower, such difference might be a ground for rendering the transition more gradual; and the degree or extent of difference should serve as a guide for determining the gradations by which that difference should be reduced. But from all the information which I have been able to collect, not omitting that which the agricultural reports of 1833 and 1836 by the committees on agricultural distress of the House of Commons, and of 1836 by the committee of the House of Lords, are calculated to afford, I am firmly persuaded that the difference is very inconsiderable, so inconsiderable as not to form a valid objection to a very early resort to the only system which can hold out the prospect of security, to farmers in their leases, to landlords in their incomes, and to the public in having their supply of food divested of an impost which is felt grievously by the consumer (not to mention the other grievances attending it), while it adds little, if at all, to the permanent income of the producer.

SECTION 6 *Effects which a bounty would have had*

If then the system of corn laws from 1815 to the present time has so signally failed to control, as on each occasion it was the professed object to do, the range of fluctuation, or to secure what was considered to be a remunerating price, it may be asked whether, admitting the justice and expediency of the principle of monopoly in behalf of the landed interest, the objects proposed were or are attainable by legislative regulation. The answer must be in the affirmative, on the supposition, however, that the principle is acquiesced in, and the regulation submitted to by the public.

The failure of the present, and the still more signal failure of the former corn laws, has arisen from the circumstance, that while possessing the power under certain conditions of artificially *raising* the price to a given height, there has been no provision in them for the application of a *sustaining* power. In order to be effectual in maintaining, as well as in merely occasionally raising the price, it is absolutely essential that there should be a bounty on exportation. In the case of a total prohibition of importation up to so high a rate as 80*s.*, the quantum of bounty on exportation that should have been effectual in keeping the price up to that level, would have been something so extravagant as not to be thought of; and the bounty which was provided by the law which previously existed, viz. 5*s.* per quarter on wheat when the price was at or under 48*s.*, appeared so insignificant in amount, and dependent upon a contingency so improbable, that it was not thought worth retaining. The promoters, therefore, of the law of 1815 abandoned that part of the provision of former laws. At the same time, if the promoters of that measure had been at all aware of all its consequences when unaccompanied by a bounty, they would not only not have abandoned, as they did, the principle, and the previously existing rate of bounty, but would have made a considerable struggle not only to maintain the principle, but to increase the rate. If the proposed increase had been only to 10*s.* payable when the price should be at or under 60*s.*, it is highly probable that they would have been successful. And it is quite clear that such a bounty, however insignificant it would have appeared at the time (as no one contemplated that with so high a prohibitory rate of import as 80*s.*, the price was ever likely to fall so much below the remunerating rate, which was then held to be 96*s.*, as 60*s.*), would have become operative before the expiration of many months after the passing of that bill, and it would have been effectual in preventing the low range of prices between 1820 and 1825.

But when the principle of prohibition, upon being found to be not only ineffectual for its professed object, but in the highest degree injurious to all parties affected by it, was abandoned, and the plan promulgated, upon which the law of 1828 was eventually framed; if the landlords who were then as now all powerful in parliament, had been intelligent enough to perceive the inefficacy of a duty on importation without a bounty on exportation, instead of exerting their influence as they did in procuring the very impolitic alteration which was made in the House of Lords, whereby the pivot price, as it was called, namely, the rate at which the high duty of 20*s.* 8*d.* should attach, was raised from 62*s.* to 66*s.*, they had made the concession, apparently great, of restoring the provisions of the Act of 1804①, with the

① By the Act of 1804, the duties on foreign wheat were, —

			£	s.	d.
When under 63*s.* per quarter	–	–	1	4	3
At or above 63*s.*, but under 66*s.*	–	–	0	2	6
At or above 66*s.*	–	–	0	0	6

Bounty on exportation of wheat when at or under 48*s.* per quarter, 5*s.* per quarter.

Exportation prohibited when above 54*s.* per quarter.

On other corn the duties, and bounty, and prohibition, in proportion to wheat.

alteration only of raising the rate of the bounty on exportation from 5*s*. per quarter on wheat to 10*s*. , and raising also the average price to which it should attach from at or under 48*s*. to at or under 55*s*. ; there is fair ground for supposing that, so great being apparently the concession, such a measure would have been more readily acquiesced in by the public than that which was adopted, and which has continued in force to the present time. And there cannot be a doubt, that under the provisions of such an Act as 1804, with only the alteration supposed of 5*s*. additional to the bounty, and 7*s*. additional to the price at which it would attach, the fluctuations of prices, would have been within a very small range compared with those which we have witnessed.

While, however, it must be obvious, from this view, that the landlords would have been great gainers, if, instead of standing out, as they did in 1828, for a higher import duty, they had made the great apparent sacrifice of a lower maximum price in consideration of a bounty on the export; there is no cause on the part of the public for regret, that they were so short-sighted on that occasion; inasmuch as there is every reason to believe that the average price to the consumer would have been higher in the case supposed, and the public would, moreover, have been subject to additional taxation for defraying the bounty, when it became, as it would have become, operative. Happily, bounties are now so much out of fashion, that there is no longer any chance that this mode of encouragement to agriculture can again be resorted to.

SECTION 7 *Suggestion of the substitution of a fixed duty*

There is a very prevalent opinion even among those who are

supporters of the principle of monopoly, or, according to the more palatable term, of protection in favour of the home grower, that a moderate fixed duty would be preferable to the present shifting scale. And among those who claim, on the part of the public, an abolition of the corn law, there is a large proportion who, if a total abolition were unattainable, would prefer a fixed duty. But there is a very wide difference among those who prefer a fixed to the sliding duty, as to what the fixed amount should be.

If it were to be determined merely on the only correct principle, namely, that of countervailing any charges falling exclusively on the home grower, or in a greater proportion than those paid by the rest of the community, the minimum duty of the present scale, namely, 1*s.* per quarter (which, under any circumstances, it would be desirable to maintain, if only for regulation and statistical purposes), would amply answer the justice of the case. But in the absence of any principle, the quantum of duty, if the change were made, would be a compromise of some medium rate between what the landlords might conscientiously consider themselves entitled to claim, and what the public would submit to pay. It strikes me that any thing under 8*s.* per quarter would not to the landed interests appear to be worth having; and I have no idea that the public would consider any thing above that rate to be a change for the better. Assuming, 8*s.* as the rate fixed, subject, however, to a reduction to 1*s.* if the price reached 56*s.* or 60*s.*, the change from the present system would be a great improvement in more points of view than one.

In the first place, the averages, and the uncertainty and manoeuvring connected with them, would be done away with, as would, likewise, the mischievous anomaly which, by the effect of low condition on the averages, excludes foreign wheat precisely at the time when it is most wanted for mixture with our own.

In the next place, this country would present a constant market, instead of the present capricious one, and would afford an opening for returns for exports beyond that which at present exists, except in the uncertain intervals when the duty is approaching its minimum, and there would be less liability to disturbance of the value of the currency.

SECTION 8 *Conjecture as to the prices at which wheat would range in the event of a free trade*

It may be expected, that in a treatise like this on prices, since so much of the discussions both in and out of parliament has proceeded on the question of the probable range of the prices of wheat in this country in the event of a free trade (by which I mean the retention of the duty of only 1*s*.), a conjecture should he hazarded of the effect on prices of such an alteration.

One among the great difficulties in the way of forming a conjecture on this point is that of taking a sufficient number of years, which should not appear unreasonably long, for the purpose of forming anything like a fair average. A single season like that of 1816, or a recurrence of such at near intervals, like those at the close of last century, which extended their desolating effects over the whole of the continent of Europe, as on the other hand a series of favourable seasons, would make a great difference in an average of ten years. But barring any extraordinary difference in the seasons, I should expect that the price here, with the ports always open at a duty of 1*s*., would, in a series of years of some length, average about 43*s*.

The quantity which we might look to import at an average of the price that I have named, might approach to from 1,500,000 to 2 millions of quarters. If there were to be a fixed duty of 8*s*. the quarter, I very much doubt whether the annual importation would reach that quantity; and, at any rate, if the average price in this country should, that duty existing, be under 45*s*., the probability is, that a great part of the importation would be bonded. Indeed, with the ports always open, even subject to a fixed duty of 8*s*. on entry for consumption, I believe that this country, but more especially the port of London, would become the emporium of the trade in corn with Europe and America; and we should thus, independently of the great accession of trade so afforded, be assured of a large available supply, in the event of our own crops being deficient.

To enter into all the grounds on which this estimate of probable prices is founded, would require a treatise devoted to that object, and is beyond the purpose of this work.[①] I can only say, for the estimate which I have formed, that it is derived from the experience that I have had in the corn trade, and from the best sources of information that I have been able to

---

① Among other reasons, however, there are two which may be noticed as having considerable weight in favour of the supposed tendency of prices to vibrate upon a rate of about 45*s*. The one is, that from the experience of the three years during which the price in this country was on an average under 45*s*., there was no apparent tendency to diminished or deteriorated cultivation in this country; and the other is, that at about that price there are fair grounds for supposing that a moderate, and by no means overwhelming, annual foreign supply would be imported.

meet with. Before quitting this point, however, I must observe that my estimate of the price at which a foreign supply might be expected of the extent supposed, may be considered by some of the opponents of the corn laws as strengthening the ground for the supporters of them, inasmuch as such statements may be made to work upon the minds of the farmers, in frightening them with the prospect of cheap foreign corn. And it is partly, perhaps, from an apprehension of this kind, that some of the most distinguished of the opponents of the law have been at great pains to prove that the foreign growers could not afford an annual supply of wheat under a price standing in this market 50*s*. or upwards, exclusive of any duty on importation. If they had any sufficient grounds for such estimate, which I am persuaded they have not, the arguments for an abatement of the monopoly would be weakened, inasmuch as there would be so much less to contend for. If a free trade would not afford a supply under 50*s*., while the average price under the monopoly did not, for some years, materially exceed that rate, the argument against the monopoly would be confined to the objections arising out of the extreme fluctuations, and the other inconveniences distinct from price; such as disturbance in the direction of capital, and derangement of the circulation, to which the present scale of duty exposes the country. Those objections are, of themselves, of great weight; but the substantial and enduring ground of objection is, that while subjecting the country to these inconveniences, it artificially raises the price of food to the community, who suffer a loss by it, much greater in amount than the utmost gain derived from the monopoly by the classes in whose favour, and by whose preponderance in the legislature, it is inflicted.

SECTION 9 *On the effect of the prices of provisions on the condition of the working classes*

The state of prices of provisions, and of the rate of wages in the two last years, strikingly confirms the deductions from previous experience of the little tendency which exists in wages to follow a fall or rise in the prices of provisions except at long intervals, and then only in a degree far short of such fall or rise. When treating of the great fall and cheapness of the prices of provisions in 1833-1834-1835, I took occasion to observe, that, "the extension of trade, the general but not speculative improvement of the prices of commodities, the undoubted and substantial prosperity of the manufacturing and mining interests, the general employment of the working classes at full wages, and the increase of the revenue, accompanied a great fall of the prices of provisions, but more especially of the price of wheat, which was lower at the close of 1835 than it had been in the last seventy years; thus furnishing a fresh and decisive negative of the often repeated, but perfectly unfounded assertion, put forth by parties interested in the corn monopoly, that high prices of agricultural produce tend to increased demand for other productions, and to extended employment and higher wages to the working population." With the state of things then described as exhibited at the close of 1835, what a contrast, as regards the working population, is that which is presented at the close of 1839.

In a few instances the wages of agricultural labourers have been raised, but in a very trifling proportion to the rise of necessaries; and in cases where an advance of wages has been granted, it has been rather from motives of fear or humanity on the part of the employers, than as a legitimate consequence, on principles of business, of an improved demand relatively to the supply of labour. While in the manufacturing districts there is not only no increase of money wages, but there is a falling off of employment, so that while the prices of provisions are in some instances nearly doubled, and while several other necessaries, and more especially the secondary necessaries, such as tea, sugar, and tobacco, are at a considerable advance, the earnings of the work-people are reduced; they are thus suffering cruelly under the twofold evil of having their little income less, and of finding that reduced income going a much less way in the supply of their most urgent wants.

The present state of things, therefore, furnishes fresh proof, if additional proof had been wanting, of the negative of the dogma of the advocates for restrictions on the corn trade, that the landlords and farmers getting higher prices must be the better customers and employers of the manufacturers, shopkeepers, and labourers; and in that way to hold out more than compensation for the higher prices which the latter classes are obliged to pay for their food. I do not mean to say that in the present case the high price of provisions is exclusively attributable to the corn laws, but it is here adduced as adding, to all former experience, a striking instance of the utter want of foundation in fact, as well as in reasoning, for the supposition that a high price of food can be a cause of increased employment and advanced real wages to the working classes.

CHAPTER Ⅱ

ON THE PRICES OF PRODUCE, OTHER THAN CORN

The state of prices of raw produce, and of commodities generally, as likewise, indeed, of labour, in the two last years, viz. 1838 and 1839, is pregnant with illustrations of the theory which, with reference to the practical working of the system of our currency, as it has existed, both during the bank restriction and subsequent to the restoration of cash payments, it has been the purpose of the former part of this work, as it is of the present continuation of it, to establish.

In the preceding chapter it has been seen how little of the fluctuations in the price of corn could be traced to the state of the circulation as a moving force; and it will be found that a reference to the prices of other produce and of labour will equally prove the absence of any direct agency of that cause.

When giving an account, in the preceding part of this work, of the state of the markets, and of the disturbed state of credit in 1836 and part of 1837, it was observed, that those articles only which had manifestly been the subjects of exaggerated demand in the branches of trade, to which alone a great abuse, that is, an undue extension of credit, had applied in 1835 and the earlier part of 1836, were observably depressed by the great contraction of credit in the last six months of 1836, and the first half of 1837; such contraction of credit being confined, as the previous extension had been, to the American and East India trades, but principally to the trade with the United States of America.

As, according to the general laws which govern markets, such articles as have risen beyond the due level, from an exaggerated demand, or, in other words, from anticipation of higher prices on grounds not warranted by a correct appreciation of the proportions of supply and demand, (such exaggerated anticipation of demand being favoured by an undue extension of credit), usually fall in nearly an equal degree below that level; so, when any particular market has been depressed by a failure of credit, and by an exaggerated apprehension of further fall, there is a rebound which not unfrequently proves to be beyond the occasion. This was the case with several articles of American and East India produce, which having been unduly depressed by the failure of credit in those branches in the first six months of 1837, rallied towards the close of that year, and attained prices which, when the supplies for the season came forward, could not be maintained. There was, accordingly, a considerable degree of dulness, and a drooping tendency of markets for those descriptions of produce in the spring of 1838; and, excepting in the corn markets, the rise of which has been the subject of explanation in the preceding chapter, there was a general character of quietness prevailing in the markets for commodities through the greater part of that year, with a tendency, however, towards the latter part of it, to an advance in the price of several articles, besides corn, of which the supplies proved to be below expectation. This is the more to be observed, inasmuch as the period of the greatest dulness, or at least of the most completely quiet markets, and the lowest prices of commodities, in the summer of 1838, were coincident with a greater amount of Bank of England notes in circulation than there had been for many years before; the amount, according to the return dated 24th August, 1838, was 19,481,000*l.*, while in the three months ending 8th March, 1836, when there was so much excitement and overtrading, it had been only 17,439,000*l.* Here was an increase of 2,000,000*l.* in the circulation, while the market rate of interest was, for the best bills 3 per cent, and in some instances as low as $2\frac{1}{2}$ per cent; and during the progress to this state of things in the money market, the markets for produce, with the exception of corn, were dull, which is another word for absence of briskness of demand. This being the state of the markets for commodities, and the state of the money market, in the summer of 1838, as exhibited by the amount of the circulation, and by the rate of interest, it may be not uninteresting or uninstructive to compare those several conditions with what they were in the corresponding season in 1839.

The markets for produce in the summer of 1839, (subject only to the usual oscillation incidental to the supply and consumption of most articles of raw produce,) after having maintained a remarkably steady tendency to advance coincidently with a progressive though slow reduction in the amount of the circulation, and with a very decided and unusual increase in the rate of interest and discount, were, with exceptions not worth mentioning, at a higher range of prices than they had been at the corresponding time of the preceding year.① During the whole progress of the recent pressure on the Bank of England there was no period in which more alarm and anxiety prevailed in the money market than in the middle and latter part of July last, when the apprehension entertained by the directors themselves was evinced by their desire of selling their dead weight, and when it was known that they had, in the alternative of not effecting such sale, applied to the Paris bankers for assistance. It was known, too, that the Bank rate of discount, which had already been advanced to 5 $\frac{1}{2}$ per cent, was to be raised, and it was apprehended that the advance would not stop at 6 per cent., to which it was raised on the 1st of August. For some weeks before, and during the progress of this pressure, the newspapers were teeming with forebodings, according to the currency theory, of the result of such measure by the Bank for its safety, in knocking down prices, by forcing sales of commodities. And, in fact, it was given out to

① It may not be uninteresting to see the impression which was made by this state of things while in progress. I therefore insert the following extract from the city article in the "Times" of the 6th July, 1839, which gives, as I considered at the time, and believe it to be, a very correct representation.

"With respect to the state of money, there is no material alteration, but confidence is diminishing in the symptoms of improvement manifested early in the week. All the portfolios of the leading merchants are full of foreign bills to an unusual degree, while our trade exportations do not by any means supply a substitute for them as they arrive at maturity, so that a further drain of bullion is thought to be inevitable. *The restraining measures at the Bank have not had the effect of lowering the prices of any articles of commerce*, with the exception of cotton; and with respect to that, it is now very generally ascribed rather to the diminution of consumption to which the spinners in self-defence have resorted than to any other cause. It follows, consequently, that though the financial crisis is a severe one, and places the Bank of England, in particular, in a most embarrassing situation, the merchants are, comparatively, quite at their ease. The foreign exchanges have not at all improved this afternoon, and the rates on Paris and Hamburg are both lower. The quotations were — Amsterdam, 12 $\frac{1}{2}$ to 1; Paris, 25 15 to 20 (short); Hamburg, 13 10 $\frac{1}{4}$ to $\frac{1}{2}$ at 3 months."

be the creed of the Bank directors that they could not be expected to stop the drain on its coffers without forcing down the prices of commodities. As far, therefore, as an actual reduction of the circulation, a great and very unusual rise in the rate of interest, and an almost universal opinion, which, of itself, is sometimes of powerful operation in realising the result to which it is directed, could be supposed to have a direct influence on the markets for commodities, it might be imagined as an inevitable consequence that those markets must of necessity be much lower in August, 1839, than they had been in August, 1838. But how stand the facts?

By the Bank returns, the circulation, which had been on the average of 3 months, in August, 1838, 19,481,000*l*., was in August, 1839, 17,969,000*l*. The Bank rate of interest and discount, which had been $3\frac{1}{2}$ and 4 per cent, was raised to 6 per cent, but the market rate, which in the first six months of 1838 had been one per cent, below the Bank rate, was in the summer of 1839 considerably above it; and good bills, which were not within the date or other rules prescribed by the Bank, and consequently not discountable there, were not convertible but on terms which, whether charged as discount merely, or with commission in addition to discount, amounted to 7, 8, and in some instances, I believe, to 10 per cent, per annum.

Under these circumstances, a comparison of the prices of commodities at the two periods is peculiarly calculated to serve as a test of the currency theory. In the list of articles which may be considered as showing the general state of prices, if I were to give the quotations from those which will be found in the Appendix to the present, in continuation of the former part of this work, I might be liable to the supposition of being under a bias in the selection, and in straining the quotations of prices, as is too often done when a purpose in controversy is to be answered. I therefore here give a list of articles and the prices attached to them, exactly as they are stated in a very useful weekly publication, very ably conducted by Messrs. Henry Burgess and Co., entitled "The Circular to Bankers."

If any considerable proportion of these articles had fallen in price under circumstances the reverse of those which had raised them, such fall would infallibly have been set down to the operation of the currency as an originating cause. There can be no doubt that if there had been an excess of supply of any of the articles, and if that excess, or a part of it, had been imported or held on credit, or, which is the same thing, on capital borrowed for a limited period, the fall from mere excess of supply would be aggravated, that is, would be more abrupt, and to a lower point of depression in a contracted or difficult state of the money market, or, in other words, in a state of discredit, and a high rate of interest. Thus, in the case of the depression of the markets for particular descriptions of produce in the summer and autumn of 1836, the articles which fell in price were nearly all connected with the overtrading of that period in the American and China trade, and the fall was from excess of supply, and from the failure of credit of the importers or holders, as also from falling off of demand from the United States. The proof that such had been the causes, was in the fact that the markets, which were unconnected, directly or indirectly, with those branches of trade did not participate in the depression.

Such, however, is the tendency to infer the relation of cause and effect from mere coincidence, that, as I had occasion to observe when treating of that period, the fall of prices was said, and commonly believed, to be general; and to have been exclusively caused by the state of the money market. Thus, in a Tract which I have before referred to, on "The Causes and Consequences of the Pressure on the Money Market in 1836," it was observed, — "The fall in price of almost all the articles of raw produce (sugar, coffee, tea, silk, cotton piece-goods, metals, drugs, &c.), from the 1st July last, when the rate of interest was first advanced, has not been less than from 20 to 30 per cent." Now the advance in the Bank rate of discount in July of that year was only to $4\frac{1}{2}$ per cent, and afterwards to 5 per cent, and the market rate had not advanced in any thing like the proportion that it did in 1839; moreover, the markets in which there was no notorious excess of supply, and which had not been under the influence of the exaggerated demand from America, were not more disturbed by the pressure on the money-market in 1836 than they have been in 1839, — why, therefore, should the smaller rise in the rate of discount in 1836 produce such an effect?

So prevalent has been the notion of an intimate and necessary connection between the state of the money market and the prices of commodities, that the general high range of the markets for produce throughout the whole of 1839, the firmness of nearly all of them, and the buoyancy of many of the most considerable of them, during the period of the greatest pressure, has been a constant matter of surprise, and has puzzled most of the persons who are under the influence of the currency doctrine, to account for. The most general explanation that I have heard attempted has been, that there was a scarcity of commodities, and that, if it had not been for the pressure on the money market, there would have been speculation, and still higher prices. But if the money market had been easier, and if, in consequence of such greater facility, prices had risen last summer higher than they did, the effect, by this time, would have been larger supplies, or a diminished consumption, or both; and in that case, prices, with the utmost facility of the money market, would be lower now than they arc. Sufficient proof, however, has been afforded in the article of Tea, how little the money market deters speculation where real grounds, from actual or apprehended scarcity, exist for the anticipation of a considerable advance of price. The market for this article had been, during the first six months of 1839, in a quiet and rather dull state. But upon the arrival of the accounts from China of the seizure and confiscation of the opium, and of the violent proceedings of the Chinese government, causing a suspension of the shipments of tea from thence, with every appearance of an interruption for a considerable length of time, if not a total cessation of the trade, a speculative demand arose. In a few weeks, the prices of the descriptions constituting the bulk of the supply advanced by no less than 120 and 150 per cent. And during the progress of that advance, the market exhibited all the character of wildness which has been ascribed exclusively to the state of markets during the Bank restriction①, or more recently in 1825. But, in point of fact,

---

① It is surprising how unconscious the public, or at least the reasoners among the public on alterations in the value of the currency, are of the complete analogy which the recent rise of 150 per cent, in the bonded prices of Tea exhibits to the rise of prices which occurred during the war in various articles of which it was apprehended that all future supply would be permanently cut off, such rise of prices being supposed by those persons to have been *caused* by the Bank restriction.

The following account of the rise and progress of the Tea speculation is extracted from the supplement to the "London Price-current" for the year 1839.

"Tea. — The past year has been remarkable for an extraordinary rise in the prices, the consequence of a speculative demand, founded on an anticipated diminution or cessation of supplies, by reason of the interrupted trade between the Chinese and English merchants since the extensive seizure of opium at Canton. The market continued generally steady until July, by which month and in August a rise of 2*d.* per 1*b.* took place in Congou. In October the prices paid were 5*d.* higher. And at the December sales, when the highest prices were paid, Congou, which at the beginning of the year was dull of sale at 1*s.* 1*d.*, realised 2*s.* 7*d.* to 2*s.* 8*d.* per 1*b.*"

there was no such speculative rise in any of the markets for produce (the limited and comparatively insignificant article of spices excepted) in 1825, as has recently been witnessed in Tea, an article in which very large capitals are invested. I have been assured that some parcels, during the progress of the rise, changed hands at least eight times.

The fluctuations in the cotton market, and the causes of them, namely, the deficient crops in America in 1838, and the exaggerated anticipations by the planters of such an advance in price as, in their opinion, cotton ought to fetch in this country, —those exaggerated anticipations having been promoted and rendered operative by the assistance and participation of the United States Bank, and other banks in America, —are matters of such notoriety, and have been so often referred to, and so fully described in connection with the deranged state of the southern and western banks of America, as to supersede any detailed description of them here. The highest elevation of prices under the influence of the operations for artificially enhancing the value, by undue banking aid and participation, was attained in the early part of the spring of 1839. The decline from that price has been ascribed in some of the American newspapers to "the putting on the screw" (according to the slang term) by the Bank of England. But, in point of fact, the decline in the price of cotton began before any advance in the rate of interest by the Bank, and for a very sufficient reason, namely, that the manufacturers, finding that the stocks of yarn and cotton goods had, in consequence of the great additional power which had been applied, by the erection of new mills in 1836, 1837, and 1838, outrun the consumption, very naturally, and as they would and must have done in their own defence, even if the utmost facility of the money market had prevailed, determined to work short time. They have thus succeeded in tiding over the effects of the deficiency of the cotton crop of 1838, and are enabled, by the return of abundant supplies at moderate prices, to be in train for resuming full work, with the restored prospect of a steady trade.

There are two reasons which are unanswerable against the assertions put forth on the part of the American cotton speculators, that it was the putting on of the screw by the Bank of England that disconcerted their operations, by causing the decline of the prices in this country. In the first place, the decline of prices from their highest artificial elevation, in March, 1839, had begun, and the failure of the speculation had become evident before the Bank had shown the least disposition to put on the screw; indeed, the cheapness of money at that time is, as will be seen, one of the charges that have been brought against the Bank of England. And, secondly, if the putting on of the screw was solely, or even mainly, or *at all*, *a cause* of the fall in the price of cotton, how happened it that the same screwing process did not affect other raw materials in this country at the same time? But, indeed, a further question may be asked, and that is, —if the mere action of the Bank of England is considered as having caused a fall in the price of cotton in this country, how is the fact to be accounted for, that at the end of July, 1839, when the screw was in its fullest operation, the prices of cotton were higher than they had been in July, 1838, when the money market was in the easiest possible state?

During the few weeks at the close of 1839, there has been a decline in some of the articles; and the quotations on the 31st December last are lower than those in December, 1838. But as the markets were advancing at the close of 1838, in consequence of the stocks (of which comparative statements, at that time of the year, are usually made) being found to be rather below expectation, so, in December, 1839, the markets, in some instances, have declined upon its being found that the stocks were larger than they had been at the corresponding period of 1838. As far as I can learn or judge, there is no fall of prices in any description of produce from pressure of sellers, or in any degree beyond what might be expected, in the easiest state of the money market, from a mere reference to the supply compared with the estimated rate of consumption. But there is this further most important consideration, as bearing upon the question of the connection between the prices of commodities and the state of the circulation, that the state of prices, taking the great majority in point of bulk and value of the articles, at the close of December, 1839, was higher than it had been in August, 1838; the comparison of the circulation stands thus,

August 21. 1838	19, 481, 000*l*.
January 7. 1840	16, 366, 000*l*.

The Bank rate of interest and discount having risen in that interval from $3\frac{1}{2}$ and 4 per cent, to 6 per cent, and the market rate from 3 per cent to 7 and 8 per cent.

Again, if we take prices as they stood two years ago, and compare them with present prices, we shall find that, with exceptions hardly worth mentioning, they are higher now than they were then; the intermediate variations having been in a very extraordinary degree in a direction precisely opposite to that which, according to the currency theory, would have been inferred. Thus, while the circulation had been increasing between December, 1837, and August, 1838, by about 1, 500, 000*l*., and the Bank rate of discount had been reduced from 5 to 4 per cent, and the market rate in a still greater proportion, the markets for the majority of articles of produce at the latter date were drooping; as, on the other hand, we have seen that while the circulation was in a slow but progressive reduction to its recent comparatively low amount, and while the pressure on the money market was becoming most severe, prices were rising; the advance of prices applying to a larger number and value of the articles which are considered as indicative of the purchasing power of money, than will be found to have been the case in any two previous consecutive years.

It is difficult to conceive grounds of presumption stronger than these of the absence of the necessary connection which is so constantly supposed and asserted to subsist between variations in the amount of the Bank of England issues, or in the state of the money market, and the state of prices.

It may be contended, however, as it has been on former occasions of controversy on the question of the influence of the currency on prices, when the discrepancy, by a reference to the Bank of England issues, was too great to be got over, that it was the country banks, which, by their inordinate issues had caused a great rise of prices, and by their subsequent contraction a great fall of prices. I have examined that point at some length in former parts of this work; and I may have occasion, when treating more distinctly hereafter of the state of the circulation, to refer to the question of the connection between the country bank issues and the state of prices. I will here only, therefore, observe that a reference to them will not explain the phenomena of the state of markets for produce, inasmuch as the great increase of issues had been in 1838, when nearly all articles, corn excepted, —which exception will of itself go a great way towards explaining the cause of this increase, —were lower than in 1839; and the greatest reduction of issues was in progress between June and September, 1839, when the markets for nearly all descriptions of produce ranged very high. Having given the foregoing general view of comparative prices, relatively to the amount of the Bank of England and country bank issues, I propose in the following chapter to examine more particularly the causes and effects of the variations which have taken place in the circulation in the last two years.

CHAPTER Ⅲ

ON THE STATE OF THE CIRCULATION IN 1838 AND 1839

The state of the circulation has undergone, within the two last years, such variations in its relation of cause and effect with the exchanges, with the rate of interest, with commercial credit, and above all, with the position of the Bank of England, that a painful degree of public attention has necessarily been fixed upon it: and independent of the generally prevalent anxiety to investigate the causes of these variations, and to provide, as far as practicable, a remedy against their recurrence in such a degree as that in which they have recently been experienced; an examination of the circumstances which have given rise to them, and of their actual and probable consequences, forms an essential part of the subject of prices, to elucidate which is the object of the present publication, as it was of the work of which this is a continuation.

The most convenient mode, as it strikes me, of conducting the examination of the several questions to which the phenomena of the circulation, in the period under consideration, naturally give rise, will be to enquire, —

1. What have been the causes which, independent of the Bank's regulation of its issues, have operated on the exchanges in such a degree as

to produce a strong tendency to an efflux of bullion?

2. How far, if at all, the Bank's regulation of its issues has been connected by the relation of cause and effect with the depressed state of the exchange, and the consequent drain of bullion?

3. What has been the influence, of the Bank's regulation of the paper currency on the variations which have occurred in the prices of commodities, and of shares in joint stock companies, and on the rate of interest; or, in other words, on the markets for produce and for shares, and on the money market?

4. How far the regulation of the paper and credit part of the currency admits of being conducted without a recurrence of the danger of suspension of cash payments?

SECTION 1 *Causes of the recent depression of our foreign exchanges, and the consequent drain on the coffers of the Bank of England*

When treating, in the foregoing chapter, on the state of markets for agricultural and other produce, it was observed that, with the exception of the great rise in the price of wheat, and the disturbed state of the cotton trade, and, more recently, the great rise in tea; the two years since the close of 1837 have not been marked by any spirit of speculation in goods, or by any elevation of prices, beyond such as a fair mercantile view of the relative state of supply and demand fully warranted. Nor, with the single exception of corn, have the prices of commodities in this country, as compared with those abroad, been, during that interval, or in any part of it, at such a relative rate as to indicate, by that criterion, any diminution in the value of our currency, compared with the currencies of foreign countries.

It is very material to bear in mind this circumstance, as it furnishes a striking illustration of a position which I have before had occasion to advance, namely, that, although the prices of commodities form the medium through which the tendency to a level in the distribution of the precious metals in the commercial world operates, in the long run, there are disturbing causes which may, during very considerable intervals, act powerfully upon the exchanges, and induce, in a convertible state of the currency, a strong tendency to an efflux of the metals, to counteract which, extraordinary efforts may be requisite on the part of the regulator of the currency, which, in this country, is the Bank of England; while, during the whole time, there may have been no intermediate derangement of the ordinary level of the prices of commodities.

The prices of corn, indeed, advanced in the course of 1838 very much beyond their ordinary level, of late years, in this country, and beyond the level of prices abroad, so as to induce an unprecedentedly large importation; the payment for which has been one of the depressing causes operating upon the exchanges: such occasional necessity for extraordinary payments abroad being one of the many evils attendant on the corn laws. But, as the rise in the price of corn was not caused by an enlargement of the circulation—such rise having been proved to be justified by a great deficiency of our own crops—and the importation not having exceeded what was necessary to make up for that deficiency, it must be regarded, not as an indication of a circulation depreciated by excess, but as a disturbing cause, operating on the balance of foreign payments, much beyond what would otherwise have been the balance of trade, in the ordinary state of the circulation, such as it then existed. However, the extra payments for foreign corn, large as they have been, and sudden as the call has been for them, have not been of such magnitude or duration as alone to be sufficient to account for the long-continued depression of the exchange, and the consequent uninterrupted drain on the coffers of the Bank. The value of the foreign corn imported in the two years 1838 and 1839 may be computed at about 10, 000, 000*l*. But there was a considerable excess of exports from this country in those two years, particularly in 1839. And although it is probable that, as usual, a considerable part of those exports may have been for account of the manufacturers or shippers on this side, and therefore not immediately available as payment for the corn imported; yet a part of that excess of exports must have gone towards that payment, the whole of which, therefore, cannot have operated in creating the adverse balance of payments. Whence, then, the continued heavy pressure on the exchanges, which so nearly had the effect of draining those coffers dry? In former instances, the large and long-continued balances against us of foreign payments, which, on two memorable occasions previous to the Bank Restriction Act, nearly exhausted the stock of bullion before the exchanges had turned, were plain and palpable causes, and so obviously violent in their operation, that it is matter of wonder they could be counteracted and surmounted; for surmounted they were, and the exchanges were effectually turned by a resolute and extraordinary degree of contraction of the circulation. I allude to the instances in 1782-1783, and 1795-1796, when the payments for importations of foreign corn, though large for that period, formed only a small proportion of the payments abroad, for the maintenance and pay of troops and transports, such payments, in the latter period, being increased by remittances to foreign powers for subsidies. In 1799 and

1800, and again from 1809 to 1814, foreign extra payments for corn, and for military purposes were on a still increased scale, and the paper, being no longer convertible, the increased value of the foreign currencies, from these causes, was shown in a great depression of foreign exchanges. In 1818 there were large importations, not only of foreign corn, but of nearly all other descriptions of foreign produce; and to the payments for these were added the remittances for the large foreign loans negociated, for the greater part, with capitalists in this country. In this instance there was some efflux of the metals; but the remainder of the effect of the adverse balance of payments (the paper not being then convertible) was felt in the exchanges; which were hardly so much depressed (about 8 per cent) as might have been expected from the operation of such powerful causes: and yet their mere recovery, upon the cessation of these causes, in 1819, is implicitly believed to have been the exclusive effect of Peel's bill.

The derangement of the circulation, and the drain, nearly to exhaustion, of the Bank treasure in 1825, was the result of many concurrent causes, which rendered the whole of the circulation redundant in such a degree as fully accounted for the sudden and extensive pressure on the exchanges, and the consequent efflux of bullion. These causes I have pointed out, in a former part of this work, and I shall have occasion to refer to them hereafter more particularly.

In the interval from 1828 to 1832 there was a considerable fluctuation of the Bank treasure. Twice, during that period, the drain proceeded to a great extent. The causes, however, admitted of sufficient explanation, which already has been given, in treating of the circulation during that period. In each of those cases, between 1828 and 1832, the drain was surmounted without effort, and without any occasion for raising the rate of the Bank discount above 4 per cent; consequently without any observable disturbance of the money market.

On the minor fluctuations of the treasure, between 1832 and 1836, it is unnecessary to dwell, as they entailed no consequences worth mentioning. The circumstances connected with the reduced state of the stock of bullion in 1836 and the early part of 1837 were, —

1. The excessive credits to the United States of America, creating a temporary balance of payments against this country for American accounts.

2. The negociation of Dutch and other foreign securities attracted by the low rate of interest here.

3. An internal demand, although to no great extent, for Ireland.

If to these had been added a demand, in the autumn of 1836 for foreign corn, by a deficiency of our own harvest, the coffers of the Bank would have been in as imminent danger of exhaustion in 1837 as in 1839.

Of the causes of the heavy balance of foreign payments, which have recently so nearly run the Bank aground, those which have been most distinctly operative may be classed under the following heads: —

1. The large importations of foreign corn, the computed amount of which, in the two years, was to the amount of about ten millions sterling.

2. The state of financial and commercial relations with the United States of America.

By the financial slate, I mean our over-importation of American securities, which were created chiefly by bonds of the separate states, and by the United States Bank, and other American banks and joint stock companies.

By the commercial state of our relations with that country, as having contributed to the recent derangement, I mean, not only a renewed tendency which there might be to an excess of mere mercantile credits, but mainly the peculiar circumstances of the cotton trade. ①

3. The state of credit on the continent of Europe.

It is well known, that in France and Belgium, three or four years ago, the system of joint stock banks was brought into operation on a very extensive scale; not only for purposes of deposit and discount, and the ordinary functions of mere banking, such as the safe and economical transmission of funds from one part of the country to another, by bills of exchange and credits, but also for the circulation of notes payable on demand. There was, besides, in both those countries, a very general spirit

① The peculiar circumstances to which I allude, were the unjustifiable and extravagant operations of the United States Bank, followed by the banks of the western and southern states, in making advances on cotton to the planters (if not, as reported, taking the cotton off the hands of the latter), with a view of withholding it from the manufacturers in this country, unless it should reach a price adequate to the exaggerated notions which prevailed on the other side, of the increased value which the article ought to bear, in consequence of an ascertained deficiency of the crop.

The shipments of cotton, when they did take place, after being held back some time, were consigned to agents on this side, for the account of shippers on the other side, but were still held by that factitious assistance of spurious banking credit; so that, our manufacturers, although mostly out of stock of the raw material, bought most sparingly, reducing their mills to working short time. This struggle, which was of a kind that commonly takes place whenever raw produce is held at what the manufacturers consider an exaggerated rate, became, in this instance, of importance only from the magnitude of the space in our manufacturing industry which is occupied by raw cotton. In the struggle, the manufacturers succeeded, as they always do when it so happens, as it did in this instance, that the stock of wrought goods (in their various stages from yarn to the finished article) in hand, both in this country and abroad, had outrun the consumption. In truth, to our manufacturers the insane attempt at artificially enhancing the price was the most salutary occurrence imaginable, as it compelled them to reduce their work; and they thus escaped a loss which they must have sustained if they had got into stock at the moderate advance which in consideration of the deficiency of the crop they might have been induced to give.

But the effect, as regarded our exchanges, was a reduced amount of manufactured cotton goods for exportation, while the importation of the raw cotton had been mostly paid for by advances which the consignees on this side obtained upon it. I mention this as one, although a minor item, in the account of the causes of the balance of payments against this country.

of speculation and over trading, which prevailed in various ways, one of which was manifest in a remarkably great extension of joint stock companies for different purposes.

The effect of these operations, according to their extent, and in the degree in which the additional medium of paper and credit outran the power of absorption without diminished value, must have tended, in various ways, to displace a portion of the metals equivalent to the excess of paper. And it is probable that some part of the tendency to an influx of bullion, which set so strongly into this country during the twelve months from May, 1837, to May, 1838, may have arisen from this cause. But in the autumn of 1838, the Bank of Belgium failed, and there was a severe run upon Lafitte's bank in France, accompanied by a considerable revulsion of commercial credit, the extent and degree of which are attested by the number of bankruptcies in those countries in 1838 and 1839, and by a much more severe pressure on the trade and manufactures in those countries than has been experienced here.

The inevitable effect of the derangement of commercial credit in France and Belgium was an increased value of the precious metals; which, through the medium of their foreign exchanges, would therefore be re-imported, and in part, if not chiefly, from this country.

There appear likewise to have been causes in operation in the interior of Germany tending to an absorption of the metals, but whether to replace paper in discredit, or to answer financial purposes, does not appear. A letter, dated Frankfort, September 8th, 1839, inserted in the Times of the 14th September, alludes to the prevalence of a report "that some bankers were on the point of answering orders from their south German correspondents for a supply of silver coin." There have likewise been, from time to time, other allusions to a demand from the same quarter for silver in exchange for paper.

The Russian government appears to have found an increasing degree of inconvenience from its almost exclusive paper currency, however carefully regulated, for some years past; and accordingly, by an ukaze issued in July last, it has restored the former nominal standard, making the late paper ruble convertible at the rate of three rubles and a half into the silver ruble, which is intrinsically worth 3*s.* 3*d.* With a view to this alteration, there is reason to believe that there has been, chiefly through Amsterdam and Hamburg, and from the interior of Germany and Prussia, a considerable absorption of the metals in the two last years.

In some of the German papers, too, mention is made of the suspension of specie by the Bank of Batavia (Island of Java), caused, it is there said, by an unusual demand for silver for China. The peculiar state of things in China, connected with the proceedings of the government of that country against the contraband trade in opium, may have added to the causes of demand for silver there.

Not any one of the causes enumerated under the foregoing heads would singly have been sufficient to produce such an effect on the exchanges as to have required any very considerable effort on the part of the Bank to counteract it, or, in other words, to have occasioned any difficulty in the regulation of its issues. But, combined, as those causes have been, with the addition, probably, of others too deep-seated and remote to admit of being clearly traced, they required, on the part of the Bank, a considerable vigilance to perceive the indications, and much promptness and firmness of purpose to apply timely and effectual precautionary measures. In what degree the Bank's regulation of its issues can be considered as having originated and aggravated or counteracted and mitigated, the operation of those causes, will form the subject of the following examination.

SECTION 2 *On the regulation of the bank issues in 1838 and 1839*

The state of the circulation, which had been partially disturbed in 1836 and 1837, had, at the commencement of 1838, been restored to a perfectly sound condition.

The position of the Bank, on the average of the three months ending April 3rd, 1838, was, —

		£			£
Circulation	-	18, 987, 000	Securities	-	22, 838, 000
Deposits	-	11, 262, 000	Bullion	-	10, 126, 000
Liabilities	-	30, 249, 000	Assets	-	32, 964, 000

Here the bullion was in the proportion of more than one half to the circulation, and had reached the full amount, which, according to the system professed by the directors in their evidence in 1832, was held to be the desideratum, namely, the proportion of one third of their liabilities, or perhaps, more properly speaking, in the language of that evidence, what was considered as a full currency. But however satisfactory was the position of the Bank, if viewed with reference merely to the perfect solidity and safety of the then existing state of the currency, the accumulation of so large a portion of unproductive stock, while the securities had been so considerably reduced on a comparison with what they had been for some time before, gave rise apparently, in this instance, to the impatience which has been almost uniformly manifested on the part of that establishment on similar occasions, to find means of employing a portion of it productively.

In order to the more ready reference to the position of the Bank of England at the different periods which will be the subject of comment and comparison, a table of the Monthly Gazette returns is inserted.

Average op Three Months

	Circulation	Deposits	Securities	Bullion
1838	£	£	£	£
9th January –	17, 900, 000	10, 992, 000	22, 606, 000	8, 895, 000
6th February –	18, 206, 000	11, 266, 000	22, 569, 000	9, 543, 000
6th March	18, 600, 000	11, 535, 000	22, 792, 000	10, 015, 000
3rd April	18, 987, 000	11, 262, 000	22, 838, 000	10, 126, 000
1st May –	19, 084, 000	11, 006, 000	22, 768, 000	10, 002, 000
29th May	19, 018, 000	10, 786, 000	22, 648, 000	9, 806, 000
26th June	19, 047, 000	10, 426, 000	22, 354, 000	9, 722, 000
24th July	19, 286, 000	10, 424, 000	22, 601, 000	9, 749, 000
21st August	19, 481, 000	10, 298, 000	22, 747, 000	9, 746, 000
18th September	19, 665, 000	10, 040, 000	22, 846, 000	9, 615, 000
16th October –	19, 359, 000	9, 327, 000	22, 015, 000	9, 437, 000
16th November	18, 900, 000	8, 949, 000	21, 171, 000	9, 339, 000
13th December	18, 469, 000	9, 033, 000	20, 707, 000	9, 362, 000

Continued

	Circulation	Deposits	Securities	Bullion
1839				
9th January –	18, 201, 000	10, 315, 000	21, 680, 000	9, 336, 000
5th February –	18, 252, 000	10, 269, 000	22, 157, 000	8, 919, 000
5th March	18, 298, 000	9, 950, 000	22, 767, 000	8, 106, 000
2nd April	18, 371, 000	8, 998, 000	22, 987, 000	7, 073, 000
30th April –	18, 350, 000	8, 107, 000	23, 112, 000	6, 023, 000
20th May	18, 214, 000	7, 814, 000	23, 543, 000	5, 119, 000
25th June	18, 101, 000	7, 567, 000	23, 934, 000	4, 344, 000
23rd July	18, 049, 000	7, 955, 000	24, 905, 000	3, 785, 000
20th August –	17, 969, 000	8, 029, 000	25, 588, 000	3, 265, 000
17th September	17, 960, 000	7, 781, 000	25, 936, 000	2, 816, 000
15th October –	17, 612, 000	6, 734, 000	24, 939, 000	2, 522, 000
12th November	17, 235, 000	6, 132, 000	23, 873, 000	2, 545, 000
12th December	16, 732, 000	5, 952, 000	22, 764, 000	2, 887, 000
1840				
7th January –	16, 366, 000	7, 136, 000	22, 913, 000	3, 454, 000

The opinions of the mercantile part of the public were strongly expressed, through the medium of the newspapers and banking circulars, in favour of efforts to be made by the Bank to get rid of some part of their large stock of bullion. And the directors seem to have participated in these views; inasmuch as they were induced, after having reduced the rate of discount in February, 1838, from 5 to 4 per cent, to adopt the very anomalous proceeding of shipping bullion (gold, it was said) to the United States of America.

It was reported, at the time, that the amount to be shipped would reach 2,000,000*l*.; but, from what cause was not stated, the total sum so sent fell short of 1,000,000*l*. In point of amount, therefore, as the treasure of the Bank appears at that time to have been about 10,000,000*l*., the transmission of a sum under 1,000,000*l*. would not, of itself, call for any special remark, but for two reasons. The one is, that it forms an additional instance of the impatience which, as exhibited on former occasions, the Bank seems to have felt whenever there has been an accumulation of treasure in its coffers, and of its resort to some unusual effort to get rid of it. The other, and more important purpose in here referring to the transaction, is to notice the motive assigned for a proceeding so unusual, namely, to afford to the United States Bank, and the other American banks which had suspended their cash payments, the means of accelerating their resumption of payments in specie, and thus to hasten also a revival of the trade with this country. ①

However desirable it might be that the American banks should fulfil their engagements to their creditors, by paying in specie, it was no part of the business of the Bank of England to hasten their doing so, nor was it for the real interests of the American public that the restoration of cash payments should be thus artificially accelerated; for, in proportion as the exertions of the banks for their resumption, by the reduction of their securities, or, in other words, by the contraction of their loans and discounts, was

---

① The measure was greatly applauded by the numerous persons on both sides the Atlantic who are of opinion that the forcing operations of banks are properly applicable to the direct purpose of promoting the commerce, manufactures, and agriculture of the country, by facility of advances; which must mean, on securities more slender, or at a rate of interest lower, than, with a due regard to the interests of their proprietors and depositors, they would be justified in taking.

superseded by the extraneous assistance then afforded them, so was the ground for their future course less secure: in proportion as they found more facility, and less discredit, in getting over the effects of their previous overbanking, in so far would they be the less likely to be deterred from the repetition of the conduct which had brought them into that predicament. And, as to accelerating the revival of the trade between the United States and this country, and consequently the demand for our manufactures, such being professedly the ulterior purpose of this quixotic measure of the Bank of England, any proceeding on the part of that body, with such a view, is most earnestly and strenuously to be deprecated and reprobated.

The trade of this country requires no such fostering and forcing process, by operations of the Bank of England, or any other banks, in its behalf. An improvement, produced by such means, cannot be sound, and still less can the Bank which professes to hold out such artificial means and resources to trade be considered to be under salutary or safe regulation. It is neither more nor less than a system of officious interference, unbottomed on anything like correct principle, and coming properly, therefore, under the designation of mere quackery.

The result, indeed, proved to be so; inasmuch as the United States Bank, had it not received the countenance and aid of the Bank of England, would not have been in a condition so soon to renew its reckless course, and would not, in all probability, have been enabled to aid and abet the southern and western banks in their preposterous attempts to obstruct artificially the legitimate operation of supply and demand in the article of cotton; an attempt which, in its failure, recoiled with especial force on the parties to it, and was also productive of injury to the commerce of this country, to favour which was the object of the Bank of England in aiding the American banks.

Excepting this eccentric operation of the Bank of England, in the early part of 1838, its movements, during the remainder of that year, were apparently under correct regulation; or perhaps, more properly speaking, the action of the public upon all the elements of the position of the Bank was so equally distributed, that, without any effort on the part of the directors, the bullion, although under a process of gradual reduction, preserved its due proportion to the liabilities, which underwent a reduction, in a nearly corresponding ratio.

By the following comparative statement, from the monthly Gazette returns of the quarterly averages, it will be seen that the state of the currency, as exhibited by those returns, from March, 1838, to January, 1839, varied little, if at all, from what it would have done if the issue of the Bank notes had been under separate management, and made to vary with the demand for gold.

	Circulation	Deposits	Liabilities	Securities	Bullion	Assets
Apr. 3rd, 1838,	18.987, 000	11.262, 000	30, 239, 000	22, 838, 000	10, 126, 000	32, 964, 000
Jan. 9th, 1839,	18, 201, 000	10, 315, 000	28, 516, 000	21, 680, 000	9, 336, 000	31, 016, 000
Decrease	786, 000	947, 000	1, 723, 000	1, 158, 000	790, 000	1, 948, 000

According to this comparison, the circulation had, within a difference not worth noticing, of 4000*l*., decreased in the exact proportion of the decrease of the bullion. The *proportion*, however, of bullion to the liabilities had been highest, and the amount of securities lowest, at the time of the return of the 21st December, 1838, when they stood thus, —

		£			£
Circulation	-	18,469,000	Securities	-	20,707,000
Deposits	- -	9,033,000	Bullion	- -	9,362,000
		27,502,000			30,069,000

According to the principle on which the actual amount in each month is computed from the three preceding averages, the securities were at their lowest point in November, 1838, when they are reckoned to have been about 20,300,000*l*. There is nothing, therefore, in the position of the Bank thus far that can, in any way, be considered to have been indicative of any excess in the circulation; meaning by the term excess such an enlargement of the issues beyond the due proportion to its bullion as to be in itself an originating cause of a depression of the exchanges, and of the consequent efflux of bullion. It is, accordingly, from this time, and from this state of the securities, that the question arises, how far the management, such as it has been found to be, was calculated to aggravate, and did aggravate, the tendency to an efflux of bullion: such efflux having been the proximate cause of the inconvenient pressure on the money market, which became necessary in order to counteract that drain. And also, how far the measures taken by the Bank to stop the drain were judiciously chosen.

The reduction which took place in the securities, to the comparatively low amount at which they stood in November, 1838, being so much below that at which they had ranged for some time before, is accounted for by the circumstance that, while several of the securities upon which advances had been made to the Northern and Central Bank, and to the American houses in 1836 and 1837, must have been running off, there was no equivalent supply of fresh ones offering, because the market rate of interest had fallen below the rate charged by the Bank. When the reduction of the Bank rate of discount from 5 to 4 per cent, was announced, in February, 1838, the market rate had fallen on bills of the same description to 3 $\frac{1}{2}$ per cent; and, as the spring advanced, there was a further decline of about $\frac{1}{2}$ per cent. The period when the market rate of interest seems to have been at its lowest point was in the early part of the summer of that year.

Henceforward there seems to have been a tendency to an advance in the rate of interest, although very slow; and until nearly the close of the year it did not reach the Bank rate. By that time, however, it became evident to those who paid any attention to the signs of the times, that events were in progress which should enjoin caution on the part of those whose business it was to regulate the circulation.

The circumstances which, as causes of a probable drain, strongly indicated, towards the close of 1838, the expediency, on the part of the Bank, of keeping a look out a head, and of taking precautionary measures against the highly probable increasing demand for gold, have already been stated, under three separate heads.

These causes were manifesting themselves in combined operation towards the close of 1838, and presented signals, which could not be mistaken, of impending drain on the coffers of the Bank, requiring strong precautionary measures of counteraction. But the directors had before, upon principle, disclaimed to act upon anticipation; and the interests of the proprietors were opposed to so low a state of their securities. Instead, therefore, of reducing them, or at least keeping them down, the Bank met the increasing demand for money (as a rising rate of interest is technically called) by increased facilities to borrowers; inasmuch as, in the periodical notice issued on the 29th of November, advances were offered till the 23rd of January following, at $3\frac{1}{2}$ per cent, per annum, not only upon bills of exchange, to which the former notices were confined, but on Exchequer bills, East India bonds, or other approved securities.

The market rate of interest having, by this time, become rather higher than the Bank rate, this notice of increased facility, so unaccountably timed, inevitably increased the amount of its securities, which, in the course of the following three months, were considerably enlarged. Notwithstanding this increase of the securities—notwithstanding the steady advance in the market rate of interest—notwithstanding the increasing manifestation of the progress of circumstances requiring counteraction by a reduction, which could now be effected only by means much more forcible and inconvenient than would have been requisite a few months sooner, —and above all, notwithstanding that there had been a diminution of upwards of two millions of treasure, the Bank, instead of taking warning, and retracing its steps, by a forcible reduction of its securities, actually, on the 28th of February, 1839, issued a notice offering advances until the 23d of April, and on similar securities, at the same low rates as by the notice of November preceding. And notwithstanding an advance which was still in progress in the market rate of interest, with a declining state of our foreign exchanges, and a consequent increasing drain on its treasure, such was the apparent utter unconsciousness, on the part of the Bank, of approaching disturbance of the circulation, and still more, of circumstances threatening its stability, that not a single step appears to have been taken which had even the semblance of an attempt at precaution, until the 16th of May following, when a notice was issued raising the rate of discount to 5 per cent. The effects of this total disregard of the indications, which prescribed a course totally opposed to that which was pursued, are exhibited in the following comparative view of the position of the Bank.

	Gradation.	Deposits.	Liabilities.	Securities.	Bullion.	Assets.
Dec. 21. 1838,	18, 469, 000	9, 033, 000	27, 502, 000	20, 707, 000	9, 362, 000	30, 069, 000
May 28. 1839,	18, 214, 000	7, 814, 000	26, 028, 000	23, 543, 000	5, 119, 000	28, 662, 000

Here we have the circulation kept up within 250, 000*l*. of what it had been at the close of 1838, while the securities had been increased by upwards of 2, 800, 000*l*. , and the bullion diminished by upwards of 4, 000, 000*l*.

But, in fact, if the amounts of the securities and of the bullion were taken according to computation of what they stood at in the months instead of the quarterly averages, the contrast would be still greater, inasmuch as it would appear that the securities were increased by upwards of 3, 000, 000*l*. , while the bullion had been reduced by upwards of 5, 000, 000*l*.

It is not easy to conceive bow it happened that the Bank should have suffered such a state of things to take place, and to be in progress for six months, with every appearance of a feeling of perfect security. Such apathy under the increase of its securities, while the bullion was fast flowing out, is the more remarkable, since it was, in a two-fold point of view, at variance with what has been understood to be the system by which the Bank professed to be regulated, according to the explanations of that system, in the evidence on the Bank charter in 1832. For it was not only stated that the securities ought not to vary materially in amount, but that it was of importance that the Bank rate of discount should be kept generally above the market rate, *except* in periods of discredit or scarcity of money.

The exception, in my opinion, vitiates the rule; as I shall by and by have occasion to remark; but that is not here the question: because from November, 1838, to May, 1839, there was neither commercial discredit nor any such scarcity of money as to justify, even according to that exception, an increase of securities, by keeping the Bank rate of discount under the market rate, as was the case during the whole of that time. Indeed there can be no stronger evidence of the fact of the Bank rate having been below the market rate, than the very increase of the securities, which, there is reason to believe, were wholly commercial. When at length the continued drain of bullion seems to have roused the directors to a sense of the necessity of adopting some precautionary measures; and when, accordingly, on the 16th of May last, they raised the rate of discount to 5 per cent, this advance which, if it had taken place a few months sooner, might have had some influence in keeping down the securities, had now no such effect; for the obvious reason that the market rate had advanced still more. So unconscious were the directors apparently of the utter inadequacy of this measure, so hesitatingly and tardily applied, that, on the 30th of May, being the usual period for shutting the books for the dividends, a notice was issued from the Bank offering advances at 5 per cent, till the 23rd of July, on the same general description of securities as in the two preceding notices.

There cannot be a better commentary on the shortsightedness which then prevailed in the regulation of the currency than that, within three weeks after the issue of this notice, and while more than one month was unelapsed of the period to which the operation of it was announced to extend, it was found that the demand thence arising for advances on securities was such as must increase the circulation exactly at the time when, from the state of the exchanges, there was an imperative call, then become too urgent to be mistaken, for a decided reduction of it. The following notices were accordingly issued: —

No. 1. — "At a Court of Directors, held 20th June, 1839, Resolved, that the rate of interest on bills of exchange and notes discounted at the Bank of England be 5 $\frac{1}{2}$ per cent, from this day."

No. 2. — "The Governor and Company of the Bank of England do hereby give notice, that all further advances which may be made, in pursuance of the order of the Court of the 30th ult., will be at the rate of per cent., from this day, and that such advances will be made on bills of exchange only."

A considerable sensation in the money market was excited by these notices, inasmuch as by the first of them the charm was broken of the supposed impassable line of 5 per cent; and by the second there was an *exclusion* of securities, other than hills of exchange, such other securities having been *included* in the notice of the 30th of May.

This exclusion had the immediate effect of reducing the price of Exchequer bills, and, indeed, of the public funds generally, by the uncertainty which the holders of them were suddenly thrown into, as to the power of raising money upon them in case of emergency; the resource of application to the Bank being thus cut off. Without, however, entering into the question of the wisdom of these measures, I mention them here as showing how unaware the directors must have been of the force of the causes operating as a drain on their treasure, which was rapidly tending to exhaustion, to have been obliged thus suddenly to adopt a measure so stultifying of that which they had announced only three weeks before. As notwithstanding the unusual steps thus haltingly taken, the drain upon the coffers of the Bank outran them, a measure was announced on the 13th of July, which, if it had been sincerely intended, and consistently carried into operation, was best calculated for the effect proposed.

The measure here alluded to was a notice issued by the Bank of its being ready to receive tenders, on the 17th of July, for the purchase of the annuities known familiarly as the dead weight, to be made either in money or in the 3 or $3\frac{1}{2}$ per cent, stocks. There was a strong suspicion, on the part of the public, that the Bank was not sincere in this announcement of an intention to part with its dead weight; and that it only made the demonstration with a view to make it appear that it was doing all in its power to reduce the circulation, while, in fact, it was not disposed to make any real sacrifice for the purpose. The event has given countenance to that suspicion; for when the time arrived for making the tenders, it became manifest that so high a minimum price had been set by the Bank for these annuities as to afford no chance that the biddings, for any amount worth mentioning, could come up to it. Accordingly nothing was done. The announcement proved to be, as seems to have been intended, a mere bru-tum fulmen; and here a grave charge rests upon the management.

Instead of the plain straightforward course of converting the dead weight securities at a small abatement from the highest nominal value, the directors resorted to the discreditable expedient of applying for assistance to a set of Paris bankers, who, after much hesitation, and much humiliating inquiry, consented to grant it. ① The assistance thus resorted to, and the

① This arrangement transpired about the 24th of July.

accommodation granted, consisted of credits by twelve of the leading firms in Paris to the extent of 50, 000, 000 of francs, or 2, 000, 000*l*. sterling, to be drawn against for account of the Bank of England.

If, after selling a portion of their dead weight, and whatever other convertible public securities they held, with such accompanying restriction upon discounts as might be rendered necessary, in order that the securities should not increase through that channel in proportion as the public securities were diminished, the contraction of the circulation had been still found, although this is highly improbable, insufficient to stop the drain; then, and not till then, as a last resource, in the clear alternative of a suspension of cash payments, which would be the greater evil, would a resort to such an arrangement as that with the Paris bankers have been justifiable.

But this extraneous and extraordinary resource could not, of itself, be relied upon for turning the exchanges, which still were such, as with short intervals of rallying, continued to favour the efflux of bullion. The Bank, therefore, with a view to keep down the applications for discounts, which were still increasing, and thus counteracting its endeavours to contract the circulation, raised, by a notice dated 1st of August, 1838, the rate of discount to 6 per cent.

The lowest amount of the treasure of the Bank was, according to the Gazette returns, on the average of the quarter ending 15th of October, when it appeared to be 2, 525, 000*l*. ; but the lowest actual amount was computed to have been about 2, 300, 000*l*.

There was no further advance of the Bank rate of discount beyond 6 per cent, which seems to have been effectual in keeping a strong pressure on the money market; and this, with the aid of drafts against the credit of the

Paris bankers, appears to have been sufficient, with the quantity of bullion before exported, to stop the further efflux of bullion after the middle of September.

It is, doubtless, a great point gained, and is justly a matter of congratulation for the public, that the imminent danger of suspension of cash payments has been passed; and it must, in fairness, be admitted that, as I have already shown, the circumstances leading to the recent difficulty were not, in their origin, attributable to any undue enlargement of the Bank issues. But the escape has been a narrow one, and attended by circumstances of almost national humiliation in the application of the Bank of England for assistance from France. Credit, indeed, is taken by the Bank of England, for having, although at the risk of suspension, preserved the commerce of the country from the injury to it which might have resulted from earlier and more effectual measures for the contraction of the circulation. But there is every reason to believe that earlier measures for contraction, on the part of the Bank, would have obviated the necessity for more stringent ones later, and that the commerce of the country would now be in a more satisfactory position if the proper legitimate measures for regulating the exchanges had been sooner adopted.

There has been a degree of uncertainty and well-founded apprehension, under the too tardily adopted measures of precaution, which need not, and probably would not, have existed, if the Bank, upon the first indication of a decided demand upon its coffers, had taken measures for reducing the securities, or, at any rate, keeping them down instead of enlarging them as it did.

The Bank of England cannot, in the recent instance of pressure, reasonably charge the country banks with having unduly extended their part of the circulation, so as to counteract the measures of the Bank of England for correcting the exchanges; for it appears by the Gazette returns, that, in the quarter ending 29th September, 1839, there was a reduction of their issues of nearly 1, 200, 000*l*. , while the reduction of the Bank of England issues, in the same interval, was only about 300, 000*l*.

And there is another important consideration which renders the state of jeopardy into which the Bank had fallen still more distinctly referable to omission of early precaution; namely, that the whole of the drain has taken place through the medium of the exchanges, without the slightest extra internal demand, whether from political causes, as in 1831-1832, or from commercial panic and discredit, as in 1825, or more partially by a demand for Ireland as in 1836. On the contrary, instead of a demand for gold from the country, there was, as I understood, through a great part of the summer a tendency to an influx of gold from the country to the London bankers. More than usual, too, it was said, of gold was paid into the bankers' hands by the smaller traders in London, in discharge of the bills on them; and my impression, from what I collected at the time, was that the London bankers paid more gold into the Bank than for internal purposes they took out of it. If so, it should seem that a part of the foreign demand was supplied from the internal circulation of gold, thus proving practically one of the advantages of having a considerable portion of gold as currency, and at the same time leading to the inference that the demand for exportation has been greater than appears by the mere difference in the stock of bullion, as stated in the Gazette returns.

Now, according to the system professed on the part of the Bank, in the examination before the committee on the charter, in 1832, it was stated that although against the effects of political discredit and internal demand, the Bank could not be perfectly secure, *the foreign exchanges could always be rectified without a crisis*[①]: by crisis being understood, as I conceive, a near approach to, but not actual suspension.

How then has it happened that, without wars or revolutions abroad, and without commercial discredit or political convulsion or panic leading to an internal demand for gold, the Bank has not so regulated its issues as to rectify the exchanges which, according to the system propounded in 1832, it would be able to do under any circumstances but those of political discredit or internal panic ?

It is quite clear that no system at all has been followed, and, what is more, no system has existed. The principle which is supposed to have been propounded by the directors in 1832, and which has been reasoned upon in the controversies to which the partial disturbance of the circulation gave rise in 1836-1837, will be found on examination of the terms in which it was announced and explained to be nothing like an intelligible principle. The exceptions and reservations overlay the rule, and leave the management, such as it has been, clear of the charge of inconsistency, simply, because no consistent principle has been laid down for its guidance.

The rule or principle which was understood to be laid down by the evidence of the Bank directors was, that their securities should be kept at a nearly uniform amount, and their bullion at about one third of their liabilities.

Such is the general impression as to the rule supposed to be laid down; but, upon a nearer view of that evidence, it will not be found to bear out that impression. With regard to the supposed rule of keeping the securities

---

① Evidence of J. H. Palmer, Esq., question and answer 673.

even, there is nothing in the evidence from which it can be inferred that it is considered by the Bank as its duty so to keep them. All that appears about the proportion of one third of bullion to the liabilities, is, that when that proportion exists, it is considered to be a full currency, and a desirable state of it; but not a syllable is said of the necessity or expediency of any effort for preserving it, still less for recovering that proportion.

It appears, moreover, upon reference to that evidence, that the directors, conceiving that among the duties of the Bank of England is that of accommodating the commerce and supporting the credit of the country, consider themselves bound, whenever there is a pressure for money, to come in aid of the mercantile interests. Thus it occurs that, as soon as anything like a pressure for money, or simply a rise of the market rate of interest takes place beyond what happens to be the Bank rate, and which pressure for money, if allowed to take its course, is calculated to correct the exchanges, the Bank, upon the plea of accommodation to the commerce of the country, presents a source, through the medium of discounts, which effectually counteracts that process. If Exchequer bills, under such circumstances, are sold by the Bank, the reduction, thus effected, of the securities, on one hand, is compensated, and sometimes more than counterbalanced, on the other hand, by an increase of discounts; and there is hence an increase of securities at the Bank, precisely when there ought to be a diminution of them. This assumption of a duty, on the part of the Bank, adds greatly to the difficulty and delicacy of its position.

It is difficult enough to reconcile, in all cases, the interests of the proprietors with the interests of the public; but when, in addition to these two sometimes conflicting interests, the claims of merchants seeking loans or discounts are allowed as a matter of right, it is no wonder that no consistent rule is followed; or rather, I might say, that there is some consistency in always increasing the securities when, according to the system professed, they ought to be reduced. Indeed, it is obvious that this must generally, if not always, be the case, inasmuch as, among the three branches of duty which the Bank thus has to perform, the increased applications for loan or discount are always favourable to the interests of the proprietors. The applicants, therefore, for discount, being supposed to represent the commerce of the country, are placed in the fore ground as opposed to the reduction of securities, or, in other words, to an effectual contraction of the circulation, when the interests of the public, in the maintenance of the convertibility of the paper, require it.

In order to avoid the possibility of my misstating the rule, and the exceptions and qualifications, I will quote those parts of Mr. Horsley Palmer's evidence that relate to the points in question, constituting the whole of the grounds on which have proceeded the controversies that have more or less occupied the attention of the public respecting the conduct of the Bank during the last four years. In the extracts from, and comments upon, that evidence, which I am about to make, I wish it to be distinctly understood that I do not, in the slightest degree, propose to detract from the justly merited encomiums which have been bestowed on that evidence, as containing an admirable and luminous explanation of the working of the system of the Bank in all its parts. It is only on one or two points of principle that I venture to dissent from the views stated in that evidence, as they are of great importance in the question of management. Some years having elapsed since the evidence was given, every allowance is to be made for possible changes or modifications of opinion from subsequent experience.

But consideration for the commerce of the country has, avowedly, on the part of the Bank, so much influenced its proceedings, in its very irregular management of the currency within the last four years, that, whether Mr. Palmer adheres or not to the doctrine expounded by him in his evidence, it must be looked upon as having been adopted by the Bank.

The first question asked relating to the principle of regulation was in the following terms (the italics are not in the original, and are intended to mark the passages which appear to me to be deserving of special notice): —

"72. What is the principle by which, in ordinary times, the Bank is guided in the regulation of its issues? —Answer. The principle, with reference to the period of a full currency, and consequently, a par of exchange, by which the Bank is guided in the regulation of its issues (excepting under special circumstances) is, to invest and retain in securities bearing interest, a given proportion of the deposits and the value received for the notes in circulation; the remainder being held in coin and bullion: the proportions which seem to be *desirable under existing circumstances* may be stated at about two thirds in securities, and one third in bullion: the circulation of the country, so far as the same may depend on the Bank, *being subsequently regulated by the action of the foreign exchanges.*"

Mr. Palmer, in a subsequent answer (293), said, "I wish the committee to understand, that when I used the terms two thirds and one third, I meant to allude to the period of a full currency, prior to the commencement of a demand; the progress of a demand reduces the proportion; *but when the demand ceases, and the exchanges reassume a favourable character*, then we are in a progressive state to reassume our proportions."

Hence it appears, that when the proportions are reduced by a demand for bullion, there is no effort on the part of the Bank to restore those proportions, trusting to a spontaneous turn of the exchanges for a return of the bullion.

A rule or principle like this, applied only to ordinary times, and guarded by the reservations which I have marked with italics, amounts, it will be observed, to little or nothing. The witness, however, after explaining that the liabilities included the deposits, is further asked, —

"78. According to your description of the prin-ciple upon which the affairs of the Bank are conducted, do not the directors of the Bank of England possess the power of regulating the whole circulation of the country? —Answer. The Bank is very desirous not to exercise any power, but to leave the public to use the power which they possess of returning bank paper for bullion."

"79. Would the exchanges be corrected if the amount of currency was left wholly in the hands of the public? —Answer. *They have been principally corrected under that management.*"

"80. Is the Bank exposed to no inconvenience by waiting to have the correction applied in this manner, in preference to itself interfering, by that power, to diminish the circulation in case of a fall of the exchange? —Answer. —No; provided they are *adequately supplied with bullion* when the exchanges are at par, and which "proportion I have stated to be about one third."

"81. Does not the Bank, if it thinks proper, possess the power of extending the currency, or of diminishing it, without waiting for the interference of the public? —Answer. It has the power."

"82. Would the Bank forcibly contract their issues by a sale of securities during an unfavourable course of exchange with foreign countries; and would they forcibly extend their issues by the purchase of securities, when the exchange was favourable ? — Answer. I think not, *except under special circumstances.* "

"83. You mean to say that the Bank would not forcibly do that, but that it would leave it to the public to act upon the Bank, and produce the effect at which it would arrive? —Answer. I do. "

"It appears, by the accounts before the committee, that, for the four last years (1827 to 1832) the amount of securities varied very little; do you consider it important in the management to keep the securities at nearly the same amount? — Answer. *As nearly as the same can be managed.* "

The fact noticed in the last question, namely, that the securities had varied little during the four years preceding May, 1832, is material; because a reference to it naturally led to the supposition that the comparative equableness of the amount had been the result of management, and had, according to answer 79, *corrected the foreign exchanges*, under considerable variations in the amount of bullion; and this impression added great weight to the announcement of the principle by which it was supposed to be effected. But in truth, the Bank was nearly passive as to all the elements of its position①, in those four years, with the exception of

① The expression of elements of the position of the Bank is, I am aware, open to criticism as being an unusual application of the terms. My excuse for the employment of them is, that I cannot readily find others which so compendiously and clearly convey the meaning which I here attach to them; a meaning which must often be referred to. By the position of the Bank, I mean its situation or condition with reference to the four circumstances entering into the view of it as presented to the public by the monthly returns, namely; the circulation and the deposits on the one side, and the securities and the bullion on the other. Those four circumstances I designate as the elements, and the state of the Bank, as composed of those elements, I consider as its position. With this explanation, it will be found, that although this use of the terms is somewhat strained, it has the redeeming quality of being concise and distinct.

some remittances of silver to Paris in exchange for gold. The securities were preserved from great variation by two causes: 1st, the very large stock of bullion before the drain commenced. 2nd, the market rate of interest never rose above the Bank rate of 4 per cent.① The applications, therefore, for discount were on a restricted scale, and the conflicting duty imposed upon itself by the Bank of accommodating the commerce of the country did not come into play.

I have before remarked at some length upon the state of the circulation in those four years, and upon the apparently satisfactory working of the supposed rule.

It appears by the following answer, that the term "*regulation* of issues, according to the foreign exchanges," ought rather to have been that, in such cases the foreign exchanges *regulate the issues*; but, even in those cases, there must be an implied assumption that the securities are unvaried.

"122. How do you regulate your issues according to the foreign exchanges? —Answer. By the notes being returned for gold or silver for export."

"123. Do you regulate them from the returns you have of what the foreign exchanges are, or from the action which takes place upon the Bank? —Answer. The action which takes place upon the Bank."

"124. Do you find that the alteration in the action upon the Bank is simultaneous with an alteration of the rate of the foreign exchanges; and

① Mr. Gurney, in his evidence, *Bank Charter Report*, 1832. — "The value (interest) of money was $2\frac{1}{2}$ per cent, in London up to the end of 1830; then it rather suddenly jumped up to 4 per cent; and it has ranged between 3 per cent, and 4 per cent, ever since, rather tending downwards to 3 per cent."

that it is the case invariably ? — Answer. Certainly. "

Then comes a question, the answer to which is worthy of notice.

"125. Do you not sometimes anticipate the actual action upon the Bank, by the demand for gold, when you see there is a tendency in the foreign exchanges to produce that action ? —Answer. No; we wait for the actual demand. "

The disclaimer, therefore, of the directors, in 1836, of being bound to anticipate and consequently to reduce, instead of extending, the securities, from a view of circumstances which they already foresaw must lead to a considerable demand for gold, was perfectly consistent with the practice here explained.

The committee, after several intermediate questions on other points, very naturally come to inquire how the Bank manages to keep its securities nearly even.

"148. You stated that the principle was to keep the amount of securities in your hands nearly the same; do you, in order to effect that, restrict your discounts upon the bills of private individuals? —Answer. No. "

"149. Does it ever occur that the amount of private bills accumulates beyond its average amount? —Answer. Yes. "

"150. In such case, how do you keep the whole amount of your securities at the same amount? —Answer. By a sale of part of the government securities. "

"151. Then, when you said that you have never forcibly contracted the amount of currency, you do not mean to exclude your selling securities in the market, in case the securities accumulate in your hands? — Answer. If there be a demand for an increase of the issues upon commercial bills, the Bank find the means of supplying the demand by a sale of part of their government securities[①], thereby *providing that the amount of their securities be not increased, but merely their character changed.*"

This last answer is the only one which is not so guarded by qualifications as to convey nothing like a distinct rule. Here it is clearly admitted, as the duty of the Bank, in regulating its issues, with a view to correcting the exchanges, to sell government securities corresponding in amount with the increase through the medium of commercial bills and it remains with the Bank to explain why this was not done, as there is no question that the resort to such sales, in sufficient amount, accompanied by an advance in its rate of discount, would have superseded the unfortunate necessity of recourse to the humiliating expedient of assistance from the Paris bankers.

The conduct, indeed, of the Bank in July last, with reference to the dead weight, is quite decisive of glaring inconsistency with this clearly laid down rule; and never was there occasion more urgent for adhering to it. For how did the matter stand? By the public notice from the Bank, inviting tenders for the dead weight, there is the most unequivocal proof that, in the opinion of the directors, a sale of a part of those securities, sufficient to meet the increase of commercial bills, was desirable for a contraction of the currency, with a view to abate or stop the rapid drain on their coffers. If there had been no offers, or, in other words, if those securities had proved upon that trial not to be marketable, the inability to sell would have been an available plea. Or, even if the terms offered, or likely to be obtained, had been so ruinously low as to have entailed a heavy loss upon the terms on which the annuities had been purchased from the public,

---

① In answer to some previous questions, Mr. Palmer had stated that the dead weight annuities were marketable securities.

there might have been something like an excuse, although not a valid one, for hesitation in effecting the sale.

But there was no such excuse. The securities were ascertained to be perfectly marketable on terms which left a large profit on the purchase, and it was only a question of a quarter, or at the utmost, of half a year's purchase, that stood in the way of realising a sufficient amount. The Bank is, therefore, reduced to this dilemma; the conversion of a part of these securities was, or was not, desirable with a view to the due regulation of the currency. If it was not desirable for that purpose, why announce an intention of sale, for there could be no other purpose in it? If it was desirable for the public interest, with reference to the state of the currency, how can the difference of a quarter or half year's purchase, a difference which could not in the slightest degree affect the public interest, be urged as a plea for foregoing the sale? It is hard, indeed, to believe that, on this most important occasion, the interests of the public were not sacrificed to the supposed interests of the proprietors; I say supposed, because it may well be doubted whether the alternative resorted to, of assistance from France, will not, in all its consequences, prove more injurious to the interests of the proprietors than the sale of even a considerable portion of the dead weight.

SECTION 3 *Doctrine of the supposed duty of the Bank of England to accommodate the trade, and to support the commercial credit of the country*

Previously to giving the questions and answers which relate to the supposed duty of the Bank to extend its discounts in periods of pressure on the money market, it may be desirable to point out an ambiguity in the use of the term accommodation, as applied to banking.

Its original and legitimate signification applies simply to the *convenience* of banks as places of safe deposit for money, and for the convenience of making payments by cheques; also for the transmission of sums for account of its depositors to different parts; and, in some cases, for finding suitable investments. The safety and facility with which the banks answer the several purposes of convenience, required by their customers, form the measure of the *accommodation* for which they are instituted and supported: and that is the only sort of accommodation which they are bound to afford *as a duly.*

The terms upon which the accommodation is afforded are commonly determined by competition, and consist, for the most part, in the power which the banks have, by consent or custom, of employing on discount or loan such part of the monies lodged with them as, upon an average, or according to stipulation, is not likely to be called for by the depositors. It is, in these cases, essential to the bankers, as remuneration for their trouble, and the expenses of their establishment, to lend the surplus funds on available securities. It is their *interest* to lend as much as they can venture to do with safety; but it is no part of their *duty*, and it is only a part of their functions, because they could not otherwise so well accommodate their depositors.

With regard to banks which issue promissory notes, the privilege is granted them by the state for the purpose of having a more convenient circulation than that of gold, and equally safe, for payments of 5*l.* and upwards; and the manner in which the banks obtain a profit on the issue, is through loans or discounts. They lend for the interest to be derived, and not as a part of their duty. ①

It is common, when a person applies for discount or loan, to speak of his being accommodated with the advance; and the facility of borrowing is no doubt an accommodation to those who have occasion to avail themselves of their securities or credit, for the purpose of raising money upon them. Hence a vague notion prevails, that when the accommodation of banking is talked of, it is supposed to be an institution for the purpose of enabling persons to borrow②, instead of being merely for the purpose of affording safe custody, and more convenient channels for the employment of deposits, than the owners could conveniently find for themselves; or of administering to the public a convenient and safe substitution of paper money for coin.

The effect of this vague notion of accommodation is, that there seems to be a claim of right, or something very like it, on the part of merchants and traders for loans from bankers, with an implied assumption that such applications should be complied with, in cases where the wants of the applicants may indeed be urgent, but where also the bankers have not the

---

① Bankers may, indeed, enter into stipulations, or allow it to be understood, with persons who give them their business as depositors, that a certain amount of advances, either on personal security or by the way of discount, will be granted to such depositors; and so far it may be of the nature of a duty towards such parties. But prudent bankers take care not to commit themselves to stipulations of that kind, so as to interfere with the *paramount duly* of fulfilling their own engagements. And at any rate, this is widely different from the notion that banks are institutions for the benefit of borrowers.

② There are striking instances of this notion in the evidence before the committee on the Bank of Ireland charter, some of the witnesses examined making it a matter of serious charge against that bank, that it would not always give sufficient accommodation, or rather the accommodation required, in the way of discount for other banks; while it may be observed, by the way, that it is rather questionable whether it is quite right or creditable that one bank should apply to another bank for discount at all, except under peculiar circumstances, which might carry the excuse for such a course along with them.

money to lend without endangering their ability to fulfil their engagements — their primary and paramount duty to their depositors, and the holders of their notes. It is commonly said on such occasions, that the banks, and more especially the Bank of England, are bound to make an effort, and depart from their usual course of prudence, for what, in the phraseology of this doctrine, is called the support of commercial credit.

In the following extracts, the judiciousness of the answers, *saving only the exceptions of discredit*, contrasts strongly with the glaring misconception which the questions involve of the object of discounts in the business of banking.

"173. Do you not hold that the discount of private paper is one of the worst means which the Bank, as a bank of issue, can adopt for re-gulating its notes? —Yes; provided they are adequately supplied with other marketable securities."

"174. Upon what grounds do you form that opinion? — Because *such a system materially interferes with the action of the private bankers of London*; and further, it tends in my opinion to *that extension of the circulation which might prove prejudicial to the Bank.*"

"175. Then your answer applies only to a state in which discounts can be easily obtained from private bankers? —It applies to those periods."

"176. Would it not have a *considerable effect upon the commerce of the country*, if there were a scarcity of cash for discount in the market, and the Dank of England did not come in to supply that deficiency? — I know no scarcity, as affecting the circulation of the Bank of England except discredit, and such as may arise out of the foreign demand for bullion in times of an unfavourable exchange."

"177. In case of *a deficiency of capital for carrying on the concerns of the country*, and that it cannot be procured from private bankers or brokers, would not *the aid of the Bank of England, in discounting bills, be very advantageous to the country*? —I do not know what is meant by a deficiency of capital as respects the Bank. *In a time of discredit*, it is extremely desirable that the Bank should grant *the requisite aid to the public by an increased issue of their notes*; and there are times when the Bank may afford considerable facilities to the commercial interests through discounts, by changing a part of their Exchequer bills into securities of the former character."

"178. Then you think that the Bank of England should be a bank of discount only in cases of emergency? —I think so, with the exceptions above referred to."

"179. Is not the *accommodation of discount to the commerce of the country* one of the main objects for which the Bank has ever been instituted, *and for which all banks are instituted*? 1 —As an exclusive bank of issue in the capital, it appears to me that it cannot beneficially conduct a discount account to any great extent with individuals, except in times of discredit. *When the circulation is full, a competition with the bankers would, in all probability, lead to excess, in addition to other difficulties which would occur in the attempt, on the part of the Bank of England, to regulate their issues through that channel.*"

There cannot be a more striking commentary than the concluding sentence of this last answer, on the advances by the Bank to the money-brokers in the autumn and winter of 1835-1836. The circulation was then *full*, and the competition with the bankers, by this use of the extra deposits, as they were called, led to excess, not in the issues of bank notes, but in the extension of credit; and thence the difficulties which occurred in the attempt on the part of the Bank to regulate their issues *through that channel*, namely, of the discount market.

It is impossible to convey in clearer terms than in the following answers, the legitimate functions of the Bank of England, and in the questions, the doctrine of the ultra currency theory.

"181. What do you consider as the principal function which it is the duty of the Bank to per-form? —Answer. To furnish the paper money with which the public act around them, and to be a place of safe deposit for the public money, or for the money of individuals who prefer a public body like the Bank to private bankers."

"182. Are not those functions the functions of a government rather than a private company? —Answer. That is for the government to determine."

"183. Then the benefit conferred is merely the substitution of paper money in the place of specie, and not from *accommodation to the industrious classes.* —Answer. I think the Bank cannot satisfactorily offer that accommodation while their circulation is so employed by other establishments."

"184. What establishments do you allude to? —Answer. The bankers of London and the country."

"193. Do not you think that the Bank of England would have very little answered the purposes of its establishment, *if it had not been prepared to give circulation to the commerce of the country by means of those discounts*? —Answer. I hold it to be impossible that the Bank *can ever with any propriety issue upon discounts below the market rate.*"

Then, however, comes a question, the answer to which conveys the assumption on the part of the Bank to consider as one of its functions that of upholding the credit of the country.

"198. You do not mean to say that one of the objects of the Bank of England is not to afford accommodation to the commercial classes, but what you mean to say is, that you do not consider it advisable that the Bank should found their issue upon commercial discounts, that that is a bad means of establishing the issue; but that, under peculiar circumstances of pressure, the Bank may come forward and assist most materially by discounting private paper? —Answer. That is precisely my view. The Bank of England is required to provide a requisite supply of paper money for the average circulation of the sphere on which it acts, and to uphold public and private credit when called upon. When commercial credit is affected, it is in such times that the credit of a great body like the Bank of England is available, and has the power to uphold the credit of the country."

This self-imposed duty of the Bank to uphold the credit of the country would, in my opinion, be found, under many conceivable circumstances, to be incompatible with the maintenance of its own credit, that is, with the fulfilment of its own engagements to pay its notes in coin.

Mr. Palmer, in a subsequent examination, gave the following explanation of the main points of the principle which he had wished to convey in his former evidence.

"477. In answer to a question by the committee, you are supposed to have stated it as your opinion that the Bank of England ought to confine itself to public transactions and the management of the currency of the country, and not to interfere with the general commercial discounts in the metropolis: is that your opinion, or do you wish to give any explanation upon that answer. — Answer. With reference to the answers which I have given in the former examination, I am apprehensive of having been misunderstood with respect to the opinion I entertain of the functions of the Bank in London, as a bank for commercial discounts; my intention was to impress upon the committee an opinion, that in ordinary times, the leading functions of the Bank of England have been to furnish, upon a stated principle, an adequate supply of paper money convertible into coin and bullion upon demand, and to act as a bank for safe deposit of public and private money; and in so acting, that it is not deemed to be desirable to attempt to regulate the amount of issues of the Bank in London through commercial discounts, but that there are occasions and circumstances when the functions of the Bank, as a bank for commercial discounts in the capital, have been, and ever must be, of the first importance to the country. *The reasons which appear to me to exist against the regulation of the amount of issues through commercial discounts in London arise from the magnitude of the deposits in the possession of the bankers of London and other individuals seeking employment with which the Bank ought not, in my opinion, to interfere.* The Bank fixing a public rate of interest, at which it may be willing to discount all approved bills of a given description, and being the only body issuing money adlibitum, within the sphere of the circulation of such bills, thereby fixes the maximum of the rate of interest during the existence of such notice, and consequently, all persons having money already in existence to employ, must necessarily offer to lend it under the Bank's public rate, except in times of actual scarcity or deficiency of money currency. If the Bank were required to hold no other securities than commercial bills, they would be under the necessity of acting in common with all other parties, viz., by competition in the purchase of bills of exchange at the existing market rate of interest. *It is that competition with private bankers and individuals in London which seems to me to be so objectionable*; and if the plan hitherto acted upon answers the public objects, I can see no benefit in a change. In order to place that part of my opinion clearly before the committee, which has reference to the period when the action of the Bank, as a bank for commercial discounts in London, is one of the greatest public importance, I beg to state that those functions of the Bank are exhibited when a scarcity of money, or discredit, exists in the London commercial money market. The market rate of interest will then advance to that previously fixed by the Bank, as their public rate for commercial bills, which will occasion such bills to be immediately sent to the Bank for discount. The Bank then becomes the *main support of the commerce of the country*, A material difficulty exists, under the present system, of affording, during the period of a scarcity of money, that quantity of issue which the commerce of the country might in such time require, viz. the limitation by law of the rate of interest to 5 per cent, per annum; it being evident that, in the event of the foreign exchanges being adverse, the Bank might not only be under the necessity of raising the rate of interest to that *maximum*, but afterwards, as the only resource left, *be compelled to limit the quantity or description of bills to be tendered for discount*; *either of which last measures would be equally detrimental to the commerce of the country.*"

Here is the same assumption on the part of the Bank of a duty *to support the commerce of the country.* There was, indeed, so far a reason for it under the circumstances at the time when this evidence was given, that the usury law then existed in all its rigour and impolicy. Still the opinion is expressed in the foregoing evidence, that limiting the quantity or description of bills to be tendered for discount would be detrimental to the commerce of the country.

This doctrine is specious and popular, and the motives of the directors, in being guided by it, may be praiseworthy, but it is essentially unsound and unsafe; and as long as it is entertained and acted upon, at *least without a very much larger amount of bullion than has hitherto been retained*, there can be no consistency in the regulation of the issues, nor can there be any security against a frequent recurrence of the danger of suspension of cash payments.

The commerce of the country is, happily, of such vigorous growth, both in its root and branches, as not to require for its protection, from the adverse contingencies inseparable from all trade, the special protection of the Bank of England; the prospect of protection so held out being neither more nor less than a resource against the effects of overtrading.

Now in all cases of overtrading, the parties, as they took the chance of gain on capital beyond their own, are bound to abide the inconvenience, or loss, incidental to disappointment in the continued use of borrowed capital, after the expiration of the time for which it was lent. An advance in the rate of discount is, doubtless, disadvantageous, being either a deduction from profit, or an aggravation of loss to those merchants and traders who are obliged to borrow (for discounting is a form of borrowing) when there is an advance in the rate of interest; but, on the other hand, there is a corresponding advantage on a fall in the rate of discount, and this is among the inevitable elements of uncertainty attending all engagements for future payment, in cases in which the means of discharging pecuniary engagements involve a necessity for the conversion of securities. ①

The case of the increased issues of the Bank, at the close of 1825, when its treasure was reduced to the lowest ebb, is commonly adduced as an instance of beneficial interference in support of credit; such enlarged issue being at decided variance from the principle which enjoins contraction of paper in proportion to the demand for bullion. The circumstances of that case were so peculiar, the impending and paramount evil of suspension was so imminent, that resort to some *desperate* remedy might be considered to be justifiable. And as the foreign demand for gold had ceased, and the internal demand had arisen chiefly from the discredit of the country circulation, there were reasonable grounds for anticipating a degree of benefit which might be allowed to outweigh the objections on general grounds to such a measure. But the precedent is a dangerous one, and rather than leave to any directors the power of judging of the propriety of departing from the general rule which should determine the amount of their issues of paper, it were better that some other provision were hereafter made (supposing any such provision necessary, which assuredly I do not admit) against the occurrence of a similar crisis; a crisis, however, which could not have occurred at that time, nor would be likely to occur again, without previous mismanagement, in a great enlargement of the securities held by the Bank, precisely at the time when the propriety of diminishing them had been urgently indicated.

---

① As far as relates to our foreign commerce, the utmost probable fluctuations of the rate of interest are of very inferior importance, and a source of much less uncertainty, and perplexity, and risk of loss, than variations in any marked degree of the exchanges, such as occurred in this country during the war, such as have recently occurred in the United States, and such as are perpetually occurring in the states of South America.

There is, indeed, no point connected with the regulation of the currency upon which I have a stronger conviction—a conviction in which I am fortified by the concurrence of several of my mercantile friends who unite a knowledge of principle with great experience in business—than that the directors of an establishment, which is entrusted with the administration of a sound paper circulation ought not to be allowed to consider themselves at liberty to depart from the strict rules laid down for regulating it, in consequence of any views which they may entertain, of the claims of the mercantile interests for accommodation, or of inconvenience to trade from not regarding them.

There is, moreover, reason to believe that the trade and manufactures of the kingdom would be generally in a sounder state if they depended less upon what is called banking accommodation; and that they have been more injured than benefited on every occasion in which (with the single exception under the special circumstances just now referred to of 1825) the Bank has departed from its own supposed rule of regulating its issues by the exchanges, in order, as alleged, to prevent inconvenience or discredit to the commerce of the country. To prevent inconvenience to the commerce of the country, from an undue contraction of the circulation, was the professed object of applying the extra deposits on the West India loan to an increase of securities in 1835; a measure which, as I have already had occasion to observe when treating of that period, contributed in no small degree to the undue enlargement, and subsequently to the contraction and disturbance, of commercial credit in 1836-1837. And the interference of the Bank in behalf of the Northern and Central Bank, and of the American houses in 1836, however well intended and however it may have averted heavy losses to eminent firms at the time, may be considered, in several points of view, as having tended to aggravate the recent mischief arising to the trading and manufacturing interests from the extravagance of American banking. The effect of that interference was, to skin over the sore in American trade and banking, and so to allow the constitutional disease (of abuse of credit) to proceed to a greater extent and depth, till it should break out with increased virulence, as in the recent instance; not to mention the anomalous position in which, in consequence of that interference, the Bank of England was placed, of having to send an agent to America to collect the debts which it had made its own, and of being thus placed in intimate communication, which was anything but desirable, with the United States' Bank. Among the effects of that communication seems to have been the transmission of bullion thither in the spring of 1838, upon which I have already remarked. In short, I am not aware of any instance (with the single exception already noticed) in which, however well intended the deviation of the Bank from its straight course, with a view *to benefit commerce*, has not been attended with more harm than good to the trade which it has been its professed object to support.

SECTION 4 *Result of the review of the management of the bank in 1838 and 1839*

As the result of the impartial review in the preceding pages of the management of the Bank, in as far as a judgment can be formed of it from its public measures, and from the monthly Gazette returns of its liabilities and assets on the average of the three months preceding, the following appear to be the main points open to criticism.

1. The impatience manifested at the commencement of 1838 to reduce

the stock of bullion.

2. The forcible operation towards the close of 1838 for the purpose of extending its securities by increased facilities for loans, at a time when the market rate of interest was rising above the Bank rate, and when the proceedings of the banks in America (particularly with reference to the cotton trade), and the state of commercial credit on the Continent, were calculated to suggest, as a measure of precaution on the part of the Bank, rather to reduce than to extend its securities.

3. The continuing, during nearly six months, namely, till 16th May, 1839, the same relatively low rate of interest, and the extended facilities for loans, notwithstanding the continued rise in the market rate of interest, and notwithstanding the notoriety of the large importations of American securities then in progress, the negociation of which was of course greatly promoted by the comparatively low rate of interest and discount charged by the Bank. The effect of this state of things being, that the Bank had by the end of May lost 5 millions of treasure, while its securities had increased by upwards of 3 millions.

4. The inefficiency of the measures taken between May and July to stop the further progress of the drain.

5. The hesitation and inconsistency of the proceedings of the Bank in respect of the dead weight.

6. The recourse to the bankers of Paris for assistance: a measure, the resort to which could not be justified on any ground but that of its being considered as the only remaining resource against a suspension of cash payments; and doubtless, it was the lesser evil; but so discreditable an expedient ought not to have been resorted to until the dead weight, or a considerable portion of it, had been converted, and such conversion found

to be ineffectual.

The general conclusion, with reference to the management of the Bank being, that while, à priori, the inference is irresistible, that there must be something essentially erroneous in the system or in the regulation by which, in a state of profound peace, and without any counteraction from the country banks, the Bank of England should have sustained so narrow an escape from suspension of cash payments; so it appears, by a reference to particulars, that the measures of the Bank were characterised by anything but a due and vigilant regard for the interests of the public in the maintenance of the convertibility of Bank paper, or for its own credit, which has been much impaired in public estimation both at home and abroad, by its resort for aid to the bankers of Paris.

SECTION 5 *Vindication of the bank from some groundless charges*

While, in pursuance of the design upon which this work has been from its origin conducted—an essential part of which has been to give an account of the state of the circulation, with such remarks as were suggested by a view of the mode in which it had been regulated by the Bank of England—I have found myself under the necessity of animadverting on the management of the Bank, such as it has appeared, on grounds open to the public; I have now to offer some remarks upon charges, very groundless, in my opinion, which have been brought against it.

This I feel myself bound to do, not only in fairness to that establishment, but also with a view to point out what appear to me to be very erroneous impressions, mixed up with those charges of the effects of variations in the elements of the position of the Bank, on the rate of interest, and on prices, and on the connection between the rate of interest and prices — impressions which, being extensively entertained by persons who take great pains in inculcating them upon others, and who are likely to take an active part in the forthcoming discussions in parliament on the subject of banking, have an importance which might otherwise not belong to them.

Such is the prevalence, almost universal, of the currency theory, namely, of the theory which ascribes to the regulation of the Bank issues a direct influence, as an originating cause, in producing great variations in the prices of commodities, as well as in the rate of interest and in the markets for shares, that the most exaggerated and extravagant declamations on the power exercised by the Bank directors in enlarging or narrowing the circulation, and thus raising or depressing all markets ad libitum, are uttered with the most perfect confidence, and are generally allowed to pass current without question. And perhaps they would not be worth questioning, were it not that the implicit belief in them may be calculated to he attended with a practical influence in the discussion on the renewal of the Bank of Ireland charter, and probably on banking generally in the United Kingdom, in the course of the present session. As a specimen of the extravagance of exaggeration, introduced as it is into one of our most respectable journals, I have preserved, and now insert, the following extract from the City article in the *Morning Chronicle* of the 3rd of June, 1839.

"In a commercial country like Great Britain, the management of the paper circulation is necessarily one of the most important trusts that it is possible to repose in any body of men, for the most vital interests of the community depend on its proper administration. Our present system of national banking is, however, replete with errors, which it is to be hoped the legislature will in course of time remove. The charter of the Bank of England has not many more years to run, while the term of that of Ireland has already expired, and the endeavours, therefore, of the commercial interests of the sister kingdom are strongly exerted to prevent the renewal of the monopoly which it is declared has been, and now is, one of the greatest obstacles to Irish prosperity. The evils to which we allude are in the conflicting motives between public and private advantage, which, it cannot be denied, must more or less exist in the minds of those who have the direction of the banks of England and Ireland. In both countries they are for the most part influential, wealthy men, who carry on private operations on an extensive scale, and to whom, therefore, the rise or fall in the value of commodities is a most material consideration. Individually, perhaps, they are no worse than others would be, similarly situated but it is the fact of their being so circumstanced as to be obliged to choose between duty and interest, that forms one of the strongest arguments in favour of the separation of the issue of paper from the rest of the banking business. In Ireland, notwithstanding that operations are on a less extensive scale, and that the country is poor, the mischiefs arc of a grosser nature and more severely felt than here, where, on account of the disasters which have already ensued from Bank mismanagement, the eyes of the people are opened, and the manoeuvres of the Bank parlour being severely scrutinised into, the projected evils are either nipped in the bud, or, from previous preparations, fall comparatively harmless upon the mercantile community. A check of this sort is beginning, however, to be apparent likewise in Ireland, and the defects of the system have begun to be pointed out by many of the Irish papers. The Bank directors have it in their power to create a rise or fall in the price of most articles of trade, by an expansion or contraction of the circulation; and being themselves, moreover, greatly interested in the slightest fluctuations, they must, as a matter of course, according to the laws of human nature, lean to those measures which most accord with their own mercantile views and expectations. The directors besides have a very unfair advantage over their competitors in trade; for the knowledge which they possess as to when the screw is to be put on or taken off, enables them in the first place, greatly to extend their operations; and in the second place, to saddle others with goods at high prices at periods of animation, and be enabled to purchase at the lowest mark during times of depression; thus, in fact, driving less well informed operators out of the field of competition with them. The sphere of the movements of the Irish Bank directors being so limited, comparatively, the effect is more apparent and harder to be endured. *The Dublin Pilot*, on this head, says, in one of its recent numbers —

"The 'Bank directors' in London and Dublin know when panic is approaching, and of course know when *to sell out*; and if the panic should not come fast enough, they know how and are willing enough to hasten it. Very well; by the same knowledge they can foresee whereabouts 'an improvement in the times' sits — that is to say, free discounts, expanded issues of paper; and they prepare for it by times by purchasing up all the mercantile property they can lay hands on at the previously depressed prices—*depressed by themselves' mind.* Three or four months of free discounts will bring an advance of twenty to thirty per cent, in the value of the leading article, and what with newspaper aid of one sort or another, they are enabled to sell out again at immense profits, so that the fortunate monopolists contrive to realise princely fortunes in a few years. Of course their operations are not so clumsily managed that vulgar eyes can perceive them, but they flow on as we describe, nevertheless. We have often given utterance to these opinions in one shape or another. We have bellowed in the ears of our statesmen the injustice of conferring on any body of men the power of contracting or expanding the measure by which the value of all men's property is to be sold. Mr. O' Connell told a story at a late meeting of the tyrant Procrustes, who invented an iron bed of that peculiar construction that it could be extended if the condemned victim to be placed upon it were shorter than others, and if longer the legs of the victim were cut off. The twenty-four gentlemen who manage the Bank of England, and the fifteen gentlemen who manage the Irish concern, conduct them just as Procrustes conducted his iron bed. When they want commodities cheapened they can chop off the legs of the circulation, and then 'money is scarce', and 'times are bad and when they want to raise prices, they stretch out the paper issues to extraordinary dimensions, prices rise, money is plenty, and while all is apparently smooth these favoured gentlemen monopolists, or some of them, as we have already shown, may 'sell out'.

"As a proof of the want of confidence which is the result of the present system, in any times of peculiarly severe pressure, merchants and men of business, instead of looking for and expecting relief from the banks of either country, are only anxious, on the contrary, to ascertain whether the operations of those establishments may not further perplex and embarrass them. This is a state of things which ought not to be, and more particularly from institutions that are meant, and ought to be, of national use and benefit."

It must, of course, be evident that the foregoing extracts were written with reference to the discussions pending in last session of parliament on the question of the renewal of the charter of the Bank of Ireland. To enter on that question would be foreign to my purpose; I would only incidentally observe, that if no weightier reasons exist against the renewal than the supposed power, and the sinister exercise of it, by the directors here described, there would not be much difficulty in deciding upon it: and widely as I differ from the writers on ail the assertions advanced by them, there is none on which I differ more widely with them than in that which relates to the greater influence ascribed to operations of the Bank of Ireland, within its sphere, than to those of the Bank of England. The same sort of reasoning unquestionably applies to both, but in an infinitely smaller degree to the Bank of Ireland than to the Bank of England; and to neither will the attributing of the power, or the charge of the abuse of it in the manner supposed, be found, with the slightest semblance of truth, to apply.

As regards the Bank of England, Mr. Hume has, by his speech in the House of Commons on the 8th of July last, of which a copy, revised by him, has been extensively circulated, given his support to a great deal of the same sort of exaggeration of the influence of the regulation by the Bank of England of its issues upon prices, as well as upon the rate of interest.

SECTION 6 *Examination of the effects imputed by mr. hume in his speech of the 8th of July, 1839, to the management of the Bank of England*

It appears to me, that while Mr. Hume is correct, as might be expected, in his figures and tabular statements, he draws inferences from them perfectly inconsequent, and entirely misconceives the working of the system of the Bank as deducible from those very statements. It must be said, however, in justice to him, that the errors and fallacies which pervade his reasoning are not peculiar to him. But they are put forth with rather unusual distinctness and prominence, and present, therefore, a better than ordinary opportunity for an endeavour to clear the ground of them, as well both in fairness to the Bank as with a view to future discussion of the subject.

The main sources of error here alluded to may be classed under he following heads: —

Ⅰ. The use of the terms abundance and scarcity of money, dearness, and cheapness, and value of money, to signify chiefly variations in the rate of interest, although occasionally and without distinction applying them to the purchasing power of money. To this ambiguous use of the term is probably owing Mr. Hume's frequent reference to variations in the prices of public securities, and in the prices of commodities, as being produced by the same identical operations of the Bank.

Ⅱ. The blending of the deposits with the amount of Bank notes as a criterion of the quantity of paper money in circulation, emanating from the Bank of England; in other words, blending under one common term, and ascribing the same general effects to the circulation and the liabilities of the Bank.

Ⅲ. A shifting of the criterion of the quantity of money, as depending upon the Bank, and operating upon prices, from the deposits and circulation to the securities and bullion, or assets, and sometimes to the securities alone.

Ⅳ. An assumption that it is in the power of the Bank to regulate the market rate of interest.

Ⅴ. The theory that the markets for commodities are directly influenced by every alteration in the quantity of money in the hands of or emanating from the Bank, or by every marked variation in the rate of interest.

Ⅰ. *Ambiguity in the use of the term Value of Money.* — The practice of using the terms, abundance or scarcity of money, low or high value of money, and cheapness or dearness of money, and more or less of demand for money, synonymously with a low or high rate of interest, has of late years become very general, not only on the stock exchange and among the money dealers, with whom it had for some time previously been in general use, but amongst bankers and merchants. Mr. Hume is not, therefore, chargeable with introducing any novelty by such use of the terms, but he has suffered himself to be led into no little confusion in their practical application by not distinguishing between their technical and comparatively modern use, and the more general signification attached to them, of purchasing power or exchangeable value, as applied to commodities and labour. The whole train of his reasoning upon the consequences which he ascribes to the quantity of money as emanating from the Bank assumes the identity of their operation on the money market, and on the markets for produce; that is, on the rate of interest and on the prices of commodities.

Thus after going back, as he does, for the last twenty years, and showing that in 1822 there was an increase of money as compared with 1819, Mr. Hume proceeds to observe —

"It was in consequence of this greater *abund-ance of money*, and a greater stability of things resulting from a return to cash payments, that the government was able in 1822 to reduce 160, 000, 000*l.* of 5 per cent, to 4 per cent, stock, which it had not been able to effect during the eight previous years of peace, while the suspension of cash payments continued. It was also owing to the greater abundance of money that the Bank in 1822 reduced the rate of interest in its discount from 5 to 4 per cent. Another proof of the greater abundance of money is in the comparative prices of 3 per cent, consols, which, in August, 1819, stood at $71\frac{1}{2}$ per cent, and rose in August, 1822, to $80\frac{1}{2}$ per cent."

Now, admitting as I do, that the quantity of money in February, 1822, was greater than in 1819[①], I have to observe that the effect here ascribed to abundance of money is a fall in the rate of interest, and the proof of the greater abundance is the fall of the Bank rate of discount, and the rise of consols. It is hence evident that abundance of money is, in the effects here ascribed to it, applied in the sense of value of money in use or on hire, the measure of which value is the interest or net rent stipulated for such use.

It will be seen, that in the subsequent passages of the speech the term is

① The contrast is, indeed, not a little amusing between Mr, M. Attwood labouring to show that money was less in quantity, and that the very low and falling prices of commodities in 1822 were not; from their abundance, but from the scarcity of money; and Mr. Hume, who shows that money was increased in quantity, and adds as a *proof* of abundance of money that the rate of interest had fallen.

applied *indiscriminately*, as suits the purpose, in both senses, and so as to include under the same category consols and commodities: hence not a little of the confusion that pervades the whole of the reasoning; a point which it is very material to bear in mind with reference to the further conclusions.

Ⅱ. *Deposits, considered as a part of the Circulation of the Bank of England.* —With reference to the deposits, Mr. Hume states, — "He would not admit it to be a question whether or not deposits should be a part of the circulation; for as they were payable by the Bank on demand, he must consider them equally so as the paper in circulation." He accordingly blends them under the common terms of paper money and circulation, and considers the variations in their amount as coming under the direct influence of the Bank.

That the deposits in the hands of the Bank, and the promissory notes actually issued by the Bank, agree in some important particulars is doubtless true. The Bank is *liable* to be called upon for the payment of the deposits, or the greater part of them, on demand; and agreeing in that particular, the amount of them and of the Bank notes issued is properly designated under the common term of *liabilities.* But the probability of the demand from the one or the other is different, according to the character of the deposits①; and the deposits differ from the Bank notes issued, inasmuch as the former, while they remain in that state, that is in the hands of the Bank, consist of money, indeed (not, however, created by

① The different character of the deposits, and the circumstances by which the variations in their amounts are determined, have been so fully and clearly stated by Mr. Pennington, in a letter from him, inserted in the former part of this work, as to supersede the necessity of entering into them here more at large.

the Bank), but of money that is unemployed and inert. Whereas, the Bank notes issued are so much money, all, or the greater part of which, is in actual employment, as a part of the medium, with the metallic circulation, for current payments.

There may be causes of variation in the amount of the deposits on a very large scale, while the circulation undergoes a comparatively trifling alteration.

The amount of the government deposits[①] is influenced to a considerable extent by an increasing or failing revenue, or by special financial operations. The deposits of bankers[②] are under a direct influence from the foreign exchanges, the market rate of interest, and the state of credit; while the amount of the circulation may be uninfluenced, or only in a very inferior degree, by any of these circumstances; and the variations of it are to be considered as the consequences, rather than the causes, of variations in the amount of pecuniary transactions.

The blending, therefore, of the deposits with the Bank notes, under the term of paper circulation, and treating of them as in their origin proceeding from designed operations of the Bank, and as being identical in their action upon prices both of securities and of commodities, or, to speak in language less technical, on the rate of interest and on the prices of produce, leads inevitably to confusion, and is quite incompatible with any consistent application of their variations to elucidate the working of

---

① The government deposits, according to an account in the Appendix to the Bank Charter Report, varied little above or below 4 millions, from 1826 to 1831, both years included.

② The deposits belonging to London and other bankers are stated by Mr. Horsley Palmer in his "Tract on the Causes and Consequences of the Pressure on the Money Market in 1836", as varying from 3 to 4 millions.

the system.

Mr. Hume, however, makes this confusion of terms instrumental in a charge against the Bank of excessive fluctuations in the amount of the currency. Thus, —

"He (Mr. Hume) asserted, that the directors had acted in 1835-6, and again in this year, contrary to that understood principle; and, so far from steadiness in the currency having been obtained through the agency of the Bank, he would show, that by every one of its operations, there had been a continual fluctuation, perpetual ups and downs, without any apparent or discoverable principle. And to show the extent of these, fluctuations, he would now state some of the changes in the amount of Bank notes and Bank post-bills in circulation in different years, as follow: —

		£		£
Dec. 20.	1823	17, 575, 000		
Dec. 24.	1825	25, 611, 000	Increase of Bank notes and Bank post bills in 24 months	8, 036, 000
Jun. 16.	1827	20, 503, 010	Decrease of Bank notes in 18 months	5, 107, 960
Apr. 18.	1829	20, 750, 60	Increase of Bank notes in 20 months	247, 022
Jun. 26.	1830	19, 978, 550	Decrease of Bank notes in 14 months	771, 510
Feb. 4.	1832	19, 156, 990	Decrease of Bank notes in 20 months	821, 560

"But the extent of the fluctuations in the issues of paper by the Bank would appear more clearly when he afterwards stated the amount of bullion and of securities. The circulation and deposits of the Bank, from 1834 to this time, had fluctuated greatly. In 1834, on the 1st of July, the amount was 33,991,000*l.*; and, on the 16th of December, 30,560,000*l.*, a decrease of nearly four millions. In 1835, on the 28th of July, the amount was 29,833,000*l.*; and, on the 15th of December, it was 35,050,000*l.*, an increase of more than five millions. In 1836, on the 8th of March, the amount was 34,705,000*l.*, and on the 15th November, it was 30,225,000*l.*, a decrease of near five millions. In 1838, on the 1st of May, the amount was 30,090,000*l.*, and on the 25th of June, 1839, 25,668,000*l.*, a decrease of four and a half millions — thus always varying, often within a few months, to these great amounts. Let the House compare these fluctuations just enumerated with the comparatively slight change in the amount of the circulation of joint stock banks and of private banks in the same period, and then say how far the joint stock banks deserve the censure cast upon them for overissue of paper. The honourable member read the following table: —

Return of the Circulation of Private Banks and Joint Stock Banks, three months, ending

		Private Bank		Joint Stock Bank		Total
		£		£		£
1833 Dec. 28	-	8,836,803	-	1,315,301	-	10,152,104
1834 Jun. 28	-	8,875,795	-	1,642,887	-	10,518,682
Dec. 28	-	8,537,655	-	2,122,173	-	10,659,828

Continued

				Private Bank		Joint Stock Bank		Total
				£		£		£
1835	Jun.	27	–	8, 455, 114	–	2, 484, 687	–	10, 939, 803
	Dec.	26	–	8, 334, 863	–	2, 799, 551	–	11, 134, 414
1836	Jun.	25	–	8, 614, 132	–	3, 588, 064	–	12, 202, 196
	Dec.	31	–	7, 753, 500	–	4, 258, 197	–	12, 011, 697
1837	Jul.	1	–	7, 187, 673	–	3, 684, 764	–	10, 872, 437
	Dec.	30	–	7, 043, 470	–	3, 826, 665	–	10, 870, 135
1838	Jun.	30	–	7, 383, 247	–	4, 362, 256	–	11, 745, 503
	Dec.	31	–	7, 599, 942	–	4, 625, 546	–	12, 225, 488
1839	Mar.	30	–	7, 642, 104	–	4, 617, 363	–	12, 259, 467
	Jun.	29	–	6, 917, 657	–	4, 167, 313	–	12, 275, 818
The lowest, Dec. 28. 1833						–	£	10, 152, 104
The highest, Jun. 29. 1839						–	£	12, 275, 818
Increase					–	–	£	2, 123, 714

"It thus appeared that the greatest variation in the amount of private and joint stock circulation in the seven years, 1833 to 1839, was from 10, 152, 104*l.* to 12, 275, 818*l.* , or 2, 123, 714*l.* It was wonderful, considering what the conduct of the Bank had been in forcing out money — considering what temptations it had held out to private banks to extend their issues, and to individuals to engage in wild and hazardous speculations—that both joint stock banks and individuals had not yielded to the temptation to a much greater extent than they had done. All these statements were drawn from public documents, from reports of committees, and other official sources. *He put forward nothing in the way of figures that he believed could be disputed*; *and*, *resting upon these proofs*, he asserted that the Bank of England had acted in a most injurious manner, and widely different from what ought to have been the conduct of a great public body, having full power confided to them over the currency of the country, and holding the influence which the Bank held."

In order to avoid the imputation of giving a garbled extract, I have inserted the entire passage, although a part of it, namely, the reference to the amount of Bank notes and Bank post-bills in circulation between December, 1823, and February, 1832, is not strictly relevant to the examination under the present head. But irrelevant as it is to the more immediate topic, it is worth a passing notice here as showing that when it answers the purpose of a charge against the Bank, the circulation of Bank notes can be distinguished from the deposits, which are in all other instances blended.

And with reference, moreover, to the extent of the fluctuations in that interval, Mr. Hume must surely have been aware that, at the close of 1825, the derangement of the circulation, and more especially of the country circulation (how occasioned I have elsewhere shown, but it is not now the question), was such as could only be remedied, and remedied it was, by the very great addition made for that very purpose by the Bank of England. And the subsequent subsidence to the usual amount was the necessary effect of the restoration of confidence, and of the general circulation to their ordinary state.

But the immediate purpose, in referring to this quotation from Mr. Hume's speech, is to point out, more especially, the mode in which the blending of the deposits with the circulation of the Bank of England is made subservient to the establishing of a comparison injurious to the Bank of England in contrast with the private and joint stock banks. Surely, if the circulation only of the latter is to be taken for the purpose of any inference of the regulation of their issues, the same rule should, in fairness, be applied to the former. And if the circulation only of the Bank of England, at the dates nearest to those selected by Mr. Hume, be taken, it will appear that the fluctuation was much less in proportion than that of the country banks.

I am not disposed to think that, as regards the mere amount of the circulation of the country banks, there is any fair ground of charge against them, of having unduly extended it, but still the fact is that the fluctuations of it were much greater than that of the Bank of England. And I am inclined to think, that if the liabilities of the private and joint stock banks were made known, the variations would have been found (with the exception, perhaps, of the distinct effect of the East and West India deposits) to have been still greater in proportion.

There needs not, it is to be presumed, any more striking instance of the confusion of reasoning and the inconsequence and unfairness of inference to which the blending of the deposits and the circulation is calculated to lead; the deposits being, moreover, an element of its position over which the Bank has no control whatever. And yet it is with reference to such statements, that Mr. Hume adds, —He put forward nothing in the way of figures that he believed could be disputed; *and resting upon these proofs*, he asserted that the Bank of England had acted in a most injurious manner."

I believe that the Bank, in employing a part of its deposits as it did in 1835-1836, acted injudiciously; but that is a point belonging to the question of investments in securities by the employment of deposits, and is quite wide of anything that Mr. Hume seems to have had in view in this statement, which refers simply to the amount of the deposits blended under one head with the circulation.

As to the charge of excess in the circulation, properly so called, the answer of the governor of the Bank, Sir John Rae Reid, to that part of the Speech of Mr. Hume just quoted, is quite decisive. "I have here," he said, an account of the circulation of Bank of England notes, showing the average of seven years from 1833 to 1839, ending the 5th of April in each year. The amount of circulation was,

On the 5th of April	1833	–	£ 18, 900, 000
—	1834	–	18, 400, 000
—	1835	–	18, 500, 000
—	1836	–	18, 400, 000
—	1837	–	18, 300, 000
—	1838	–	18, 300, 000
—	1839	–	18, 400, 000

"Now it really does appear to me (and I hope the House will think so also), that seeing the nearness to which the circulation in each of these respective years approached the other, no complaints can be made on this particular score, as having been the cause of any particular over-trading. I take the average amount of circulation for thirteen weeks previous to the before mentioned dates, from April, 1833, to April, 1839, in each year; and without troubling the House by going into particulars, I must say that the difference is so small that it is not worthy of notice; and that, with all the disposition to find fault, there is no opportunity for doing so." —*Mirror of Parliament*, July 8.

1839.

It is impossible that there could be a more complete case to show that, whatever may have been the causes of the phenomena in the rate of interest and in the state of trade, the origin of them, their moving force, could not, with any semblance of reason, be referred to any undue increase in the circulation. And although I do not think that there is, under the circumstances, any fair ground of charge against the country banks for having unduly extended their part of the circulation, it is not easy to conceive any conclusion less warranted by facts than the statement, that the *circulation* of the Bank of England exhibits more fluctuation than that of the country banks.

Ⅲ. *Securities held by the Bank of England, with or without the Amount of Bullion, considered as tests of the Increase of Bank Notes.*

A further fertile source of inconsistency of reasoning is, the shifting of the test of increase of Bank notes from the liabilities to the securities and bullion, in the first instance, and subsequently to the securities alone. Thus, Mr. Hume had said,

"I may repeat that the amount of securities held by the Bank is, with the amount of bullion, the true and only tests of the increase of Bank notes."

And then after showing the great variation in the securities from May, 1832, to June, 1839, he goes on to observe, —

"It ought particularly to be noticed, that on the 11th of December, 1888, the amount of securities in the Bank was 20, 707, 000*l*. ; and, although the exchanges were against England, and the bullion going abroad, the directors continued to issue money at 3 $\frac{1}{2}$ per cent, on approved securities; so that, when the last return was made on the 25th of June, 1839, the securities had increased to 23,934,000*l*. In other words, they had forced out money, and increased the paper circulation to the amount of more than three millions, although, during all that time, the "exchanges were against England; and he believed that, if there had been weekly returns, it would appear that the circulation had been increased by nearly four millions during the first part of that period. *One of the immediate effects of this increase was, by creating speculation, to raise the price of corn, and of every other article: for example, of upland cotton in the Liverpool market from fid. in December to* 9 $\frac{1}{2}$ *d. per* 1*b.*, *and corn from* 73*s.* 6*d. to* 81*s.* 6*d.* &c."

The extraordinary reasoning by which the increase of the securities between December, 1838, and June, 1839, is assigned as a cause of the rise of cotton and corn, I shall have occasion to remark upon hereafter. In the mean time, my insertion of the foregoing extract is for the purpose of showing that here, because, on the above comparison, there appears to have been an increase of upwards of 3 millions of securities, money is said to have been forced out, and to have constituted an increase of the paper circulation by an equal amount, notwithstanding that the actual circulation of Bank notes was less by upwards of 300,000*l*., and the deposits were reduced by upwards of 1,400,000*l*. So that, while by the definition, in the passage of the Speech before quoted, the circulation and the deposits together, that is, the liabilities, constituted the quantity of paper money as regarded the Bank of England, and while, according to this definition, the quantity of money in June, 1839, was less by 1,700,000*l*. than in December preceding, the adoption in the subsequent passages of the securities as a criterion, makes the increase of the quantity of money in circulation upwards of 3 millions. ① This is, indeed, a specimen of blowing hot and cold with the same breath. And however convenient for the purposes of the speaker such a mode of reasoning may be, it is conducive to anything but clear and just conclusions.

The increase of the securities by the Bank, in the interval here referred to, forms undoubtedly a ground of objection to the management; but not for the reasons stated by Mr. Hume. It did not force out money in the way supposed by him, so as to add to the circulation, which was in fact diminished; but it counteracted the effect which the demand for bullion ought to have had, in contracting the circulation, at a time when the coffers of the Bank were experiencing a rapid drain.

Ⅳ. *Assumption that it is in the power of the Bank of England to regulate the market rate of Interest.*

Mr. Hume, throughout the whole of his speech, seems to be impressed with, and to inculcate, the opinion that the Bank of England, by its several notices of the rates at which advances on loans would be made, or bills discounted, really could or did originate or cause the variations in the rate of interest and discount; upon the extent of which variations he descants, as being productive of the most injurious consequences. Of those several notices from the Bank, which I have before adverted to, a correct account is given in the speech.

After contending for the proofs which those measures and the low stock of bullion afford of mismanagement by the Bank of England, he proceeds,

---

① And a note at page 18. notices that, on the 17th September, 1839, the amount of securities was 25, 936, 000*l*. , so that the circulation, according to Mr. Hume's doctrine, was increased, as compared with December, 1838, by upwards of 5 millions.

in the following extract, to contrast with it the management of the Bank of France; and, passing a high eulogium on it (not higher than, I believe, it deserves), he lays particular stress upon the circumstance of its having, for many years, preserved a uniform rate of interest, namely 4 per cent, blaming the Bank of England for not preserving the same uniformity.

"He would state to the House how very different had been the conduct of the Bank of France in times of difficulty. It appeared from the evidence of Mr. A. Baring, before the Lords' committee of 1819, that even in a period of panic and considerable pressure, the Bank of France never reduced or increased the rale of its discounts of commercial bills. All it did, in order to check excessive speculations, was, to reduce the period of discounts from ninety days to sixty; and for a short time to forty-five days. From the year 1819, until the present time, the Bank of France had never increased the charge for discounts, but had preserved an uniform rate of 4 per cent, all that time, and had never refused to discount any amount of commercial bills with proper indorsement; and he believed, that the Bank of France really gave much more assistance by discount to the commerce of the country than the Bank of England did. During the whole of the political disturbances in France in 1830 they had steadily continued in that course. He had lately examined that bank, and lie would mention to the Chancellor of the Exchequer, the answer of the governor to him, when he asked whether there would be any objection to his seeing the accounts of the Bank — 'None at all; our house is a house of glass. Every man may see our transactions.' In fact, the transactions of the Bank of France are every day printed, and returns of them made to the Treasury. These accounts are regularly made up, and printed, showing every shilling received and paid during the day, and the amount of discounts under every head; in short, the whole daily transactions of the Bank are regularly entered for inspection, and also published yearly to the world; so that there is no mystery, and the greatest confidence in the operations of the Bank accordingly existed in France. Whilst, as regards the proceedings of the Bank of England, all is secrecy, mystery, and consequent want of confidence. On a late occasion, when the Belgian Bank failed, a run took place on the banks in Paris, in consequence of the erroneous principles on which Lafitte's bank was for a time conducted, and there was considerable pressure in the money market in France: but all that the Bank of France did, was to re-discount some of the paper held by Lafitte's bank at forty-nine days' date, and thus it gave efficient assistance, and stopt the run. That was all that had been done to place the currency of Paris in its proper state, while we were undergoing most severe attacks upon our property, occasioned by the most erroneous currency arrangements of the Bank of England, which was the parent, instead of being the preventor, of speculation. While the Bank of England had been discounting and lending at $3\frac{1}{2}$ per cent, 4 per cent, 5 per cent, and $5\frac{1}{2}$ per cent, the Bank of France, avoiding such variation and its evil consequences, had continued its discounts at 4 per cent. When commercial men in France wanted money, they went to the Bank of France and got discount without difficulty; the result of which was that the amount of commercial discount by that bank was much more in proportion to the commerce of the two countries than that of the Bank of England. *He complained, that the Bank of England, by lending money at times at low interest, often lower than the market price, on stock and other securities, did, in reality, urge to over speculation by merchants, and to over issues of paper by joint stock banks*;

and, having got the country into great excitement of high prices and apparent prosperity, altered their plan, when their coffers were emptying, —reduced their discounts, —*raised the interest, and, to prevent the exhaustion of their bullion, suddenly cramped the whole of the commercial transactions of the country. The Bank of France did no such thing.*"

The cases, however, of the Bank of France and the Bank of England are very far from being sufficiently analogous to justify such inferences.

The currency of France consists, in a very large proportion, of the metals; and its foreign commerce forms a very small proportion of the transactions in which that currency is employed. Very different is the case in this country, where the metallic part of the currency is so much smaller, and the commerce so much larger. It may therefore be, and probably is, a comparatively easy matter for the Bank of France to collect and retain a larger amount of bullion in proportion to its securities; and, as I shall have occasion hereafter more particularly to observe, a large stock of bullion is the only means of avoiding the necessity of operating forcibly on the securities when a decided drain manifests itself. The paper circulation of the Bank of France, moreover, is relatively small. Under these circumstances, there can be no great difficulty in preserving a uniform rate of discount. But I should apprehend that the Bank of France cannot maintain that uniformity of rate without great variations in the amount of securities or of bullion; and Mr. Hume overlooks the necessary inference, from the very circumstance which he notices, that in two instances which he mentions they did what was equivalent to an advance in the rate of discount, namely, that in 1818 (in order, not as Mr. Hume supposes, consistently with his theory, to check excessive speculations, hut to counteract the drain of specie)① they reduced the period of discounts from 90 days to 60, and, for a short time, to 45 days, and on a recent occasion to 49 days. Now, as regards accommodation to the mercantile classes, I am strongly of opinion that a reduction by the Bank of England of the length of the commercial hills which it would discount to 45 days, preserving the rate at 4 per cent, would have been felt as a greater inconvenience, a more severe pressure than an advance of the rate to 6 per cent, for the longer term.

Still greater would he the inconvenience to the trading community, and more effectual, consequently, for the recovery of the exchanges, would he a limitation of the amount of hills to be discounted. This was the expedient adopted by the Bank of England in 1795. But in proportion as it would be more effectual, by so much the more distressing it would be to the mercantile classes, than a considerable rise in the rate of discount.

If the usury law had been preserved in all its impolicy and absurdity to the present time, the Bank would have been under the necessity of adopting one or other of these alternatives; and it is difficult to say which of the two would have been most severely felt by the mercantile interests.

In the event of the former being adopted, the merchants would complain that, inasmuch as the course of their trade was regulated in the description

---

① The circumstance is alluded to in the evidence of Mr. Baring, now Lord Ashburton, before the Lords' committee on cash payments in 1819. "Their bullion", Mr. Baring said, "was reduced by imprudent issues from 117 millions of francs to 34 millions of francs, and has returned by more cautious measures to 100 millions of francs, at which it stood ten days ago, when I left Paris. It must, however, be always recollected that this operation took place in a country every part of the circulation of which is saturated with specie."

of the bills they received, whether as remittances which were made to them from abroad, or for their sales in the home market, by the reliance which they were led to place upon the conversion of such as had not more than three months to ran, such a measure as that of the Bank of France, of reducing the number of days, might place them, having their portfolio full of bills of a longer date, in great difficulty, from the uncertainty of being able to convert them at all.

The other alternative, of a measure similar to that which was resorted to by the Bank, in December, 1795, which I have before referred to, of limiting the total amount to be advanced, and, in pursuance of that regulation, discounting only a certain proportion of the bills sent in, without reference to the credit of the parties, would be attended with still more inconvenience, inasmuch as the merchants could not rely, however high their credit might be, upon realising, upon an emergency, the best bills in their possession. I mention these as the complaints which would have been made by the mercantile interests; not, however, admitting that, to the extent here stated, they would be well founded; or that they ought to be allowed to weigh against the claims of the public, which require that the due regulation of the currency should not be made subservient to considerations of partial convenience to particular branches of the trading community. I say partial convenience to particular branches, because it cannot be too often repeated, that an interference with the due regulation of the currency can never be for the general benefit of trade.

The Bank adopted, in 1795, a further limitation, which was to confine the accommodation to each firm within a certain amount, taking into consideration the bills running upon, as well as those proposed for, discount. , Such rules were more readily submitted to at that time than they would be now, when so much larger interests are at stake; but even then the remonstrances were, as I have before described, loud, and from powerful parties, against such restriction.

The Directors of that time were not influenced by the modern doctrine of the claims of the mercantile interests, at the expense of the claims of the public. They accordingly continued the process of contraction of the circulation. But the pressure was very severe. While the Bank rate of discount for bills so limited was 5 per cent, the real price paid for loans, and for forbearance, was uncommonly high, much higher than any within the experience of modern times: and sacrifices, much beyond any rise in the rate of interest that we have lately witnessed, were submitted to in the difference between the credit and ready money prices of stocks and commodities. I mention this only to show that Mr. Hume's *beau ideal* of a uniform rate of discount by the Bank may be attended with much more inconvenience than he seems to be aware of.

There were periods, indeed, even during the restriction on cash payments, when a rate of discount by the Bank of 8 or even 10 per cent, would have been considered preferable to some of the limitations which then prevailed; and among others, the length of the bills being confined to 61 days, instead of the present limit of 95 days. At the same time, I am not at all prepared to say that there are not some advantages attending this more severe mode of limitation. In an ambitious and enterprising commercial community, among whom there is generally a tendency to outrun the due bounds of credit, inevitably leading to a reaction, it is desirable to hold out a constant memento against the risks of over-trading; and this is most effectually done by the occasional recurrence of periods in which there is a difficulty, or at least a diminished facility, in realising the best securities.

This, however, is not the general opinion; and those who contend for facilities to the commerce of the country, which in more homely terms means merely greater facilities to the merchants borrowing, ought to consider the relaxation of the usury law, which has allowed the Bank to raise its rate above 5 per cent, and at the advanced rate to discount the bills, provided they are of the prescribed description, to an unlimited amount, as a great boon to the commerce of the country. And I have not heard of any instance in which the working of the amended law has been otherwise than beneficial. ①

The class of persons who are supposed to have received the greatest benefit from the relaxation of the usury law, are the smaller description of tradesmen. Many of these, it has been observed, if the law had existed in its former rigour, must have failed, in consequence of being forced to sell at ruinous prices, upon the occurrence of the late pressure, from their not being able to raise money upon bills, not of first rate, but of fair security, at 5 per cent. Tradesmen of this description, by getting their bills discounted at 10 or 15 per cent per annum, have in many instances been saved from making sacrifices by forced sales at 30, 40, and even 50 per cent, and have thus been

---

① It has been stated, however, and with some plausibility, that the bankers generally have been benefited more than most other classes by the relaxation of the law, and by the rise in the bank rate of discount to 6 per cent, inasmuch as, but for this alteration, they must have submitted to make advances to their customers, that is to persons keeping accounts with them, at 5 per cent per annum; whereas, ever since August last, they have charged at the rate of 6 per cent., except where confined by unexpired agreements to 5 per cent. There may be something in this view of the effect of the altered law, but not much, because the bankers would probably devote a less portion of their funds to the accommodation of their customers in the one case than in the other.

preserved from becoming bankrupts.

There is likewise another class of tradesmen who, from what I can learn, have benefited by the relaxation of the usury laws. Those whom I allude to are stated to be tradesmen of fair character and good business, who, whether for casual orders for exportation, or for the purpose of getting into stock, having occasion to make purchases to some extent, would, if taking the ordinary credit from the manufacturer, have to pay what is called the long price, from which it is customary to make an abatement for money down, of 20, or, in some cases, 25 per cent. Now, on discounting a bill or borrowing on his personal security at 15 per cent, per annum, for six months, he would have to pay $7\frac{1}{2}$ per cent, as interest or discount against 20 or 25 per cent, which he would receive by prompt payment. Indeed, it is difficult to conceive how it should ever be supposed to be an advantage to a person having occasion for a loan, to prevent him from having the greatest competition of lenders, a competition which it is the necessary effect of a usury law to restrict.

But reverting to variations in the Bank rate of discount, and to Mr. Hume's eulogy on the uniformity of the rate of 4 per cent, charged by the Bank of France, he says, — "While the Bank of England had been discounting and lending at $3\frac{1}{2}$ per cent, 4 per cent, 5 per cent, and $5\frac{1}{2}$ per cent, the Bank of France, avoiding such variation and its evil consequences, had continued its discounts at 4 per cent. When commercial men in France wanted money, they went to the Bank of France and got discount without difficulty; the result of which was, that the amount of commercial discount by that Bank was much more in proportion to the commerce of the two countries than that of the Bank of England."① The advantage then arising from this greater facility and greater extent of discount, in proportion to the commerce, might be supposed to be displayed in the greater exemption from commercial discredit, distress, and failure in France; whereas, in point of fact, it appears that the sufferings of the commercial and manufacturing classes in France, during the last twelve months, have been greater than those which have been experienced in this country during the same interval.

The following are extracts from the *Times*, August 5th 1839.

"The number of bankruptcies in Paris declared between the 1st January and the 26th July, 1839, was 607. Among them were 93 joint stock companies, whose debts amounted to 148,000,000 francs, or nearly 6,000,000*l*. sterling. The number of bankruptcies between the 1st and 26th of last month was 87."

The same newspaper, Dec. 19th 1839, after giving the tenor of advices from France, adds, —

"We lament to observe by the French newspapers, and by our correspondence, that distress prevails in France to a most lamentable extent. We have already referred to the fact, that between 60,000 and 80,000 persons in Paris are obliged to have recourse to public bounty. But we learn that this fact suggests a very inadequate idea of the extent or poignancy of the misery that prevails, and which occasions to government, and to ail who inquire into the subject, the most serious alarm for the consequences. That this melancholy state of things is not confined to the

① It might be imagined, from the stress here laid on the facility of discount at the Bank of France, that there was no such facility here. The simple meaning, however, of this difference of facility is the casual advance of 2 per cent, in the rate of discount by the Bank of England.

metropolis, we have shown by late quotations from the Lyons, and other provincial papers."

"We find in the *Capitole* the following paragraph, showing that in Normandy the sufferings of the inhabitants, already noticed, are unhappily on the increase."

"It is not only in the manufacturing towns that distress prevails. The following is extracted from a letter dated Envermen, a small village in the department of the Lower Seine."

"Misery increases daily in the rural districts. Many of the inhabitants, after exhausting their last resources, are obliged to beg. They only go out at night, and they traverse our village in bands. Some of them have not been satisfied to live on the charity of the people; but have broken open the ovens in several places, and carried away all the bread they contained."

"'Every day,' says the same paper, 'the halls of the palace of the Bourse are crowded with creditors and men of business, twenty-seven failures, one of which was for a sum of 500,000 francs, have been declared since the commencement of the month, and the furniture of 150 other debtors has been sold in virtue of judiciary decrees. Finally, the workshops are every where closing, and misery is becoming general.'"

On what possible grounds, then, can it be contended that the difference in the management of the Bank of England, compared with that of France, can be considered as having been productive of commercial derangement in this country, while the derangement and distress in France have, according to all accounts, been so much greater?

And yet the writer of a long and most elaborate letter, signed "Gresham," in the *Times* of the 30th Dec. last (the editor of which very naturally disclaims participation in the writer's opinions), after inveighing against the system of the Bank of England, observes: —

"Let us not vaunt our boasted superiority in matters of banking. Is there a country on the face of Europe where the true principles of banking are less understood, or, if understood, less acted upon? Talk of Hamburg, Paris, Amsterdam, or the confined influence of Europe operating upon our trade by an unfavourable course of exchange! Are they deranged in their operations when the exchange is in favour of England? Look at their banks and the nature of their currency, and tell us of the commercial panics, or even of the commercial embarrassments, that have convulsed continental Europe, as they have afflicted bank-ridden England with all its enlightenment on the principles of finance."

The rate of discount rose at Hamburg and Amsterdam to 7 per cent. for first-rate bills in September and October last; and yet the exchanges were in favour of both those places, accompanied by an influx of gold and silver.

It is impossible, as I apprehend, by any regulation of the paper part of the circulation, to prevent occasional, considerable, and inconvenient variations in the rate of interest. Of the causes which determine the rate of interest, I have given an explanation at some length in the former part of this work; and I have only here to add, that the circumstances which have, since that explanation was given, developed themselves in our foreign commercial relations, not only with the United States of America, but with the rest of the world, are calculated to give additional force to the causes there enumerated in disturbing the rate of interest.

A country like this, having an extensive foreign commerce, extensive beyond any of which there is an example in history, and beyond any which the most sanguine anticipations could some years back have contemplated, as within the bounds of probability, must, by its intimate relations of capital and credit abroad, participate more or less in the tendency to over-banking and over-trading, and in the consequent revulsions which may occur in the countries with which we are commercially most intimately and most extensively connected. Considering, therefore, the enormous variations in the state of credit and in the rate of interest which have occurred in the United States of America, and the variations also which have taken place, although not on so extended a scale, on the continent of Europe generally, it ought surely not to be a matter of wonder that some variation, and an inconvenient degree of it, should have occurred in this country. That the Bank of England was not the originating cause of the recent rise in the rate of interest is abundantly clear. Whether, by a different management of the Bank as to the only element of its position on which it can operate, namely, its securities, the variations in the market rate of interest may not be moderated, is a question on which, before I conclude, I propose to offer some suggestions.

Ⅴ. *Theory that the markets for commodities are directly influenced by every alteration in the quantity of money in the hands of or emanating from, the Bank of England, or by every marked variation in the rate of interest.* A principal part of the charges brought against the Bank has, however, been that, by at one time forcing out its paper, it has *caused* speculation, not only in securities, both domestic and foreign, and in shares, but also in commodities; thus artificially raising prices, and, by turning the exchanges against this country, driving out the bullion; while at another time, in order to save itself from the consequences of apprehended exhaustion of its treasure, it has suddenly and in a manner ruinous to the holders of produce, raised the rate of discount, and contracted the circulation, or, according to the modern phraseology, "put on the screw", and knocked down prices. A specimen of these sweeping charges in general terms, but in their utmost extravagance, has been given in an extract a few pages back from a daily paper. The general impression under which those charges are made is, as I have before observed, a very prevalent one.

Mr. Hume, in his Speech, states the charges more specifically, and enters into historical details to make out his case. I have already had occasion to observe, that, beginning from 1819, the rise in consols in August, 1822, is considered by him as a proof in confirmation of his statement that an increase in the quantity of money had, in that interval, taken place. He then enters into an elaborate view of the state of the circulation, and of prices, and of trade, in the remarkable period from 1823 to 1826, and attributes to the mismanagement of the Bank the whole of the extraordinary fluctuations of that period. Thus, after enumerating the purchase of the dead weight in 1823, and the paying off of the dissentients in 1824, and advances to individuals, Mr. Hume adds, that "the Bank went on making reckless advances in all these ways, until they had depreciated the currency by excessive issues of paper, and involved the country in all the evils that followed. The consequences of making money cheap, by this deviation from principle, were the foreign loans' bubble schemes and wild speculation that followed; and, in short, such a state of things ensued as had never before been seen in England." Into the particulars of that period I will not follow him, because I have already given, in a former part of this work, a full explanation of what appear to me to have been the causes leading to that state of things, and to the termination of it. I may have occasion hereafter to refer again to that period. In the mean time, I shall proceed to examine Mr. Hume's explanation of the manner in which the operations of the Bank are supposed to have originated speculations, and a consequent advance of prices, in 1835 and the early part of 1836.

It is requisite, however, on entering into this examination, to point out a very material difference which has arisen out of the circumstances attending the variations of the money market from 1836 to the present time, in the mode of accounting, by a reference to the management of the Bank, for all the fluctuations, both in the money market and in the markets for commodities, which have occurred in that interval.

Until the controversy to which the pressure on the money market in 1836-1837 gave rise, there never seems to have been a question among the partisans of the currency theory, but that the only element in the position of the Bank, affecting the prices of commodities, was the amount of the circulation, that is, the amount of notes actually issued from the Bank. Accordingly, the amount of such issues, *including the notes under 5l.*, as it stood prior to 1820, has been adduced in comparison with the amount of the circulation at subsequent periods, minus the small notes, and without allowing for the substitution of sovereigns①, in proof of the alleged great contraction of the currency, and its necessary consequence, the great fall of prices. But the theory which referred to the circulation only, as affecting prices, could not be made available to account in any degree for the state of things in the commencement of 1836. The rise of prices of several articles of produce, and the speculations in joint stock companies, and the extraordinary credits given by the American houses, occurred coincidentally with a reduced and unusually low state of the circulation of the Bank of England. The average amount of the three monthly returns ending March 8. 1886, was 17, 476, 000*l*. ② being lower than the average of any equal period in the three years preceding or succeeding; indeed, lower than it had been on an average of any three or four months in a long series of preceding years.

Mr. Hume takes no notice, accordingly, of the amount of the actual issues of the Bank, but enters into a statement of the circumstances attending the West India loan of 15, 000, 000*l*. in August, 1835, and after stating the various subsequent notices of the Bank, offering advances not only on the usual securities but also on stock, till the 15th April, 1836, when it discontinued its advances on stock, he adds, — "He had no hesitation in pronouncing these different notices to be so many puffing

---

① Without also allowing for the amount of bankers' deposits in the Bank of England. The sums so deposited were, previously to 1825, kept by the bankers in bank notes in their tills, and they then figured as a part of the circulation, which they now do not until withdrawn.

② 1836, Jan. 12th - 17, 262, 000*l*.
Feb. 9th - 17, 427, 000*l*.
Mar. 8th - 17, 739, 000*l*.

And the average of the last three months of 1835 had been but little higher, namely, only about 17, 500, 000l.

advertisements to induce the public to apply for advances; and he did not wonder that they should have had the effect first to make money plenty and cheap, which produced speculation, and then to *raise the price of articles of all kinds.*"①

On the eagerness of the Bank to invest what the directors called the extra deposits in securities, by advances at a reduced rate of interest, to the money dealers, and on the impolicy of so doing, I have before remarked at some length, and to that extent I should agree with Mr. Hume. That the measures of the Bank at that period, viz. in 1835-1836 had a most unfavourable influence, by competition with the bankers for securities, in adding to other causes of an undue extension of credit, is a point on which I have never entertained any doubt But there is no reason whatever for believing that those measures had any direct influence on the prices of

---

① Of the strange misconception by which the West India loan, and the consequent increase of the deposits in 1835, has been considered as constituting a great addition to *the quantity of money in circulation*, and thus causing wild speculations, the following extract from the speech of Mr. Williams, the member for Coventry, who immediately followed Mr. Hume in the debate, is a striking specimen.

That honourable member said, — "In 1835 there was a great increase in the issue of Bank of England notes, induced principally by the Chancellor of the Exchequer offering a higher interest than the worth of money in the market, for paying up the West India loan of 15, 000, 000*l*., nearly all of which was paid up before scarcely any of the claims were adjusted: thus interest was paid for a very large sum which was to lie idle. As an instance of the variableness of the circulation, I will state its amount at two periods of only six months from each other. In the amount of the circulation I include the deposits, which I consider, in time of pressure, to be the most dangerous to the Bank; as it is invariably seen, that when they begin to reduce their circulation, money becomes of more value, and the deposits are withdrawn; and when there is alarm, the deposits may be demanded in gold. On the 3d July, 1835, the total circulation was 29, 269, 000*l*., stock of gold 6, 219, 000*l*.; and on the 14th January, 1836, the total circulation was 36, 431, 000*l*., stock of gold 7, 076, 000*l*. This shows an increase of 7, 162, 000*l*. in the circulation, while the increase of bullion was only 857, 000*l*. This vast increase was in the deposits, to make use of which the Bank was most profuse in advancing money upon all sorts of securities. Money soon became so abundant, that any amount might be obtained upon ordinary security at 2 per cent, interest. This caused wild speculations, &c." — *Mirror of Parliament.*

commodities, for, in point of fact, there was no advance of prices at that time that could, with any appearance of reason, be traced to anything like the operation of an increased quantity of money upon the markets for produce. There was no speculation, in the correct sense of the term, in commodities upon the spot at that time, with the single exception of the operations in the silk trade by one firm; operations which ended unfortunately. Among other proofs of the absence of such speculations (in London at least), it may be observed, that with the exception above mentioned, few of the houses that failed in 1836-1837 were found to have any excess of stocks of produce on hand, nor did it appear that any of them had entered into speculations of the kind supposed: their overtrading was in credits abroad, attended with excess of exports and imports. The undue extension of credits in the trade with the United States of America, and with the East Indies and China, may indeed have operated, and did probably operate, indirectly, upon the prices of such manufactured articles as were applicable to the trade with those parts; and the raw materials of those manufactures experienced in consequence an increased demand and advanced prices; but other articles were wholly uninfluenced by the overtrading in those branches, and there was no traceable direct influence on the markets for commodities generally, in any way analogous to the effects attributable to an increased quantity of money. The fact of the progressive decline in the prices of corn to their lowest rate, during this very period, is quite decisive against the supposed direct influence of the increase of securities on the markets for produce.

By the plenty and cheapness of money referred to in the foregoing quotation from the Speech, must obviously be meant a reduction in the rate of interest, which is considered as the sole and sufficient cause of the rise of prices of articles of all kinds.

Mr. Hume then noticing the subsequent measures taken by the Bank to arrest the drain on its coffers by raising its rate of discount to 5 per cent, in the autumn of 1836, and by otherwise narrowing the facilities for borrowing, went on to say, — "The subsequent disastrous bankruptcies of so many merchants were only the results of the sudden reduction of the paper circulation by the Bank, and of the alarm thereby produced, when the directors found the bullion had almost left their coffers." Now there was no reduction whatever of the Bank issues subsequent to the spring of 1836. And during the first six months of 1837, when the pressure on the money market was at its height, and when the greatest depression took place in the markets for those descriptions of produce which had been raised by the demand from America, the issues of Bank notes were on an average full 500,000*l*. higher than they had been in the spring of 1836, when all had been excitement and prosperity. As to the bankruptcies, the most exceptionable of the measures adopted by the Bank at that time were expressly with a view to support commercial credit, and to avert or mitigate those failures. The reduction in the amount of the deposits which then occurred was the natural effect of the rise of the rate of interest, and the Bank was of necessity perfectly passive under that reduction. With regard to the securities, they would be of no avail for the support of Mr. Hume's position, because the amount of them in the first six months of 1837, being the period of the greatest pressure, was rather higher than it had been in the first six months of 1836, before any severity of pressure had been felt.

The only measure of the Bank, therefore, which, according to Mr. Hume's view, can be considered to be chargeable with the commercial reverses in 1836-1837, imputed to it, is that of having raised the rate of discount.

So again with reference to the more recent instance of disturbance of the money market, Mr. Hume seems to consider that the Bank, by its operations in varying the rates of discount, and the terms of its advances on loan in 1838 and 1839, had been the cause not only of disturbing the money market and turning the exchanges against us, but had caused speculation; of which he afterwards gives instances, in the advance of cotton and corn. For, after remarking upon the several notices issued by the Bank in the latter part of 1838, and the first six months of 1839, he observes—

"*These were examples* of the fluctuations and irregularities in the rates of discount, and in the amount and value of money, which had brought about the present existing commercial money difficulty. *It was the excessive issue of paper that, by injudicious cheapening of money and encouraging of speculation, had turned the exchanges against us, as they still continued.*"

The theory which ascribes a direct influence to the rate of interest on the markets for commodities, has been very much favoured by the modern phraseology which I have noticed, of applying the terms of abundance and scarcity of money, and the consequent cheapness and dearness of money, or a low or high value of money, to a fall or rise in the rate of interest, as in the quotation just given from Mr. Hume's Speech, where he speaks of the effect of the injudicious cheapening of money in encouraging speculation. As this theory has had, and may again have (notwithstanding the degree in which it has been shaken by the recent and actual state of the markets for produce), considerable practical influence, it may be worth while to enter into a brief investigation of the grounds for it.

The commonly received opinion is, that a low, and especially a declining, rate of interest operates necessarily as a stimulus to speculation, not only in government stocks and in snares both at home and abroad, that is in both British and foreign public and private securities, but also in the markets for produce.

With regard to speculations in securities and in shares, the inducements to enter into them, whether as investments or with a view to resale, must necessarily be influenced by the rate of interest as a primary consideration; and such investments may be speculative or not, according to circumstances; but it is with reference to the influence of the rate of interest, and of the operations of the Bank on speculations in produce, that I am more especially disposed to question the prevailing opinion.

The term speculation, in its widest sense, is, as I have before observed, applicable to nearly all transactions of purchase or sale in anticipation of the contingency of realising a profit as the result of such transactions. But this is not the sense in which the term is meant, when speculation, in the obnoxious meaning of the term, implying an undue and excessive tendency to raise prices, is referred to as having its rise or origin in an enlargement of the circulation, or in a great facility of the money market, by which is understood a high state of commercial credit, and a low rate of interest.

Speculation, in this obnoxious sense, when referring to the markets for produce, is understood to apply to purchases made either by persons in their regular trade or occupations, as merchants and dealers, but to a much larger amount, and beyond the usual proportion to their capital and credit, or, as is more commonly meant, by persons not habitually and regularly dealing in and conversant with the articles so purchased; in either case causing a marked and undue rise of price, a rise not warranted by a fair and sober view of the proportion of the supply to the computed rate of consumption. That the speculations here meant suppose that purchases are made at prices beyond those which would be warranted by a fair view of the proportion of the supply to the rate of consumption, and that such prices being artificial, must eventually be succeeded by loss and discredit, is evident: for if the prices are justifiable upon a fair view of supply and demand, they cannot be said to have their origin in an undue expansion of money and credit. It cannot, on such occasions, be imputed to the regulation of the issues by the Bank, or to a low rate of interest from any other cause, that they have produced undue speculation, the anticipation having been by the supposition, on sufficient grounds, and the result having been, as it must in such case be, beneficial to the public, by limiting the consumption or increasing the supply, or doing both, and thus preserving a due proportion, which would otherwise have been disturbed. The speculations, then, which are supposed to be detrimentally induced, or *stimulated*, by the facility of borrowing money for the purpose of purchasing commodities, must apply to persons who, it is assumed, make purchases with imperfect information, and upon insufficent grounds. There are, doubtless, persons who, upon imperfect information, and upon insufficient grounds, or with too sanguine a view of contingencies in their favour, speculate improvidently; but their *motive* or *inducement* so to speculate is the opinion which, whether well or ill founded, or whether upon their own view or upon the authority or example of other persons, they entertain of the probability of an advance of price. It is not the mere facility of borrowing, or the difference between being able to discount at 3 or at 6 per cent, that supplies the *motive* for purchasing, or even for selling. Few persons of the description here mentioned ever speculate but upon the confident expectation of an advance of price of at least 10 per cent. ①; the instances are rare in which an advance to that extent would hold out any inducement to speculate, in the sense of the word here assumed. Take wheat for example, one of the most usual and prominent of the articles of produce for speculation, and at an average price of about 50*s*. Now I never heard of any person characterised as a speculator, not a jobber, who would think the risk of loss compensated by so small an advance as 5*s*. per quarter, looking to hold it for three months. But the utmost difference between the rate of discount of 3 per cent, and 6 per cent, namely, 3 per cent, per annum, for three months, would on a quarter of wheat amount only to $4\frac{1}{2}$ *d*. per quarter, a difference which, I will venture to say, never induced or deterred a single speculative purchase. ② But, given the force of the motive, the extent to which it can be acted upon is doubtless affected as regards persons who can buy only on credit, or who must borrow in order to be able to buy, by the greater or less facility of borrowing. If, however, the mere facility of borrowing were the determining motive to purchase,

① There are in most of the markets, of any extent, for produce dealers who buy on the spot, with a view to resale in the same market, for a profit under 10 per cent. ; but these persons, a very useful class in equalising prices, come properly under the designation of jobbers, who, like those on the Stock Exchange, are commonly satisfied with a small turn of the market on each of their operations. In the daily advices of the state of the great market for raw cotton, in Liverpool, it is commonly mentioned that certain quantities have been taken on speculation, or by speculators; but this means only the purchases by the ordinary intermediate dealers, as contra-distinguished from the purchases made by the manufacturers.

② As regards speculation in corn, it is impossible that a negative more complete can be afforded of the universally received theory of the effect of an abundant circulation and a low rate of interest in stimulating to speculation, than the fact, that in the long interval of three entire years, 1833, 1834, and 1835, there was a total absence of anything like speculation, while wheat had been falling progressively from 60s. to 36s. Contrast this fact with Mr. Hume's statement, that it was speculation from abundance of money that raised the price of wheat in December, 1838, from 73*s*. 6*d*. to 81*s*. 6*d*.

there seems to be no reason why one commodity should be preferred to another; and the facility of raising money at a low rate of interest might be supposed to induce persons to enter into all markets indifferently as speculative purchasers, with a view to resale, upon no reasonable ground for expectation of a rise of price. The persons who are supposed to speculate so foolishly must be presumed to have some property, and to be holders of marketable securities; for it is not likely that they should, without having property or the reputation of it, and without good securities, be able to borrow largely on mere personal credit, for the purpose of making purchases of goods on speculation. Accordingly speculations of this kind rarely take place to any extent worthy of notice, as being in any way connected with the state of the circulation.

But while, upon general grounds, there is so little reason to suppose that the mere facility of raising money at a low interest forms a sufficient motive for persons having marketable securities, or being in good credit, to borrow for the purpose of purchasing commodities with a view to resale, or that lenders would to any extent be found to advance largely on slender security; a reference to the state of the money market, and of the produce markets at particular periods will show that, in times when the interest of money was particularly low and falling, and when commercial confidence was in the most perfect state, the prices of the largest classes of produce were low, and some of them falling, without the slightest tendency to anything like a general spirit of speculation. Throughout the whole of the interval from 1820 to the close of 1822 the rate of interest was falling, and in 1822 the market rate was nearly as low as it has ever since been; hut in all that interval there was a tendency to a fall in the markets for produce. I allude more especially to the interval of full three years, from the summer of 1832 to the summer of 1835, during which interval, with the exception of a very short -lived speculative advance, lasting only four or five weeks in 1833, on purely mercantile grounds, in colonial produce, there was nothing like what could be called extensive speculation in commodities beyond isolated instances to which every market for produce is occasionally subject At that period, any forced operation of the Bank, with a view to extend its circulation, could have had no effect whatever upon prices. Mr. Samuel Gurney, whose practical acquaintance with the working of the money market is assuredly not surpassed by that of any other individual, delivered a very clear opinion on this point in his evidence before a Committee of the House of Commons, in 1833, on Manufactures, Commerce, and Shipping.

"269. Suppose there are 50, 000, 000*l.* in circulation now, and that the Bank were to issue tomorrow 5, 000, 000*l.* more, do you think prices would ultimately rise in a corresponding proportion with that increase of money? — If the Bank of England were at this time to add 5, 000, 000*l.* to their circulation, it would affect prices only remotely; what would be its operation ? The effect of it would be, that the bankers would have more bank notes than they could use, and would lock them up in their tills; such addition would not come into actual circulation, at least no more than the transactions of London cause a demand for. And while the transactions of London are abundantly supplied, as is the case at the present time, the effect of an additional 5, 000, 000*l.* would be, that it would remain inoperative, or, rather, idle, in the tills of the bankers. I do not believe that such an addition to our circulation would affect prices at this time.

"Would it not encourage speculation? — There is every ability to speculate. As the circulation is now, individuals can get as much money as they please at $2\frac{1}{2}$ per cent; nobody omits going into a speculation now because he cannot get the means; the means are readily procured, provided it is a solid and safe speculation. If the bankers found themselves in possession, in consequence of a large issue of notes from the Bank of England, of a larger quantity of circulating medium than they had before, would they not be induced, under those circumstances, in order to make use of their circulating medium, to advance it upon slighter security; and would not that have a tendency to increase speculation, and therefore to raise prices? — The banking houses in London are conducted with so much prudence at this time, they would not, under such circumstances, make advances on slight securities.

" Do you believe that an addition of 5,000,000*l.* to a previous circulation of 50,000,000*l.* would have no effect upon prices ultimately? —I cannot give an opinion as to the ultimate remote result①,

① Mr. Gurney very properly guards himself in his answer to the question, whether an addition of 5 millions to the circulation would not have an effect upon prices ultimately, by saying "I cannot give an opinion as to the ultimate remote result." Of course he could not; for if the addition were the consequence of an influx of gold which was to remain permanently in the country as our share of a general increase from the mines, the prices of all articles, other things remaining the same, would rise in the proportion which the 5 millions should bear to the previous circulation. There can upon this point be no difference of opinion. A permanent increase of this kind, in whatever way it were introduced, would enter into and pervade all the channels of circulation, reaching ultimately wages, and thus come into contact with every description of commodities. And a government inconvertible paper, issued in direct payments not on terminable securities, and not returnable on the issuing bank, would also, if not discredited, enter into and pervade all the channels of circulation, while the increased currency and the consequent advance of prices being beyond the bullion level, would be marked by a difference of exchange, and by an agio on gold and silver.

but I am confident that should the Bank of England make such addition to its circulation, artificially, at this time, it would remain in ope-rative, the transactions of the town not requiring it. It would remain wholly unused in the bankers' tills.

"When you speak of the circulating medium, do you include that which is locked up in the bankers' tills? —The bank notes which are locked up in the bankers' tills do not, in fact, act as a part of the circulating medium. No legislative measure or forced procedure of the Bank can increase, under that view, the amount of money actually in circulation."

Under the circumstances here supposed, the bankers, instead of locking up the notes in their tills, would probably return them to the Bank as deposits.

I have extracted this evidence of Mr. Gurney for the purpose not only of showing his opinion, and the reason for it, of the powerlessness of the Bank, under certain circumstances, of adding to the quantity of money in

---

If, indeed, 5 millions of bank notes were by some magical operation to be so issued by the Bank of England, that (supposing merely for the illustration that 1*l.* notes were in circulation) 5 millions of persons of the working classes depending for the means of their expenditure on their weekly wages, should each, on rising in the morning, find himself richer than when he had lain down, by discovering a 1*l.* note in his pocket, the effect would be great and sudden upon prices. Each probably of these 5 millions of persons would immediately lay it out in purchases of articles constituting the necessaries and luxuries of those classes. And the prices consequently of food (particularly the higher descriptions of it, such as meat), coarse clothing, beer, spirits, tobacco, would rise considerably. All the markets for those articles would exhibit great briskness of demand. And as the consumption would thus outrun the ordinary supply, there would be a disposition among the producers and importers to anticipate a continuance or increased ratio of such demand. Speculation, overproduction, and overtrading, would be the consequence. But the cause of increased consumption being by the supposition not permanent, the increased supplies would prove to be beyond the demand, and losses, and failures, and discredit, would follow. And the currency having, by the rise of prices, become redundant, the paper would return upon the Bank for gold for exportation. Thus after an intermediate disturbance, the prices and the circulation would be restored to their former level.

actual circulation, but of adducing his authority for the fact that the rate of interest in 1833 was so low, and that the facility of raising money upon anything like good security was so great, as to allow the fullest scope for persons entitled to credit entering into any speculation that offered a fair prospect; but that the low interest did not operate in inducing the bankers to make advances on slight securities. Nothing, indeed, can be more opposed to historical evidence than the assumption that speculations in commodities have been produced by mere facility of borrowing. The most memorable speculations in commodities, namely those in colonial produce in 1796 to 1798, and in nearly all descriptions of produce in 1808, and in articles of export in 1814, took place when there was anything but facility of credit. The instance of the speculations in commodities in 1824-1825 is that chiefly from which the supposed connection with the state of the circulation is inferred. I have before shown, that in the origin of most of those speculations, there was sufficient motive, without supposing any influence or stimulus from the Bank circulation, although the coincident enlargement of it allowed, perhaps, a wider and longer range to them.

The speculative advance of prices in 1824-1825 was not at all to be compared to that which took place in the anterior periods referred to. But there was a feature in some of the speculations in 1825 illustrative of a state of mind among the operators, which, although of not unfrequent manifestation in the stock and share markets, has been of very rare occurrence in the markets for produce. There were some few articles, almost exclusively spices, which were the subject of successive purchases at advancing prices, without any intermediate delivery of the article, by persons, each of whom was conscious that the price at which he was induced lo buy could not be long maintained, being greatly beyond the real value; but trusted either to his own observation, or to the assurance of the brokers, or other parties interested, that he could not fail of finding persons still more credulous than himself to take it off his hands at a still higher price. Transactions of this extravagant description can only be carried on through the medium of a delusion on the part of the great bulk of the operators, which has not been improperly designated as a *mania.* This term, as being descriptive of such superlative extravagance, implying an aberration of intellect, was first applied, I believe, to the case of the remarkable speculation in Tulips, thence called Tulipomania, which occurred in Holland in the 17th century. As the accounts of that extraordinary delusion, and its attendant circumstances, are at this time probably little known, they may be worth here inserting, as given in the following extract from vol. xiv. of the *Quarterly Review*, in an article on "A History of Inventions," by John Beckmann, professor in the University of Göttingen: —

"It is well known that in Holland the tulip became, about the middle of the seventeenth century, the object of a trade unparalleled in the history of commercial speculation. From 1634 to 1637 inclusive, all classes in all the great cities of Holland became infected with the tulipomania. A single root of a particular species, called the viceroy, was exchanged, in the true Dutch taste, for the following articles: —2 lasts of wheat, 4 of rye, 4 fat oxen, 3 fat swine, 12 fat sheep, 2 hogsheads of wine, 4 tuns of beer, 2 tons of butter, 1000 pounds of cheese, a complete bed, a suit of clothes, a silver beaker; value of the whole, 2500 florins. The account of this tulipomania is so curious, and, we believe, so just, that we shall make no apology for extracting it.

" 'These tulips afterwards were sold according to the weight of the roots. Four hundred perils (something less than a grain) of *Admiral Leifken*, cost 4400 florins; 446 ditto of *Admiral Vender Eyk*, 1620 florins; 106 perits *Schilder*, cost 1615 florins; 200 ditto *Semper Augustus*, 5500 florins; 410 ditto *Viceroy*, 3000 florins, &c. The species *Semper Augustus* has been often sold for 2000 florins; and it once happened that there were only two roots of it to be had, the one at Amsterdam the other at Haarlem. For a root of this species one agreed to give 4600 florins, together with a new carriage, two grey horses, and a complete harness. Another agreed to give for a root twelve acres of land; for those who had not ready money promised their moveable and immoveable goods, houses and lands, cattle and clothes. The trade was followed, not only by mercantile people, but also by the first noblemen, citizens of every description, mechanics, seamen, farmers, turf-diggers, chimneysweeps, footmen, maidservants, old clothes women, &c. At first, every one won, and no one lost. Some of the poorest people gained, in a few months, houses, coaches, and horses, and figured away like the first characters in the land. In every town some tavern was selected, which served as a'change, where high and low traded in flowers, and confirmed their bargains with the most sumptuous entertainments. They formed laws for themselves, and had their notaries and clerks.'

"The Professor observes that these dealers in flowers were by no means desirous to get possession of them; no one thought of sending, much less of going himself, to Constantinople to procure scarce roots, as many Europeans travel to Golconda and Visiapour to obtain rare and precious stones. It was, in fact, a complete stock jobbing transaction. Tulips of all prices were in the market, and their roots were divided into small portions, known by the name of *perits*, in order that the poor, as well as the rich, might be admitted into the speculation; the tulip root itself was out of the question; it was a non-entity, but it furnished, like our funds, the subject of a bargain for time.

" 'During the time of the Tulipomania, a speculator often offered and paid large sums for a root which he never received, and never wished to receive. Another sold roots which he never possessed or delivered. Often did a nobleman purchase of a chimneysweep tulips to the amount of 2000 florins, and sell them at the same time to a farmer, and neither the nobleman, chimneysweep, nor farmer had roots in their possession, or wished to possess them. Before the tulip season was over, more roots were sold, bespoke, and promised to be delivered, than in all probability were to be found in the gardens of Holland; and when *Semper Augustus* was not to be had, which happened twice, no species, perhaps, was oftener purchased and sold. In the space of three years, as Munting tells us, more than ten millions were expended in this trade, in only one town in Holland.'

"The evil rose to such a pitch that the States of Holland were under the necessity of interfering; the buyers took the alarm; the bubble, like the South Sea scheme, suddenly burst, and, as in the outset all were winners, in winding up very few escaped without loss."

The most remarkable circumstance attending the extraordinary state of things here described, is that it should have lasted so long; and I confess myself to be utterly at a loss for a satisfactory means of accounting for the duration of the speculation; for as to the fact of the existence, and consequently of the possibility, of such delusion on the one hand, practised upon by such deception on the other, we have abundant exemplifications of it in subsequent periods; although, except in the instance of one or two of the produce markets in 1825, it has been chiefly displayed in the share and stock markets.

The South Sea scheme, and other bubble projects in 1720, form a striking sera in the history of the extravagance of which, in cases where, from the opening of new fields for enterprise, experience is not applicable, the human mind is susceptible. On a lesser scale, although of more frequent occurrence, have been the speculations of modern times in projects by joint stock companies and in foreign loans. Extravagance of speculations of this kind was exhibited two years ago, on a large scale, on the Bourse at Paris, in asphalte and railway shares. Such occasional excitement and delusion, under the influence of which interested parties have succeeded in finding dupes to bid one over another, does not seem to depend upon any particular state of the circulation, or to require, as a condition of its existence, a fall in the rate of interest. In reference to the case of the Tulipomania, there is nothing that I am aware of in the financial or monetary state of Holland, at that time, to account for it; nor if there was, to explain why the folly was not exhibited in other articles of produce.

In the case of the memorable South Sea bubble in this country, in 1720, the presumption against any influence of the state of the circulation in producing it is alluded to, and very judiciously remarked upon, by Mr. Norman, in the following extracts from his evidence before the Bank charter committee in 1832.

"2543. If, for instance, it appears there was at the period of 1825 a great increase in the amount of paper circulating in the country, and there was, contemporaneously with that, a great rise in prices generally throughout the country, do you attribute the rise of prices on that occasion solely to the increased issue of paper, or do you think that it was in proportion only to the increased issue of paper? — I certainly should not either think that it was wholly owing to the increased issue of paper, nor do I conceive that it was in exact proportion to the increased issue of paper. I consider that in 1823 a sort of moral epidemic prevailed, and that you might have the same extent of currency, perhaps ten times over, without an equal degree of commercial excitement and subsequent distress. I do not consider that at all times even a similar amount of currency will perform exactly a similar amount of work; because there may be, in periods of great commercial excitement, a considerable increased velocity of circulation.

"2544. Do you consider, then, that a spirit of speculation, engendered by particular circumstances, at any particular time, may cause a great rise of prices entirely independent of any increase in the issues of paper money? —I think there might be a spirit of speculation abroad in the first instance, unconnected with an increased currency; and when that speculation had raised prices, an increase of the circulation would probably follow, but I do not think it should necessarily, though it does sometimes, precede it.

"2545. Therefore a spirit of speculation may be engendered, and there may be a rise of prices, and that rise of prices may be followed by an increase of issue as a necessary consequence, but the original rise of prices may happen entirely apart from any increase of the circulating medium, and owing solely to the speculation itself? —Decidedly so; suppose the case of new markets opened.

"2546. Are you at all acquainted with the state of things in 1720, at the time of the bubble? —It is stated in Mr. M'Culloch's *Dictionary of Commerce*, *that the*

Bank circulation	1718	1,829,000*l.*
—	1721	2,054,000*l.*
—	1730	4,224,000*l.*

"The increase, then, from 1718 to 1721 was 225,000*l.*, or about 75,000*l.* per annum; and from 1721 to 1730 it was 2,170,000*l.*, or about 241,000*l.*

"Thus the bubble year, 1721, was preceded by a low, and succeeded by a high, rate of increase, the latter unattended by any commercial excitement; there is, then, no necessary connection between a morbid spirit of speculation and a great augmentation of Bank issues. We might, perhaps, for all practical purposes, consider the circulation of the country in 1721 to have been metallic; nevertheless, at that time the excitement that prevailed seems to have much surpassed what we saw in 1825."

It may reasonably be supposed, that although a full circulation and a low and even a falling rate of interest do not actually generate, they may contribute to extend and keep up, such a state of delusion, or, as Mr. Norman emphatically designates it, a moral epidemic. And, doubtless, such a state of the circulation and of the rate of interest is calculated to favour all projects for investment of money which hold out the prospect of increased income to the subscribers. It favours also, although it does not originate, building and land speculations, the facility of borrowing being essential to the extension of such speculations.

When the market rate of interest happens to have fallen, if there has not previously been an equivalent rise in the price of government securities, there may be such a rise of the public funds as may have the character of speculation; on such occasions, the anticipation of the prices to which they ought to attain, may be an exaggerated one, but the foundation for the rise would substantially exist in a tendency to an adjustment of the relative value of different securities for investment. On the other hand, a rise in the market rate of interest, more especially if combined with political apprehensions, has a necessary tendency to reduce the prices of all securities, quite independently of any forced contraction of the circulation by the Bank. In truth, "the putting on of the screw" by the Bank, which is the modern phrase for raising the rate of discount, is nothing more than the Bank's following the rise of the market rate; the main well-founded charge against that establishment having been, not that it raised the rate unnecessarily or too soon, but that it did not follow that rise sufficiently soon, nor with sufficient effect.

It must be quite evident that, as a fall in the rate of interest favours projects which hold out to subscribers the prospect of an improved income, so a rise in the rate of interest is necessarily attended with a fall in the value of projects in actual operation, and with discouragement to the formation of new ones. ① But these effects of variations in the circulation and in the rate of interest, on the prices of securities, have no analogy in the markets for commodities.

If there exist grounds for speculation in goods, a coincident facility of credit *may*, but will not *necessarily*, extend the range of it. It is not easy, for instance, to imagine that the speculations in Tea would have gone to

① At the same time, if any event in politics or in trade should occur, affording grounds for *anticipating* a great alteration of prices, an immediate speculation will arise, in despite of a great coincident pressure on the money market, as witness the speculation, before referred to, in September last in Spanish and South American securities.

greater length, in a state of the utmost facility of credit, and of the easiest state of the money market, than they have recently done, while the money market was in its most contracted state. Allowing, however, that, given the motives for speculation, a facility of credit, and more especially a tendency, by abuses of banking, to an undue extension of it, may admit of a greater range to speculation, it will be found that the prices of commodities are little, if at all, affected by temporary alterations in the rate of interest; whilst a *permanent* increase of the rate of interest would have effects on the prices of produce directly opposite to those which are commonly supposed. A *permanent* rise of 2 per cent, or even 1 per cent, per annum, would ultimately raise the prices of commodities, inasmuch as it would increase the cost of production, especially of articles into the production of which machinery entered.

Although in some of the foregoing remarks I have blended speculation with overtrading, as having in some points of view the same tendency, namely, that of an abuse of credit; and although, in common language, each may be resolvable into the other, there are some distinctions between them which are not without their importance in practical application.

Speculation does not necessarily involve overtrading, inasmuch as it may, in some cases, operate as a disturbing cause upon prices, without any undue extension of credit; while it is of the very essence of overtrading to be connected with engagements on credit in undue and excessive proportion to the capital requisite to provide against adverse contingencies. The instances of any general prevalence of overtrading in this sense of the term, by speculative purchases of produce with a view to resale on the spot, to such an extent as to entail, by their failure, any material derangement of commercial credit, have of late years been of very rare occurrence. In 1825① the transactions of that kind, wild as some of them were, and disastrous to the individuals concerned, were only among the minor causes of the great depression of the exchanges, and the general derangement of the circulation at that period. The main causes, as I have elsewhere described, were overtrading, in the more distinct sense of the word, both in imports and exports of commodities, and in the transmission of capital, in great part borrowed, for loans to the states of South America, and for advances in mining schemes. There were at the same time in progress loans to some of the governments on the continent of Europe; these were probably with a less proportion of borrowed capital, and therefore might not come under the description of overtrading, but they co-operated with other causes in depressing the exchanges.

The overtrading in commodities was not stimulated or induced by the facilities of the money market, but by the very low stocks of all the raw materials of our manufactures at the close of 1824, which gave occasion for orders to be sent out for purchases abroad, to an extent and at prices which the event did not justify, and in such undue proportion of borrowed capital, that by the fall of markets here, the bills for the payment of those purchases, while they depressed the exchanges, could not be fully met.

The facilities of the money market which existed in 1824 doubtless favoured this overtrading in imports; but it was still more distinctly in speculative exports that the state of banking at that period favoured

---

① In the references which are frequently made to prices, anti the state of the circulation in 1825, it is commonly assumed that the rise in the prices of produce was, strictly speaking, *general*; and thence the inference that the cause must have been general. But a material feature in that view is overlooked, which is, that the corn market and the markets for provisions were not in the slightest degree under the influence of the spirit of speculation which prevailed in some of the other markets for produce.

overtrading. The Scotch banks, especially those of Glasgow, were considered as being greatly accessary in ministering to the spirit of adventure which then prevailed in shipments to foreign parts, by advancing a very large proportion of the amount on long-dated bills. Those shipments were mostly for account of the exporting manufacturers, or merchants, possessed of comparatively slender capitals; so that in the first instance a large mass of bills was created, and as the returns in most cases were not forthcoming when the acceptances became due, the Banks refusing to renew the bills, the acceptors of course failed. In England a good deal of the same overtrading in exports took place, although not perhaps to so great an extent as in Scotland. The general exports were, at that time, on a very extended scale, but being in a great proportion for account of the shippers, furnished no immediate means of payment for the large imports both of commodities and securities in 1825, which therefore drained the Bank of England; the returns however were forthcoming, with considerable loss, in 1826; and thus, with the diminished imports, caused the tide of the metals to set in so strongly as it did after the close of 1825. Since that period, the only instance of overtrading so extensive as in its consequences to disturb or derange commercial credit, has been in the case of the American houses in 1836-1837. In fact, with this exception, there has not been, since 1825, any difficulty or disturbance of the money market till the recent instance of it, which is the subject of the present discussion.

It may appear to my readers that, admitting the truth of the position for which I am arguing, of the absence of any immediate influence of variations in the amount of the circulation, and in the rate of interest on the markets for produce, a disproportioned importance has been attached to it in this discussion. But the point in question is of more importance than at first appears. It not only enters as an essential element into all discussions which have for their object to elucidate the causes of the most striking variations which the state of agriculture and trade have undergone in former times, but has formed a prominent part in the views which have been taken of the causes and probable consequences of the recent pressure on the money market, and of the means of obviating a recurrence of them. It has been considered that a state of general prices of commodities, including corn, above the level of prices abroad, has been the main cause of the depression of the exchanges; and that no rectification of these was likely to be accomplished without bringing down the prices of commodities, so as to cause a demand for export. Whereas, in truth, the prices of securities, with the price of corn, formed the whole feature of the case. And if the Bank had earlier attended to the importance of reducing the prices of securities, instead of looking to the prices of commodities, the circulation would have been in a much more satisfactory state.

Results of the examination of Mr. Hume's Speech. — In the foregoing examination of the prominent points of the charges brought against the Bank, I have endeavoured to show, —

1. That the practice of using the terms abundance and scarcity, and consequent value of money, indiscriminately, for value in use and value in exchange, is a pervading source of error throughout the whole of the reasoning by which the several inferences are drawn, and by which the general conclusion is sought to be established.

2. That the blending of the amount of deposits with the amount of bank notes issued, as coming under the single designation of paper circulation, emanating from the Bank of England, leads to an incorrect view of the working of the system.

3. That a reference to the amount of securities, as *a criterion of the quantity of money*, leads to the most palpable incongruities, a striking instance of which is exhibited in the consequence ascribed to the increase in the securities by upwards of 3 millions in the first six months of 1839, namely, that of having made money cheap, and caused speculations; the criterion so assumed, and the consequence ascribed to the increase of securities, involving the glaring inconsistency of being in direct variance with the criterion equally laid down, and the consequences ascribed to it, of the amount of the liabilities.

4. That the market rate of interest is subject to occasional variations which it is not in the power of the Bank to control; although, for short intervals, the regulation of its securities may have some temporary effect in increasing or diminishing, and, at any rate, in accelerating or retarding, a preexisting tendency in either direction.

5. That there is no foundation in fact or in reasoning for the theory which ascribes a necessary and direct influence to the occasional expansion or contraction of the Bank issues on the prices of commodities, by generating a spirit of speculation on the one hand, or by compelling a resort to forced and ruinous sales on the other. And that, in truth, there has been no remarkable disturbance of the markets for produce during the two last years; the articles of corn, cotton, and tea, which have notoriously been under the influence of peculiar circumstances, excepted.

6. If I have succeeded in my endeavours to prove the foregoing positions, it will follow that, as they embrace the whole of the grounds on which Mr. Hume has proceeded, in stating his views on the management of the currency by the Bank, he must be considered as having failed of

establishing his conclusion to anything like the extent that he has proposed, namely, "That the evils which the commercial and manufacturing interests have experienced are attributable chiefly, if not entirely, to the conduct of the Bank."

CHAPTER Ⅳ

ON THE SEVERAL ALTERATIONS PROPOSED IN THE MANAGEMENT OF THE CURRENCY, WITH A VIEW TO REMEDY THE EXISTING DEFECTS

It is an unfortunate consequence to the Bank of England, of the position of difficulty in which it suffered itself to be placed on the recent occasion, so soon after one similar in kind, although not so striking in degree, had occurred not many months before, that not only among persons connected with banking establishments, jealous of, and seeking to participate in, the privileges hitherto enjoyed exclusively by that institution, but among many, and so far as can be judged from published and publicly expressed opinions, among a vast majority of those who, without any immediate pecuniary interest, attend to and reason upon the subject, the continued existence of the privileges of the Bank of England beyond the period to which they are limited is looked upon as an evil not to be doubted, and not to be endured.

I have never been in the habit of attributing "absolute wisdom" to the management of the Bank of England; on the contrary, I have endeavoured to point out, in a spirit of fairness, what appeared to me to have been errors in the regulation of the currency, so far as it has depended upon the Bank. One of the sources of those errors has been the too great sympathy of the directors with the claims of the mercantile community, such sympathy being, moreover, but too consistent with the interests of the proprietors. And such being the source of their errors, I suspect very much that the mercantile and manufacturing interests, which, judging from the pamphlets on the subject, and from the tone of the public press, and from speeches both in and out of parliament, manifest a decided hostility to that establishment, will find themselves woefully mistaken in the anticipation of benefit which they look to derive from so great a change of system as that of which they seem desirous. They (I mean the bona fide objectors, and not those who expect to be admitted to a participation in the advantages of issuing paper money within the circle now exclusively occupied by the Bank of England) remind me of those sagacious individuals who imputed all the evils which they felt to the too lax reign of King Log, and made a discovery of the errors of their reasoning in the greater evils which they experienced under the more rigid rule of his successor.

The specific charge of mismanagement brought forward against the Bank of England is, that by arbitrarily making money too cheap at one time, and too dear at another, or, according to more ancient but somewhat more correct phraseology, by depressing the rate of interest at one time and raising it at another, with a mere view to the interests of their proprietors, the prices of commodities and the state of credit are unnecessarily exposed to all the fluctuations consequent upon occasional excessive expansion and contraction of the circulation. I have endeavoured to show how little foundation, in fact, there is for these imputed consequences of the Bank system; the main objection to the management being the danger to which the circulation has been exposed by it, of a suspension of its convertibility; against the recurrence of which danger there is, under the present system of regulation, if regulation it can be called, too little security.

If greater security against the recurrence of the danger of suspension, which we have so narrowly escaped, cannot be provided consistently with the maintenance of the existing establishment, in its main functions, of which the most important is that of being the sole source of issue of paper money within the circle to which its exclusive privilege extends, there ought to be no hesitation in taking early measures with a view to the substitution of some other system. Of any system so substituted, the primary object should be to afford the fullest security for the preservation, under any possible circumstances, of the present standard of value, or, in other words, of the constant and perfect convertibility of the paper into gold, according to the existing mint regulations.

But the machinery of the Bank of England is so excellent, and the working of it, in all its details, so perfect; it is an institution which, in its daily operations, is so interwoven with the habits of the mercantile and banking and trading classes of the community, that it will, in my opinion, be found to be deserving of serious consideration, whether, consistently with the preservation of the present establishment and with the maintenance and, if possible, an extension of its main function of being the principal, if not the sole, issuer of paper money, it is not susceptible of such improved regulation as may afford a sufficient security against the contingency of a predicament like that in which it has recently suffered itself to be placed.

SECTION 1 *On the proposed total separation of the business of issuing bank notes from that of the deposits, and other mere banking operations*

Among the able publications which appeared on the subject of the currency on occasion of the pressure on the money market in 1836-1837, there was a great preponderance of opinions in favour of a complete separation of the business of the issue of promissory notes from that of the deposits and other mere banking operations. This separation, it has been thought, could be effected consistently with the maintenance of the establishment of the Bank of England, preserving, and, if possible, extending, the sphere of its existing privileges of issue, but keeping the department for such issue distinct and separate from the banking department. Mr. Norman, who, as a director of long experience, and possessing scientific as well as practical knowledge, is to be considered as a high authority on this subject, has, in a publication which appeared about two years ago, given his opinion that the principle of retaining a fixed amount of securities should be abandoned, and a plan, of forming two distinct departments, substituted for it. The following is the passage of Mr. Norman's tract to which I allude: —

"The principle of retaining a fixed amount of securities, lately acted upon by the Bank, had the merit of being the first, if not the only, system at all in accordance with the rules of science which have ever yet guided the conduct of any very important body issuing a paper currency; yet it is palpably faulty, as mixing together circulation and deposits things in their nature distinct; and treating an increase or diminution of the former as equivalent to an increase or diminution of the latter; it is besides, as experience has shown, of extremely difficult application, and requiring, to be understood in practice, much explanation, which may not, after all, be successful in making it perfectly intelligible to the public. Rendering full justice to the talent of those who devised this scheme, it seems clear that the time is come when it ought to be abandoned, and the plan so ingeniously explained by Colonel Torrens, viz. that of forming two distinct establishments within the walls of the Bank, of which one should form the banking, the other the circulation department, be substituted for it, provided there are no insuperable difficulties of a practical kind in the way. Upon this point, the author's acquaintance with the internal mechanism of the Bank is not sufficiently particular to enable him to pronounce a decided opinion; he can only say that, although perhaps great, he cannot think them insuperable; and that no minor obstacles in the details of the corporation, should be allowed to stand in the way of a great public good."

With reference to the opinion here stated, which is deserving of every attention, I have before had occasion to observe, that whatever the merit may have been of the principle of retaining a fixed amount of securities, there is reason for thinking that the rule was derived from the fact, and not the fact from the rule, in the only instance in which, during four successive years, the securities had been preserved in a tolerable degree of uniformity, viz. from 1828 to 1832. During the whole subsequent period, it seems to have been a rule which regulated nothing. But I do not see why it should be pronounced to be faulty, simply because it mixes together circulation and deposits, things in their nature distinct. One great objection to it, doubtless, is, that there is no clear guide to the amount which should be considered as that which it is desirable to preserve unvaried; and another objection is, that without that part of the scheme propounded in 1832, which related to the proportion of one third of bullion to the liabilities, there would never be any security from the risk of overestimating the amount that might be so held; the consequence of which might be, under circumstances suddenly operating upon the exchanges, a drain of bullion to exhaustion before an adequate contraction of the whole circulation would be effected. ①

With regard to the substitution of the plan of separating the issuing from the mere banking department, I concur in the following opinion expressed by Mr. Pennington in his letter to me: — "Although there is at present, I apprehend, no confusion of accounts between the two departments, yet so complete a separation of them as that which has been suggested could not well be effected without a more formal division of debts and assets than mere bookkeeping can accomplish." And more especially do I participate with him in the doubt which he expresses when he adds, "Whether a deposit bank, on so large a scale as that of the Bank of England, could be so conducted as to prevent considerable variations in the value of the

① Tried, however, by the proportion of bullion to the liabilities, the irregularity of the action of the Bank is still more striking than by a reference to the amount of the securities; thus, for instance —

		Liabilities.		Bullion.
		£		£
May 28. 1889	-	26, 028, 000	-	5, 119, 000
July 23. 1839	-	26, 904, 000	-	3, 785, 000

And, in point of fact, there is no part of the evidence on the Bank Charter in 1832 which warrants the supposition so commonly entertained, that the directors considered themselves bound to endeavour to maintain their bullion in the proportion of one third to their liabilities. Indeed, it was quite impossible, consistently with their qualifications of the rule, that, except by accident, that or any other proportion should be observed.

currency, I own I have considerable doubts."

If no other scheme could be devised for preserving inviolable the principle of convertibility of the paper, which I hold to be the condition *sine qua non* of any sound system of currency, there would, in my opinion, be sufficient reason for the adoption of a plan on the footing of the separation suggested. But, on the supposition of its being deemed desirable to resort to such a plan, there would be great difficulty in preserving the separation, consistently with having the control of both departments under the same body of directors. And since, in regard to the difficulties of a practical kind in the way of such arrangement, Mr. Norman, with all his experience as a director, states that his acquaintance with the internal mechanism of the Bank is not sufficiently particular to enable him to pronounce a decided opinion, it would be the highest presumption in me to hazard any conjecture upon the practicability of it.

Supposing, however, the practical difficulties of the machinery to be got over, I am very much inclined to suspcct, that the plan, in the working, would not be found to answer all the expectations entertained of it by its advocates. It would, indeed, if strictly enforced, effectually preclude all danger, under any probable circumstances, of a suspension of cash payments; and the full security on that score would, if it could only thus be obtained, be a compensation for much attendant inconvenience. But although such a separation, if it could be really and rigidly maintained, would effectually preserve the convertibility of the paper under any probable demand for gold, it might, under some conceivable circumstances, be attended with a whimsical effect. Supposing the deposit department to have no convertible capital beyond its *rest*, and to have advanced on securities an undue proportion of its deposits, a sudden demand might, under circumstances of no improbable occurrence, arise from the depositors to an extent beyond that which the reserve of notes of bullion, or of securities immediately convertible, could satisfy. In such case the deposit department, in its extremity, might apply to the issuing department for an advance of bank notes or gold; but the latter department must be supposed inexorable, and so the banking department under the same establishment might stop payment, while the issuing department would go on as usual.

The heaviest charge against the Bank, in its management of the circulation, of late years, has been that of allowing itself to be brought to the very verge of suspension; for, in other respects, it is rather in their management of the deposits, than in that of the issues, that the directors have operated inconveniently on the rate of interest. In fact, hitherto the main inconvenience that has been felt in this country, from what is called, but with no great propriety, a disturbance or derangement of the currency, during the last twelve-months is confined to the variations which have occurred in the rate of interest; for of commercial discredit, or of disturbance in the markets for produce, or in the value of property in lands or houses, nothing whatever has been experienced. But is it clear, and on what grounds can it be shown, that under a purely metallic variation there would not occasionally be very great fluctuations in the rate of interest, and under many conceivable cases much greater?

I am inclined to think, as I have before observed, that in an extended commerce like ours, in which it is inevitable that confidence must prevail in ordinary and still more in prosperous times, and that credit must consequently, in various forms, such as bills of exchange, book credits, and contracts for time, enter largely into the general transactions, overbanking and overtrading may, and among a highly ambitious and enterprising mercantile community must, occasionally take place. And although overbanking and overtrading might not, under a rigid metallic variation, proceed so far as they might in the case of an accompanying increase of paper money, the transition to a state of discredit, although perhaps, but not certainly, within a shorter range in point of time, would in some instances, be more severe; that is, the transition from a low to a high rate of interest might be more abrupt, and to a higher rate, and consequently a revulsion of credit, if there had been previous overtrading, would be more sudden, and more severely felt.

In times, for instance, when a sudden demand for foreign currency should arise, such as the importation of a large quantity of foreign corn, and simultaneously, perhaps, of several other kinds of produce, in consequence of previously short stocks, the pressure on the exchanges causing a sudden export of the circulating medium in payment, before increased exports of commodities, could be made available, (and still more, as has been the case in some instances, for example, in 1818, when large loans by the continental powers occasioned the transmission of capital from this country for investment in foreign securities), might be such as to entail a sudden and very great contraction of the currency. This would be felt most severely in transactions on credit. Large amounts of bills of exchange and promissory notes, and book credits, for transactions on an extended scale, entered into while confidence had been entire, and when new fields of enterprise had presented themselves, might just then be becoming due. At the same time the bankers, feeling immediately the effect upon their reserve of the contraction of the circulation, would call in their advances on book credits. Under such circumstances, the merchants and manufacturers, who might have to borrow or discount for the discharge of those engagements, would have to pay enormously for the accommodation, by a very high, and, it might be, a very ruinous rate of interest or discount.

It may be asked, why this should be the case? Why, or how, upon a strictly metallic basis, the transition from a low to a high rate of interest, even in the case supposed, should be likely to be more severe than under a system in which, as at present, the two departments of deposits and issues are blended? The answer to this question is, that whether it might not be more severe would depend upon the state of trade and of credit, both private and public, at the time when, from circumstances arising either at home or abroad, there should occur a demand upon the Bank for gold.

Under circumstances, for instance, like those in which the trade and circulation stood in 1838, there having been no general prevalence of overtrading, and not much observable of unduly extended credit, I conceive that the early check which, upon the plan here supposed, the first marked demand for export of bullion would have occasioned, in the contraction of the circulation, and a consequent early and decided advance in the market rate of interest, would, for the reasons before given (more especially as it would have prevented so large an importation of American securities), have obviated, in all probability, the necessity for such stringent measures as have since been found requisite to save the Bank of England from suspending its payments.

But if an examination were entered into of the manner in which the system of separation would have worked, if it had been in operation, in 1835-1836, it would be found that, while it would have presented no obstacle whatever to the phenomena of the low rate of interest, the speculations in shares, and the overtrading with the United States and the East Indies and China, and the extravagant credits granted by the American houses, it would infallibly, when the turn came, (as it must equally have come,) causing a demand for gold, both for export and for internal purposes, have been attended with a recoil much more abrupt and violent than that which was experienced.

I have before had occasion to observe, that, as far as regards the bank notes in circulation, the amount in 1835-1836 was not above that which would have existed under a separate and metallic variation; while the banking or deposit and discount department, receiving so very large an accession of deposits as it then did receive, would equally have invested the same proportion as it did in securities, the same reasons applying. Consequently, the rate of interest would have been as low, and the facilities of credit, and the motives for making use of it in overtrading, would equally have existed, without any check from the issuing department, inasmuch as gold was still flowing in till an advanced period of the spring of 1836. When, however, the demand for export of gold arose, such demand, operating in an immediate contraction of the circulation of Bank notes, would, in all probability, have rendered a considerable proportion of the immense mass of bills of exchange, both foreign and inland, inconvertible, except at a very much higher rate of interest than then prevailed. A sudden decrease of two millions, from the already low amount of the circulation, would have had a serious effect on the discount market, and perhaps on commercial credit; an effect much greater than a similar reduction under the present system.

The London bankers and the great money brokers, and consequently the country bankers, under the existing system, proceed with some degree of confidence, even in times of pressure, in advances or discounts on unexceptionable securities, at the same rate as that announced by the Bank, or, in the case of the money brokers, with the addition of a commission; because they feel assured that they can draw bank notes out on an emergency, by sending bills into the bank for discount, and so fill the void which would otherwise exist in the means of making the customary amount of payments. If no such grounds of confidence existed, the limitation of discounts or loans by the bankers and money dealers would, under the first pressure, be in a much greater proportion than that of the amount of reduction in the circulation. The deposit department might, doubtless, answer the demands of its depositors, and issue what bank notes it held to them and to applicants for discount, and so, to the extent of its stock of bank notes and bullion, might offer relief. But in the case which I am supposing as that of August 1836, there would certainly have been no bullion, and very few bank notes, to spare in the deposit department; for, upon the first feeling of pressure, the deposits would have been diminished, and the applications for discounts would have increased. Indeed, the withdrawal of deposits, large as it was, having been to the extent of upwards of five millions between January and September of that year, would have been much larger under the circumstances supposed, and could only have been met by forced sales of securities, accompanied by an extreme limitation, if not an absolute refusal, of further discounts. But it could not by those or any other means fill any void in the circulation of bank notes which the demand for bullion had caused; nor could it have interfered, as it did, in behalf of the Northern and Central Bank, or in behalf of the American houses; and it is left to the reader to judge, whether the rise in the rate of discount would not have been, in the case supposed, much greater than it actually was.

Reasonable grounds, indeed, might be shown for the opinion, that in the majority of cases of reaction from previous overtrading, against which it is doubtful whether there would be greater security, the pressure, under the proposed separation of the deposit and banking departments, would be more severe than under the present system. The greater restrictiveness, and the consequent liability, under certain circumstances, to a more sudden rise in the rate of interest, and to a more abrupt termination of unduly extended credit, ought most unquestionably not to be allowed to outweigh the consideration of the greater security which the plan proposed would afford against the contingency most of all to be guarded against, of a suspension of cash payments. But independently of the greater restrictiveness or rigidity with which the machinery of such a system is calculated to act, the anomalies and difficulties attending any attempt at carrying into effect a complete separation, such as that suggested, in the same establishment, and under the same general control, appear to be of such a nature as not easily to be surmounted.

Upon the whole I cannot help thinking, with great deference to the deservedly high authority of those persons who have recommended such separation of the business of the Bank of England into two departments, perfectly distinct and independent of each other, that if such separation could be carried completely into effect, which seems to be doubtful, the system would not be found to work so well, that is, with so little disturbance of the money market, as the system of union of the two departments, provided that the system as it exists in that respect could be guarded from such danger of suspension of convertibility as we have so narrowly escaped.

SECTION 2 *Plan proposed for retaining the present system of union of the two departments, with greater security against the risk of suspension*

There is one alteration in the mode of management, which, if the directors could be prevailed upon to adopt, with some satisfactory assurance to the public for faithful adherence to it, would, as it strikes me, afford the full advantages of the greater facility and play of the machinery attending the present system, without the liability to a recurrence of such alarm for the convertibility as has been recently experienced. The alteration which I would venture to suggest is a very simple one, namely, that discarding the rules which were professed about keeping the securities even, and of investing in a full state of the currency two thirds of their liabilities, rules which were inconsistent with each other, and were in fact never observed, the directors should undertake to hold in reserve a much higher average amount of bullion than they have hitherto considered it necessary or consistent with the interests of their proprietors to maintain: the fundamental error in the management of late years having been, that of attempting to regulate the large united amount of circulation and deposits upon too small an average reserve, partaking very much of the character of overbanking.

The opinion which I ventured to express in a former part of this work, written two years ago, "that as far as the eventful experience of the last fourteen years, viz., since 1824, can serve as a guide for judgment on this point, there appear to be good grounds for believing that not less than ten millions can ever be considered as a safe position of the treasure of the Bank of England, seeing the sudden calls to which it is liable," has received ample confirmation from recent events.

Circumstances of no improbable occurrence prove clearly, that with our present corn laws large foreign payments, in the event of a deficient harvest, concurring with other causes of an adverse exchange, may require an export of bullion to the extent of ten millions. That was the amount of treasure in the Bank coffers in 1838, and it was reduced in 1839 by actual export to little more than two millions; and if to the eight millions actually exported be added the two millions of credit which the Bank availed itself of on the Paris bankers, besides a further amount of about 700,000*l.* which were drawn upon Hamburg against a distinct credit, supposed to be for account of the Bank of England, these amounts being in lieu of so much shipment of bullion, the total balance of demand on the coffers of the Bank may be considered as equivalent to ten millions. In 1836 the stock of bullion, having been nearly eight millions, was reduced in a few months below four millions; and if the ports had then opened, as was at one time probable, for the admission of foreign corn at the lowest duty, there is every reason to believe that the Bank would have been driven as nearly to exhaustion at that time as it has recently been. The narrowness of such escapes, especially when at the expense of such an expedient as that of a resort for assistance to the bankers of Paris, is any thing but creditable to the country and to the institution.

Hitherto, at least since 1830, whenever, by the tide of the metals inwards, the amount of bullion has reached ten millions or upwards, the Bank has taken *active measures* to convert a part of so unproductive a stock into securities; and consequently the intervals during which the amount was at that high rate were very short; a few months in 1833 and a few weeks in 1838; while during 1834 the amount gradually fell from 9,954,000*l.* to 6,720,000*l.*, ranging under this last sum during the whole of 1835; and in the entire interval of the three years, 1834-1835-1836, the amount of bullion never reached one third, and was several times under one sixth, of the liabilities.

If the directors had been as much on the alert to reduce their securities when the bullion was going out as they have been impatient to increase the productive part of their assets, and so to drive back the metals when they tended to reach or to exceed ten millions, there would be something like principle in the regulation; but as it is, while they have been impatient under an accumulation amounting to ten millions, and have adopted forcible measures for reducing it, they have been perfectly passive till it got below five millions, when, as in the recent instance, the tide had already set so strongly outwards that their utmost subsequent efforts could hardly prevent a complete exhaustion of their treasure.

The plan which I would propose is, that when the tide of the metals sets fully in again, the Bank rate of discount should be kept so steadily above the market rate as progressively to reduce their securities through that channel, without increasing them by other investments. The effect of this would be to ensure a replenishment of their coffers to ten millions; and with the purpose of endeavouring to preserve that amount *on an average*, it would not be expedient on the part of the Bank to take any active measures for the increase of its securities. It is not improbable, judging by the strength and fulness of the tide with which the metals have flowed in on some former occasions, that the amount might thus reach fifteen millions, beyond which, according to analogy from former experience, if is not likely that it would go. The probability is, that in the fluctuations to which our trade, particularly that in corn, is liable, the exchanges would take an adverse turn; bullion would flow out, the market rate of interest would rise to the Bank rate, and then it would be that the advantage of the large stock of bullion would be felt; because to the extent of five millions the foreign exchanges or internal demand might be allowed to operate upon the stock of bullion, without the necessity on the part of the Bank to counteract that demand by any active measures in raising its rate of discount or selling its public securities. The quantity of money in such case in actual circulation would not be reduced, excepting in a small proportion only, to the reduction of the amount of bullion, because the withdrawal of deposits would, under the slight pressure on the money market which would attend a rise in the market rate of discount to the Bank rate, restore to the circulation an amount of Bank notes nearly equivalent to that which had been in circulation against the bullion taken out. In the majority of cases of the variations in the value of our currency relative to the currencies of other countries, whether originating on this side or the other, the balance of payments would in all probability be satisfied by the export of that amount of bullion. If the drain, however, on the coffers of the Bank should, after a reduction to ten millions, continue so as to give reason to apprehend the existence of more extensive and deeper seated causes of demand for the metals, measures might be taken for its counteraction, without producing alarm and disturbance of the money market on the one hand, or endangering an extreme and unsafe degree of reduction of the Bank treasure on the other.

A latitude for variation between fifteen millions and five millions would afford a much greater exemption from shocks on the money market than a variation, as it has recently been, between ten millions and nothing.

That the Bank might, by a regulation of its securities, maintain a high average amount of bullion, such as has here been suggested of fully ten millions, cannot admit of any reasonable doubt. And I believe that such a regulation would be more easily practicable than either that of maintaining the securities even, or of preserving the bullion in any given proportion to the liabilities. The money market would be less liable to be disturbed than under either of the two latter alternatives. The utmost alteration of the rate of discount to which the Bank might have occasion to resort would probably not exceed 1 per cent; and the occasions for an alteration even. to that extent would probably be rare. A system like this would be less restrictive, that is, the principle of limitation would operate less rigidly under such a regulation of the bullion, consistently with a blending, as at present, of the issue and deposit departments in the Bank of England, than by their total separation.

I feel strongly confirmed in this view of the greater facility, that is, of a principle of more easy adaptation, in the present system, subject only, as an essential condition, to the maintenance of a much larger stock of bullion than has hitherto been retained, by the opinion of Mr. Gurney. The following is an extract from his evidence before the committee on the Bank Charter in 1832.

3592. "Would not these fluctuations in the value (interest) of money take place even although there were no paper circulation? —I think they would take place, and to a greater extent.

"Why do you think to a much more severe extent? —Because the transactions would at times be much more cramped, a circulation of coin not giving nearly the same facilities.

"Do you think that it is possible that any system of banking could be established in the country which would prevent the variations in exchanges you have stated to exist? —Decidedly not.

"What state of currency do you think would be the state that would occasion the least fluctuation; a paper, or a metallic, or a mixed currency? —A mixed circulation has the best effect in this respect. No system of currency can be established that will prevent these fluctuations; they are in the very nature of things; you can no more prevent the value (interest) of money rising and falling, or the variations of the foreign exchanges, and their consequences, than you can prevent variations in the prices of corn.

"In a sound state of the currency, will not those fluctuations that occasionally happen be dependent altogether upon commerce? —Not altogether.

"Will they not be mainly dependent upon the natural changes in the value of commodities, foreign and domestic? —Partly, but not wholly so.

"Having stated that those fluctuations would be violent, supposing the currency altogether metallic, and that they would also occur if the currency was altogether paper, do you not think that a mixed state, such as we have now, or one similar to that, is the one most likely to prevent those fluctuations? —I think that such a circulating medium as we have now has the most wholesome effect of any in controlling these variations. ①

---

① Mr. Gurney, in speaking of the wholesome effect of the system in controlling variations in the rate of interest, was referring to the management such as it had been between 1827 and 1832, when, chiefly by the possession of a large amount of treasure, it had in two recent instances surmounted a considerable drain without any great pressure on the money market. In the former part of this work I have pointed out strong grounds for presumption, that if during that interval the variation of the circulation had been on a purely metallic basis, the pressure on the money market, which had been hardly felt, would have been very severe.

"As it is in the nature of the paper circulation, that when prices are rising there should be an increased issue of that circulation, and when prices are falling is there not a natural tendency to contract the issue; does not this increased issue of paper when prices are rising tend still further to increase the prices, and does not that reduction of paper when prices are falling tend still further to reduce the prices; and from those circumstances is it not in the nature of a paper circulation to occasion greater fluctuations than would take place if the circulation were purely metallic ? —I think not; a state of increasing prices has a tendency to increase the amount of circulation; a decrease in prices has the contrary effect; but it is an effect that operates more decidedly upon our country bank circulation. It does not operate in the same extent upon the circulation of the Bank of England, because their circulation is more fixed in its character, so much of it being represented by a debt due from government, which does not fluctuate. A country banker's circulation fluctuates wholly and solely, in my opinion, with the state of prices and the extent of transactions in his own district, and he cannot increase the amount beyond what is thus called for. ① It is a

① The tendency here observed by Mr. Gurney will go far to explain the expansion of the country bank issues in 1838, and in the first six months of 1839. The great increase of the prices of agricultural produce, but still more the great increase of transactions by the circulation of foreign corn in the interior, creating a vast mass of bills of exchange among factors, and dealers, and millers, must obviously have caused an enlarged circulation of bank notes for the liquidation of such transactions. The bank notes so created were not the cause of the rise of prices, and of the consequently increased transactions by bills of exchange and other forms of credit, but those increased transactions necessarily entailed an increase of bank notes. This was the case while the prices were rising, and while the distribution of the large quantities of foreign corn was in progress. After the bulk of that supply had found its way to its ultimate destination, and after prices had reached their maximum, the activity and extent of transactions were diminished, so that, independently of the influence which the reduction of the Bank of England issues was calculated to produce, the tendency of the country bank circulation would have been to a contraction in the last six months of 1839.

mistake when any people talk of over-issues of country bankers as being under their own control; if they did not issue their own paper, they must, when their district calls for it, issue Bank of England notes.

"In what manner then would the prices of commodities be affected if on a rise of prices taking place the country bankers did not increase their own circulation, but issued Bank of England notes in the manner suggested in the last answer? —I do not think it would affect prices at all, whether they issued a certain amount of their own notes, and added a certain amount of Bank of England notes, or whether they issued the whole amount in their own notes.

"In issuing an increased amount of Bank of England notes, do you assume that the number of Bank of England notes in circulation would remain the same, or be increased? —It depends upon the extent of their circulation; at times the amount of the notes issued by the Bank of England is more than comes into operation or circulation; the effect of this is a reduction in the value (interest) of money, and very great facilities in money transactions; this low state of money, and these great facilities, ultimately produce an extension of the amount of notes that come into operation, and extension of transactions; this extension of transactions after a time operates upon prices, but it is not a very rapid process; it is rather slow than otherwise.

"Do you think that if the country bankers issued notes of the Bank of England, instead of issuing their own notes, the effect you have described upon prices would be more gradual than by issuing their own notes? —I think it would be more sudden.

"Why do you think it would be more sudden? —Because it would then be altogether under the control of the Bank of England only; the Bank is strongly influenced by the question of gold and of the exchanges.① If it is a circulation of a country bank paper, it becomes modified in a considerable degree by the interests and wants of the particular town or district; and although it must ultimately follow a reduction of the notes of the Bank of England, it would not so suddenly follow it as if it was altogether under the control of the Bank of England. I think the effect would be more injurious to the provincial towns to be so controlled, than by leaving it in the hands of those whose business it is, and who know what is wanted in each town.

"Does it not follow from what you have said, that an over issue of notes of country bankers cannot easily be effected? —My belief is that it cannot be effected by any act of the country banker."

The opinion here expressed, that an over-issue of notes by country bankers cannot be easily effected is well worth following out. The security is a point clearly distinct from the question of undue enlargement.

My purpose, however, in giving this extract from Mr. Gurney's evidence is to adduce a very important practical authority in support of my view of the greater rigidity of the operation of the principle of limitation of a purely metallic variation, that is, of a variation in the amount of the circulation corresponding exactly with every varying turn of the exchanges, as compared with a system like that which prevails in the management of the Bank of England; a system which, if the security of a permanently

① If the case of the increase of the country circulation in 1838 were gone into, and fairly followed out, it might be shown, that if the Bank of England had been the sole issuer there *would*, and under a purely metallic circulation there *might*, have been an equal increase of the country circulation; but the reduction in 1839 would probably in the latter case have been earlier, and would most certainly have been more abrupt.

increased stock of bullion could be added to it, appears to be preferable in most points of view to any others which have been hitherto before the public. There are, however, objections to the essential condition of a greatly increased average amount of bullion, which are very formidable, and may be found to be insuperable.

Of these objections the most important are the two following: —

1. The interests or supposed interests of the Bank proprietors; I say supposed, because their real interests are bound up with the permanence of the establishment, which can only be preserved in as far as it may be found to be conducive to the public interests.

2. The country circulation, which, although I do not admit that it *has in point of fact* in any considerable degree counteracted any efforts of the Bank of England to regulate its issues by the exchanges, might be apt to extend itself at the expense, or, in other words, to the exclusion, of the Bank of England circulation, in the districts beyond sixty-five miles from London in which Bank of England notes now circulate.

The first of these objections, namely, that which may be supposed to arise on the part of the proprietors, must of course weigh greatly with the directors. The unproductiveness, in the view of immediate profit, of so large a stock of bullion as is here proposed to be maintained on an average, must of course be a serious consideration with reference to the dividend. To be liable to have a stock of bullion occasionally reaching nearly to the amount of notes in circulation is assuredly an unpromising prospect for the proprietors; and I am not at all aware of any means of getting over the difficulty hence arising, unless some compensation in the terms of the renewal of the charter were offered; a compensation which, seeing the prevailing prejudices against the Bank of England, is not likely to be granted.

The other objection is perhaps still more formidable, namely, that arising out of the country circulation. I do not at all enter into the charges against the regulation of the issues of the country banks, whether private or joint stock, as tending necessarily to surcharge the general circulation of the country, and to depreciate the value of the currency. Since the severe discipline and purification which the country banks underwent in 1825-1826 there is no distinct ground to impute to the amount of their issues either the origin or any material aggravation of the occasional variations m the state of the money market which have since occurred. Whatever of inconvenience from those variations may have been experienced is fully as much chargeable to the Bank of England as to the country banks; and in the case of neither of them do I consider that blame attaches so much to the regulation of their issues, (in which they are both limited in a degree that the public hardly appreciates), as in the management of their deposits, or rather in their advances by way of loan and discount. In the flagrant cases of the Northern and Central Bank in England, and of the Agricultural and Commercial Bank in Ireland in 1836, their extravagance was, not in their issues, but in the extent and nature of the securities on which they had advanced the monies of both their depositors and subscribers. So likewise in the more recent instances of some other joint stock banks. And as regards the Bank of England, it has been in the use of its deposits, both in 1836 and 1839, and not in its circulation, that it has been fairly chargeable with over *banking*, insomuch that if it had not had the resource of its credit in the issue of its notes the mere banking department must have stopped payment. So much I have thought necessary to state respecting the management, both by the country banks and the Bank of England, in their general business of banking, in order to clear the ground for what I have to observe relative to their respective parts in the issue and circulation of paper money. Their competition in the issue of bank notes beyond sixty-five miles from London is a good deal, if not mainly, determined by the rate of interest which they respectively charge. Now, if the Bank of England were, with a view of preserving a high average amount of bullion, to keep its rate of interest and discount permanently high, and mostly above the market rate, the effect would be, in all probability, the gradual encroachment of the country issues, and their ultimately excluding the Bank of England circulation.[①] Even on the present system of the Bank of England, of competing in the rate of interest with the country banks, the latter, there is reason to believe, have been gaining ground.

Mr. Norman, writing in 1838, took occasion to observe, — "It is the more necessary to take immediate measures for the reform of the country issues, because, as things now are, the existence of the currency of the Bank of England out of the metropolis hangs upon a thread. Even in Lancashire, which used to be supplied by it exclusively, joint stock notes are now circulated, and will gradually more and more make their way, until their rivals are entirely expelled. The final result will be to confine the latter to a constantly diminishing circle around the metropolis." — (*Remarks on Currency and Banking*, p. 104.)

There would, therefore, be no fairness in requiring the Bank of England

---

① I do not here take into consideration the arrangements made by the Bank of England with some of the country banks, for the purpose of employing its notes supplied by advances on securities below its public rate of discount. Such arrangements complicate the question, and should be separately considered.

to keep up a stock of bullion, which might, if its country circulation were so reduced, amount on an average to two thirds or three quarters of the amount of its issues of notes, while the country bankers are exempted from keeping any reserve at all of gold, and are able, by the present rapidity of communication with London, to obtain at the shortest notice a sufficient supply from the Bank of England to answer any unusual demand. Accordingly, if it should be deemed desirable by the legislature to enforce upon the Bank of England the necessity of habitually maintaining a larger amount of bullion than it has hitherto maintained, the Bank of England would be entitled to require, in the view both of compensation for the expense and of being the better able to regulate the circulation, to be the exclusive source of the issue of paper money. Whether an arrangement would admit of being made with the country banks on equitable terms to this effect I am not prepared to say. I have merely thrown out the suggestion of it, as being desirable, if practicable, with a view to the convenience of the public.

If these objections should be deemed insurmountable, as from the nature of the interests involved is but too probable, it may be considered a work of supererogation to notice two other objections, which, were the scheme otherwise practicable, would be likely to be urged against it. But as they involve questions of principle, and proceed on specious and popular grounds, they may be worth a passing remark.

One of the objections here alluded to is that of the supposed unproductiveness, in a national point of view, of so much capital locked up without employment. If the increased average amount of bullion were, which it is not, so much capital locked up from profitable employment, that consideration would not be a sufficient objection, seeing that the reason for maintaining a high average amount is to mitigate the tendency to great and sudden fluctuations in the quantity of money in actual circulation; fluctuations which, when they do occur on an extensive scale, are attended with a disturbance and misdirection of capital and industry, and with consequent losses, which in a national point of view would greatly overbalance any profit which might have been derived from the investment of that capital in securities, and thus driving the gold abroad. But in truth the stock of bullion so reserved cannot be looked upon, in any fair sense of the term, as unproductive. It is in fact a part, and upon the grounds which I have stated an essential part, of the currency circulating in the form of paper, which is substituted for its only legitimate purpose, public convenience; a purpose which would not be fulfilled if a large proportion of gold were not held, to answer unusual calls for payment abroad, to which the paper is not applicable.

The other reason that might and probably would be urged against any scheme involving so large a reserve of bullion as has here been suggested rests on the supposition, that the attracting of the extra amount must be preceded by, and attended with, an undue and unnatural contraction of the currency, the effect of which would be, a depression of prices to an unnecessary extent.

This is a consideration with a view to the public, which, coinciding as the reasoning does with the objection on the score of profit, to a large reserve, it is probable weighed with the Bank directors in their efforts to stop the influx, and to get rid of what they seem to have considered the excess, of bullion, in the spring of 1838. With reference to the influx at that time, Mr. Norman, in the tract before quoted, observed, — "It is probable that an increase will be found in the treasure of the Bank, between its lowest amount last spring and the highest just previous to the next turn of the exchanges, of from seven to eight millions. Now such an influx of treasure is unnatural, and could never occur with a metallic circulation. Its effects, greater or less in proportion to the error, will be accompanied in the first instance by a depression of prices, unnecessary in extent and continued too long, and finally by a reaction, which will occasion an equally unnecessary and faulty excess on the other."

Why such an influx of treasure could never occur with a metallic circulation does not very clearly appear. With our very extended foreign trade, which is habitually conducted on the footing of a large proportion of our exports being on long credits, while our imports are mostly paid for at short dates, and with our present restrictions on the corn trade, there might be, as there have been, on the one hand, large sudden payments abroad requiring a considerable export of bullion before any excess of merchandise exported could bring returns; and, on the other hand, when the demand for corn and for other imports, including foreign securities, ceased or abated, the returns for an excess of former exports would be coming forward, and bullion must in that case form, for want of other means, a large part of such returns. Such was the case in 1815-1816, in 1820-1822, and, excepting as regards corn, such was the case with the influx of bullion in 1826 and in the early part of 1838. If the ports should be shut against the importation of corn for the next two or three years, and, at the same time, from salutary distrust or other causes, there should be a diminished demand for foreign securities, there is likely to be a strong tendency to an influx of the metals; and it is not easy to understand why it should not be equally strong with a purely metallic variation. The Bank of England may doubtless, as in 1836 and 1838, by a competition for the investment of its deposits, create a renewed demand for foreign securities, and so stop the influx of bullion; but so the deposit department likewise might do if its functions were separated from the issuing department.

But it is to the supposed unnatural depression of prices, ascribed as an effect of the contraction of the circulation, which is assumed to lead to the influx of the metals, that my remark is directed. This hypothesis rests upon the currency theory of prices, which supposes that the contraction of the circulation, in such a case as that alluded to, reduces prices, and that the reduced prices force an influx of the metals; whereas the contraction, or rather the diminution of the circulation, is in such cases the consequence of a fall of prices from causes arising from the state of trade, and peculiar circumstances affecting the supply and cost of production on the one hand, and consumption on the other. As to an increased value of the precious metals, which might be supposed to be the consequence of retaining permanently an addition of fully five millions as a reserve in the coffers of the Bank, it would, according to any received grounds of computation, amount to so very minute a percentage, as to have no *perceptible* influence, and may, therefore, safely be neglected.

If the several objections here enumerated, or some one or more of them, be considered as placing out of the question a continuance of the present system of the Bank, with only some assurance for the maintenance of a much larger stock of bullion, and if the difficulties attending a complete separation of the functions of the Bank into two distinct departments under one establishment, be found, as they appear likely to be, insuperable, it remains to consider what are the alternatives which present themselves.

SECTION 3 *On the two schemes which offer themselves, consistently with the present standard, in the event of the bank charter not being renewed*

In the event of the discontinuance here supposed, of the exclusive privileges of the Bank of England, there appear to be only two other schemes which offer themselves for adoption, consistently with the maintenance of a system of mixed currency, consisting of coin of the present standard, and of paper strictly and constantly convertible into coin. As to any alteration of the present standard, I do not for a moment admit that the recent instances of jeopardy in which the convertibility of the paper has been placed furnish the shadow of a ground for questioning the justice and policy of maintaining it in every respect unaltered and unimpaired. I may perhaps offer, before I conclude, a few remarks upon some of the reasonings put forward against the system of the currency according to its present standard, independently of the question of the mode of administering the paper part of the circulation, such paper being required to be strictly convertible. In the meantime, supposing an alteration of the standard to be out of the question, the two schemes which offer themselves, in the event of the cessation of the Bank Charter, are —

1. A national bank, under the management of commissioners appointed by parliament, upon a footing analogous in principle to that originally recommended by the late Mr. David Ricardo. The commissioners being bound so to regulate the issues, beyond a certain fixed amount invested in securities, by exchanging notes for gold, or gold for notes, as should have

the effect of making the variations in the amount of the circulation correspond exactly with the variation which would occur if it were wholly metallic.[①]

Without entering into the details of such a scheme, which, as it has in several instances of late been propounded, is doubtless sufficiently familiar to my readers, I have to observe, on its general outlines, that it has much to recommend it, and that it would be entitled to a decided preference over any other in the event of the non-renewal of the Bank of England Charter. But, upon the grounds which I have before stated, the trading and banking part of the community would have to lay their account in a much more rigid principle of limitation to the credit part of the circulation, and a consequent occasional greater rise in the rate of interest, upon the more sudden collapse which must under such a regulation follow the reaction from any casual undue expansion of credit, than under the present system. It may be contended, that the liability to undue expansion will be less. Of this, however, I must repeat that I have great doubts. I do not feel at all sure, that upon a purely metallic basis there may not be, under circumstances favouring speculation and overtrading (such, for instance, as are constantly occurring in the United States of America), sufficient motives, in times of confidence and prosperous appearances of trade, and a great facility of obtaining credit, such an excrescent growth of credit, and

---

① The plan of a national bank, as recommended by the late Mr. David Ricardo, has been recently brought again to the notice of the public, and placed in a very clear point of view, in a tract by his brother, Mr. Samson Ricardo, with further arguments and illustrations, in the application of it to the present state of things, in the supposed event of the non-renewal of the Bank Charter. The title of Mr. S. Ricardo's publication is, "A National Bank the Remedy for the Evils attendant upon our present System of Paper Currency. 1838."

consequently a circulation of promises to pay beyond the means of payment, as would exist under the present system. But the removal of such an excrescent circulation, although cut off more completely, and therefore leaving less of the seeds of diseased growth afterwards, under a purely metallic variation, would be felt with infinitely more severity at the time than it would be under such an improvement of the present system as I have ventured to suggest. At all events, it may be right that those, whose chief objections to the present system rest on its being too restrictive, and on its consequent liability to cause abrupt variations in the rate of interest, should take this view of the effects of a more complete metallic basis into consideration.

It may readily be admitted, that, as far as relates to the mere administration of a circulation of paper money, if the desideratum be that its variations should exactly correspond with those which would be incident to a purely metallic circulation, the plan of separation of the departments within the Bank of England, or, if that should be found impracticable, a national bank, would be the only modes in which the principle could be carried into practice. But it appears to me that the propounders of the alternative of either of these schemes are not aware of some considerable drawbacks in practice from the superiority in point of principle of those schemes.

2. The only other scheme for supplying a paper circulation for the metropolis and parts adjacent, on a cessation of the exclusive privilege of issue by the Bank of England, would be that of joint stock banks in London and within sixty-five miles issuing promissory notes, either concurrently with the Bank of England, or wholly in lieu of the issues of the Bank of England, if the latter withdrew from such competition.

If the Bank of England were without the exclusive privilege to continue to issue promissory notes, I am quite persuaded that, at least for a long time to come, the attempt by other joint stock banks to obtain circulation for their notes within the same district would be abortive. The inconvenience of several descriptions of paper money entering among the multifarious and large payments of the metropolis would so infinitely outweigh any possible convenience (and I am not aware of the *slightest possible* convenience), that I am convinced that the merchants and bankers of London would have good sense and unanimity enough most strenuously to resist the introduction of so heterogeneous, so inconvenient, and so unsafe a medium for daily and current payments.

If, contrary, however, to reasonable supposition, a concurrent paper should get into circulation, the Bank of England would or might find means of confining its supply of gold to its own purposes, and of compelling the competing banks to rely on their own reserves of coin. In this case, and more especially if the paper of the Bank of England were wholly withdrawn, I have no doubt that the competition of the banks would in times of confidence tend to *minimise* such reserve. The consequence of which would be, on the eventual reaction from overtrading, a contraction by all the banks, and a suspension of payment by more than one of them. ①

---

① The Scotch banks have generally been considered as keeping very small reserves. Mr. Palmer having been asked by the Committee on the Bank Charter in 1832, —Qu. 595. "Do you think that in such a crisis (as that of 1825-1826) there would have been a tendency to general contraction among banks acting in competition with each other in the metropolis?" —Answer. I think, it would be precisely the case that does appear in Scotland. The Scotch banks are banks of great credit and great property; but whenever a demand arises upon them they have not the means of meeting it without coming to the Bank of England. Even in the last fortnight, it is very currently stated that the banks in Scotland had not the power of meeting the demand upon them. I believe Newcastle afforded some assistance; orders were also sent to Liverpool for a supply; and I know that a further supply went from London.

And as the government would not in such case be justified in interfering for their protection, if even so disposed, the circulation might be deranged in a most serious and detrimental manner; while such of the banks as might be able to stand their ground could only do so by restricting their advances in the way of discount or loan to a very contracted range. For a period of more or less duration the effect of this derangement of paper credit would be felt in a very great rise of the rate of interest, much beyond any that has recently been experienced; of which some idea may be formed by the extraordinary rate of discount in New York, upon occasion of the efforts of the banks there to maintain their ground.

After the experience of more than one of such visitations, it is possible that the management of the banks might be improved, but it would take a long time first, and not till much needless suffering had been undergone.

This I apprehend would be the result, even under such checks as the legislature might endeavour to provide. Those checks could be effectual only in securing ultimate solvency, for I doubt whether any legislative measure could be devised which should be effectual in compelling the banks to provide, and always maintain, a sufficient supply of gold to meet extraordinary as well as ordinary demands. I am here assuming, as an undoubted right on the part of the state, the principle that banks of issue are properly subjects for regulation. As to free banking, in the sense in which it is sometimes contended for, I agree with a writer in one of the American papers, who observes, that *free trade in banking is synonymous with free trade in swindling*. And as to the claim which I have seen set up, on principles of freedom of trade, for issuing notes of as low a denomination as one pound, there is no ground of principle, if the claim were admitted, why notes for one shilling, like the shin plasters (as the quarter dollar notes in the United States were called), nay, even sixpenny notes, might not be allowed to circulate.

It would be exceeding the limits prescribed for this work, and would be wearisome to the majority of my readers, if I were to enter into more detailed arguments to show, from reasoning on general principles, confirmed by a reference to the analogy of facts, that the effects of competition of banks of issue in the metropolis, if allowed to obtain circulation for their paper, whether concurrently with the Bank of England or to the exclusion of it, would be to ensure, at no long intervals, much more serious derangements of the currency, and more violent transitions in the rate of interest, than under the present system. That some adequate remedy would be found, after repeated experience of disastrous results, is reasonably to be supposed; but of this I feel sure, that the remedy will not be found compatible with the unqualified principle of freedom of action in banks of issue. The claims of right to such freedom of action in banking ought to be strenuously resisted. They do not rest in any manner on grounds analogous to the claims of freedom of competition in production. The claims for such freedom of competition are, on the part of the public, and are alone, of paramount consideration. *But the issue of paper substitutes for coin is no branch of productive industry. It is a matter for regulation by the state, with a view to general convenience, and comes within the province of police.*

It is sufficient here to notice the distinction without pursuing it further. I have only to repeat, therefore, that whether in the event of its being found that the Bank of England can offer no satisfactory security against the recurrence of such danger of suspension as we have recently escaped, or that, independently of that consideration, the legislature should determine to adopt, either a bank under the regulation of commissioners, or a competition of banks of issue, the probability is, that the variations in the rate of interest, which have been so much complained of, would be much greater under either of these systems, but more especially under the latter of them, than under the system, irregularly as it has been administered, of the Bank of England, on its present footing.

SECTION 4 *On proposed plans for altering the standard*

While one set of reasoners is arguing against the privileges of the Bank of England in the issue of paper money, and urging one of the two alternatives of a national bank or of a competition of banks of issue as substitutes for the Bank of England, —either of which systems would be more restrictive, the one constantly, the other more irregularly, but therefore the more violently so, —there are other reasoners more numerous, and more persevering, and more loud, who object to a continuance of the system on which the Bank of England has been conducted; not because it has been too lax; not because it has been too tardy in applying the means of preserving the convertibility of the paper; not because it has thus endangered the maintenance of the convertibility; but because it does not afford accommodation enough to borrowers because, having by granting too much accommodation got into danger, it has adopted means, however tardy and doubtful as to efficacy, for extrication; and because, however irregularly and insecurely, it does ultimately apply a principle of limitation to over trading and to other forms of undue extension of credit; in short, because it is too restrictive.

The persons entertaining the opinion of the too great restrictiveness of the present system, and urging alterations of the standard with a view to relaxation, may be divided into two classes.

The one is in favour of only so much deviation from the present standard as would be involved in the change to either silver as the single standard, or to silver concurrently with gold as a double standard.

The other, and much more numerous class, while objecting to a system of confining the paper to strict convertibility into either of the metals, and urging a more general facility, and a permanent enlargement of the medium of paper and credit, have not, as far as I can find, given any distinct or intelligible view of the principle of limitation which they would substitute for that which arises out of the power of the holder of the paper to demand payment of it in coin.

I propose to bestow a few remarks upon the views of each of these classes who are opposed to the present standard as it exists by the mint regulations; but before concluding the view of the alternative of the continuance of the system of the Bank of England, or of the substitution of either of the other schemes proposed, I have merely to observe, that nothing has here been said upon the question of the saving which it is supposed would accrue to the public by the institution of a national bank, both in respect of the profit now made by the Bank of England on the circulation of paper, and in respect of the charge on the management of the public debt. These, however, are points quite distinct from the questions relating to the best regulation of the currency, which have alone here constituted the subject of enquiry. I will therefore only observe in passing, that the principle of participation by the public in the profit upon the issues of paper by the Bank of England, and by other banks, is recognized by the stamps, or composition for stamps, on the notes issued. It is a question of quantum, and, with the charge for management of the public debt, must be a mere matter of bargain, and not a question of system or principle.

SECTION 5 *On the effects of a silver standard*

The alteration from a gold to a silver standard has been chiefly advocated with the real, although not always avowed, view of depreciation.

In the event of silver being valued according to the old mint regulations at 5*s*. 2*d*. the ounce, and according to the excess of that price above the actual market price of about 5*s*., at which it has ranged for many years past, the depreciation, compared with the present gold standard, might be estimated at about $3\frac{1}{2}$ per cent. A direct and clear depreciation to at least this extent is mostly contemplated by the propounders of a silver standard; but a further, although less obvious depreciation, is considered as following the substitution, namely, the effect of the disengagement of so much gold on the permanent value of the currency, deducting, however, the increased proportion of silver which the Bank of England would have to hold in reserve. On grounds which I have stated in a former part of this work, there is reason to believe that this effect would be very trifling, and hardly perceptible. But omne ignotum pro magnifico; and the advocates for the substitution are evidently under the impression of very exaggerated notions of diminished value of the currency from this cause. As far, however, as regards depreciation, there can be no doubt, that, if the silver standard were taken at 5*s*. 2*d*., there would, at the present relative market prices, be a diminished value of the currency to the extent of the difference, with some further inappreciable, and probably very trifling, depreciation, by the smaller quantity of the metals required for the circulation.

If, however, depreciation of the value of the currency were the main object of the often repeated recommendations to substitute a silver or a double standard for the present gold standard, the object might be equally accomplished, and with less inconvenience and as much honesty, by raising the denomination or lowering the standard of the present gold coins. But if the objection proceeds exclusively on the grounds generally assumed, namely, that a silver standard would admit of a larger circulation of paper with more ease and facility, or, in other words, would require less reserve to be held by the Bank than is requisite with a gold standard, I am inclined to think that, upon a closer examination than has hitherto been given to the subject, it will be found that there is little, if any, reason for this ground of preference of a silver standard.

There are three reasons, for any one or more of which it may, according to circumstances, be supposed that a less reserve will be required to be held by the Bank with a silver than with a gold standard.

One of the reasons is, that the proportion of the quantity of gold in the countries with which we hold commercial intercourse is so small, compared with the quantity of silver, having in view their respective uses, that a moderate extra demand for the former by this country is calculated to raise its value, compared with silver, in an inordinate degree. If this were the case, and if the Bank, with a considerable amount of silver in its coffers, in 1825, in 1828, in 1836, or in 1839, had experienced an inability to find a market for the silver, and so to exchange it for gold, upon any terms, or even on such terms only as would entail on the Bank a great sacrifice, some weight might be attached to this reason. But, in point of fact, the experience of each and all of those periods is quite decisive in the negative of the alleged reason; for in all and each of those cases it was found that the silver bullion was fully as available as the gold in redressing the exchanges. The Bank, in the interval between 1828 and 1832, remitted to the continent about a million of silver, which was equivalent to the purchase of so much gold. At the same time their selling the silver in this market would have been a preferable course to that of remitting it.

Another reason is, that from its less portableness there would, in the event of unusual internal demand for bullion, whether for purposes of hoarding or in consequence of discredit, be less facility to holders of notes for bringing away large sums. Contemplating, therefore, only internal demand, it may be admitted that the Bank might require a somewhat less reserve of bullion. The difference, however, in this point of view, is so little as to be hardly worth mentioning.

The third reason supposed for a less reserve is, that as the charges on the exportation of silver, the more bulky article, are greater than on gold, the expansion of paper may proceed further with a silver standard before the check operates than with a gold standard. The difference of expense on the transmission is, I believe, not so much as $\frac{1}{2}$ per cent; but it matters not in the question of the relative restrictiveness between a gold and silver standard; because, supposing a balance against this country of foreign payments, the exchange must fall sufficiently to compensate for the greater expense of transmission; and when once this is passed the drain is as great in the one case as in the other, and requires as great an effort on the part of the Bank to counteract it; while exactly in the proportion of the difference of expense of transmission, which might occasion a trifling delay before the check began to operate, would be the operation of that expense, in a contrary direction, by the delay before the turn of the exchange in our favour. The additional charges on importation would be exactly equal in retarding the reflux of the silver, thus exactly in the same proportion keeping up the pressure on the circulation.

Among other disadvantages supposed to attend the gold standard, apart from any view to depreciation by the substitution of silver, are the following: —

One of them is, that of the want of an exact par of exchange with other states, from our not having the same standard, theirs being silver. That, however, is not literally the case; because France, and recently America and Russia, have what is called a double standard, although, in point of fact, silver is alone the actual standard in France as the current money, gold hardly, if ever, entering into payment, except at an agio; while the mint regulations of America and Russia are too recent to admit of judging of their working. But supposing theirs and all the others to be strictly silver, as long as they present markets for gold, which all of them do, at a very trifling variation in the price measured in silver, or, as it is termed, in the agio, there is not the slightest difficulty or disadvantage arising from it in money dealings with the continent of Europe, or with America, or indeed with any part of the globe. But there is one point of view in which, if ours were the only gold standard, it would be an advantage, instead of the reverse, as is commonly supposed; and that is, that in the event, such as at the close of 1825 and at the close of 1839, of exhaustion, or nearly so, of the Bank coffers, the process of restoring the reflux is more easily accomplished with gold than with silver, inasmuch as in drawing gold we do not so immediately act upon the currencies of the countries from which our supplies are to be derived as we should if we required silver.

The other imputed disadvantage of a gold standard marks an astounding degree of ignorance, not only of the principles of currency but of the most commonly received principles of trade, on the part of the persons urging it. It is neither more nor less than this; that whereas gold being alone the standard, and coin being obtainable at par for gold bullion sent to the mint, silver must be sold in the market as merchandize, whether for home consumption or for exportation, because the mint is not open to it as it is for gold. It is contended by these reasoners, that this is a hardship upon our merchants, by narrowing the returns for their exports. It is no hardship at all; silver is as readily obtained and sent to this country, if the exchange answers, as gold. There is always a market for silver in this country for any quantity, and the utmost variation in the market price is very trifling; rarely so much as one per cent. ; but, for this variation, trifling as it is, the merchant shipping it obtains a corresponding abatement in the price. As to the hardship or injustice of being debarred from taking the silver to the mint to be coined gratuitously (as gold is), the Cornish miner might equally complain, that he has not the power of getting a better price for his copper, by having it coined at the mint, and made a legal tender, than by selling it in the market. And with still more reason might the exporter of goods to Chili or Cuba declaim against the policy by which the copper which he gets in return should be excluded, not only from the mint, but from any market at all, for consumption in this country. The claim is the most absurd imaginable if supposed to be on the part of merchants; and the objection, consequently, to a gold standard, on that ground, is perfectly frivolous.[①] The merchants are bound to regulate themselves by the laws as they find them; the only parties to be considered in the question of any alteration of them are the public.

So much, then, for the arguments in favour of the change to a silver standard, which are neither more nor less than pleas for depreciation, and consequently for debtors generally at the expense of their creditors, in violation of the broadest principles of justice and sound policy; while in other respects it would be the substitution of the less convenient for the most convenient description of currency.

SECTION 6 *On the effects of a double standard*

With regard to a double or concurrent standard, as it has been called, of gold and silver, it has been to me a subject of constant wonder how it could be that projects for placing our currency on such a footing should ever have been put forth by persons entitled to have any attention paid to their opinions.

There is no one more disposed than I am to admit the force of disturbing causes, in qualifying the application of general principles to the actual course of affairs; but the principle involved in the question, whether one or two (and if two, why not three or more?) metals should constitute the standard of value in the interchange of commodities, and of property of all kinds, is so wholly deducible from a clear view of the uses and purposes

① It is so frivolous and absurd, that it may be supposed that I have merely *imagined* such an objection. But I have known it repeatedly urged, and it is gravely stated and declaimed upon in a recent pamphlet, entitled, "Corn and Currency; or how shall we get through the Winter? By a Merchant."

contemplated by the establishment of any standard, as a medium of exchanges, and as the commodity stipulated in contracts, that the determination of the question, in its practical application, has been considered, by all writers of any eminence on the subject, as proceeding exclusively on general grounds of consistent reasoning, and not dependent upon particular facts, as to the position of any country with reference to its commerce or its banking institutions. It has been treated, and justly so, as determinable on scientific principles only. That one metal only should be the standard is accordingly a point upon which scientific writers, Locke, Harris, Adam Smith, Ricardo, Mill, Senior, M'Culloch, &c. , are all agreed. And to this host of authorities, in accordance, moreover, with the plain obvious purpose and meaning of a standard of value, the numerous bodies and persons who propose the change, upon the ground of the too great restrictiveness of the present system of convertibility of the paper into gold, have only to oppose the authority of Lord Ashburton.

As far as I have been able to collect of Lord Ashburton's reasons in favour of a double standard, they resolve themselves into the supposition, that it would afford more ease and facility to the Bank in maintaining a larger circulation of paper, or the same circulation with a less reserve of bullion, than under the present standard. This supposition would be well founded only if the variations between gold and silver were considerable, and alternately on one side and the other; and in this case, exactly in proportion as the facility to the Bank would be greater, by so much the greater would be the inconvenience to the public, by the uncertainty to which the option of the debtors would expose the transactions which were the foundations of the debt. Such uncertainty would be particularly objectionable in our foreign commercial relations, as it would necessarily entail a wider range of fluctuation in the exchanges than under a single standard. If, however, the variations between the two metals should be very small, in that proportion would the convenience, or, as Lord Ashburton terms it, the ease and facility, be less to the Bank and to debtors generally, and in the same degree would the inconvenience to the public be diminished. But to whatever extent the difference might be, it would still be an inconvenience. In his recommendation of the double standard Lord Ashburton referred to the example of France, in proof of the convenient working of the system; but that example furnishes no proof at all, inasmuch as the standard in France is, and has been for a long time past, for all practical purposes, of silver only, gold, as I have before observed, having been invariably at an agio or a premium upon the relative proportions fixed by the mint regulations; and if the substitution of a double standard proposed for this country were to be on the same footing as in France, the observations which I have already made on the comparative restrictiveness of a silver standard would apply to this nominal double standard.

SECTION 7 *On a system of paper circulation without a defined principle of limitation*

The most specious and the most formidable, however, of the opponents of the present system of our currency, as being too restrictive, are those who contend that an enlargement of the circulation ought to keep pace with the growth of the population, and of the wealth, and, consequently, of the trade of the community, or of the world; and that the necessity of preventing the circulation from acquiring that enlargement, by limiting the paper to so much only as can be converted at the will of the holders into the precious metals, is repressive of enterprise and industry, and of improvements of all kinds, and thus prevents the due development of the energies and resources of the community. This is the theory prevalent among landlords, merchants, and tradesmen. It includes also a great proportion of the working classes, who care not about any reduction of the prices of necessaries, but look to obtaining, as the consequence of an enlargement of paper issues, an increase of wages, in a much greater proportion than the rise of necessaries. It is the prevalence of an impression of this kind that has produced the apathy so strikingly observable in the public on occasion of the recent critical state of the Bank. So far was there from any general feeling of apprehension or distrust arising from the apparent probability of a suspension of cash payments, that it was reasoned upon with perfect coolness, and with a sort of supercilious expression of surprize at the supposition, that such an event could in any way be considered as a calamity, instead of being, as they evidently thought it, the harbinger of a better state of things, by allowing of a more permanently enlarged circulation.

Strange as it may seem, there were persons of wealth and consideration in the banking and mercantile world, who, as far as I could make out, participated in opinions, if not identical with these, very nearly allied to them. I have more than once met with persons of this description, who, in 1836, and again in 1839, when referring to an incipient difficulty in the negociation of bills and other securities, said very significantly, "You may depend upon it that there is not gold enough in the world to support the great increase of commerce." It was in vain to ask of them, upon what grounds, other than the too great quantity of paper and credit, they inferred the too small quantity of gold, seeing that a given quantity of gold would not, at the very time they were speaking, buy more silver, or so much of copper, or tin, or lead, or iron, or corn, or silk, or of most other raw materials or finished work, or of labour, as it would have purchased five or ten years ago. And when these persons were further asked, what principle of limitation they would propose to substitute for that which ultimately confined the paper and credit to such an amount as could be converted into coin, I could never make out an intelligible answer. If the want of gold alone, and not of silver, were the difficulty in maintaining an enlarged circulation, the banks of the United States, where silver is an unlimited tender, and where gold, by their new mint regulations, is also a tender, at a depreciated ratio to silver, thus affording the so-much-vaunted facility of a double standard, ought not to have experienced the difficulty which so many of them have found insurmountable.

It is impossible adequately to convey the views of the reasoners opposed to the convertibility of paper into gold or silver, without giving their own words. I therefore give, as a specimen of what is, with unessential variations of expression, the language common to this class of reasoners, the following extract from the leading article in one of our public prints.

The writer, after commenting, with considerable knowledge of the subject, on the statement which had just then been put forth of the affairs of the United States Bank, proceeded to make the following general remarks on the state of the currency in this country and in America: —

"We have shown, then, that the depreciation of American property has been caused mainly, if not entirely, by the impossibility which exists in America to represent their property in a metallic money. The property exists; there is no doubt of that; but there is a want of metallic money to represent it; and we have shown also that the want of metallic money in

America has been mainly, if not entirely, produced by the operations of the Bank of England, which has been also in want of metallic money; and which, being the stronger body, has drained the weaker one of its gold and silver. So that it appears that the obstinacy of both countries in persevering in this system of currency, which occasionally requires more than all the metallic money of the world to represent it, is at the bottom of the mischief. Thus there is a continual struggle going on in this country and in America between the industry and energy of their inhabitants; the struggle of production and the creation of wealth against the monetary system of both countries, which is continually beating down this industry and this energy, and preventing the creation of wealth by its arbitrary and absurd restrictions. England manufactures and America produces; this, the result of labour, constitutes wealth to either nation; as the population of each increases, and as the wants of the population of each increase, there is the opportunity for further manufacture and further production; but if in each country there is enacted an arbitrary law, that the value of the interchange of such manufacture or such production shall always be representable in a particular sort of money, which does not increase in the same proportion, one of two things must take place; either such manufactures or productions must be limited to the amount of money which exists to represent their interchange, or manufactures and productions, being constantly increased by the demands for them of the increasing population, their values in their interchanges must be deranged as often as the necessity occurs, no matter from what cause, of representing them by this limited amount of metallic money. And such precisely is the effect periodically; such has been the effect in the present instance of the embarrassment of the American currency. The 'law money,' the metallic money, is wanted; it is not procurable, because it does not exist; but the law is peremptory, and will have property represented by this limited sort of money; property therefore falls in value; in value as it is called, but, as we contend, in the 'law money' value only; its real value remains the same; but the effect on the holders of the property, whose business operates as compelling them to exchange for as much of the small amount of gold money as they can procure, is the loss and ruin which we observe around us. Holding these opinions, we must say, that, applying them to the case of the banks in the United States, we think their abandonment of the attempt to pay their debts in a metallic money, which is not procurable, is the best step they could take under the circumstances. Had they persisted in the attempt to pay in metallic money, they would only have increased their difficulties and added to their losses, and its effect would have been generally on America most ruinous; for the consequence of such an attempt would have been, to cause all American goods to fall to almost nothing; and the balance being against America, in favour of this country, that is to say, America being in debt to this country, which she must pay by her produce, the result would have been, that she would pay to her English creditors goods at a low price which she had contracted at a high price, and would thereby have paid her debt two or three times over in proportion to the depreciation of her produce. This would have been manifestly a cruel and glaring injustice to the Americans; for, viewing the case between the two nations as between two individuals, it would be as if the creditor, who had lent his money on the security of property estimated at a certain value, were by his superior combinations to cause that property to be depreciated to half its value, and so take double the property in satisfaction of his debt. Such would now be the injustice inflicted on America had she submitted to pay her debt at its appreciation in a metallic money value in this time of metallic money scarcity. In fact she would have to pay two bales of cotton instead of one, or some such proportion. This, we say, would be an injustice inflicted on America which we are quite sure is neither nationally nor individually desired. By the suspension of specie payment the value of all sorts of property in America will be supported, and her merchants will be better able, and more quickly, to discharge their debt to this country. We will add, that had the Bank of England been able to take this step some months ago, most of the embarrassments which have taken place throughout Europe, in consequence of the measures of the Bank of England to keep gold in this country, would have been prevented."

It is not my intention to enter into a critical examination of all the fallacies which pervade the reasoning in this extract; but as it conveys, as concisely as in any instance that I have met with, the views which prevail to a considerable extent in this country, but still more extensively in America, among the partisans of a system of currency which should have no defined principle of limitation, or, in other words, no fixed standard of value, a few remarks upon it may not be out of place, in this concluding part of my brief survey of the several schemes by which it has been proposed to supersede our existing standard of value.

I would first, however, observe on an error of fact in the assertion, that the want of metallic money in America has been mainly, if not entirely, produced by the operations of the Bank of England. This is a statement which has been prominently put forth in the several American papers on the part of the suspended banks, as a main ground of justification of their suspension, and it has been repeated in some of the newspapers and pamphlets in this country, either as espousing the interests of those banks, or as furnishing matter of charge against the Bank of England. There is not, however, the shadow of foundation for the assertion. It was the operations of the American banks in their system of reckless extension of paper and credit, —it was the overbanking and the overtrading in the United States, connected more especially with their bolstering of the cotton market (too much favoured, it is but too true, by the assistance of the Bank of England in 1837 and 1838), that contributed in a considerable degree to the inconvenient drain of the metals from this country. Not to mention the amount of bullion shipped direct thither in 1838, the payments which have been made from hence in 1839, directly or indirectly, *for American account*, to the continent of Europe, as well as to the East Indies and other parts, has greatly exceeded the sums, amounting collectively, however, to a small matter, which came from the United States as forced remittances in the last six months of 1839. And there can be no doubt that one of the principal causes of the pressure on the money market has been, the enormous amount of American securities which had been forced upon it. So much for the statement of fact. Now as to the reasoning.

The writer states the impossibility which exists in America to *represent* their *property* in a metallic money. I have always considered the term *representation* as a source of extraordinary confusion, when used, as it frequently is, in discussions on the currency. The *representation* of coin by paper money may doubtless, without any violation of propriety, be considered to convey the same meaning as *the substitution* of paper, under a principle of limitation, for coin, to serve as a medium of exchange. But what is the meaning of the inability of the Americans to *represent* their property in metallic money? The inability of the Americans, in plain and intelligible English, is, that they have given more promises to pay than they have the means of paying; and in this sense the writer says truly, that the obstinacy of both countries, in persevering in a system which calls upon the banks or individuals who have issued such promises to perform their engagements according to their tenor, (namely, to pay a certain quantity of gold or silver of given fineness), is at the bottom of the mischief, which mischief consists in the difficulty of finding in the world a sufficient quantity of the metals to enable them to discharge their engagements. If the writer has ever taken the trouble to read Adam Smith, he will find that the case of the Americans is not a new one, nor depending upon any system of currency. "No complaint," says Dr. Smith, "is more common than that of a scarcity of money. Money, like wine, must always be scarce with those who have neither wherewithal to buy it nor credit to borrow it. Those who have either will seldom be in want of the money or of the wine which they have occasion for. This complaint, however, of the scarcity of money, is not always confined to improvident spendthrifts; it is sometimes general through a whole mercantile town and the country in its neighbourhood. *Overtrading* is the common cause of it. Sober men, whose projects have been disproportioned to their capitals, are as likely to have neither wherewithal to buy money nor credit to borrow it, as prodigals whose expense has been disproportioned to their revenue. Before their projects can be brought to bear their stock is gone, and their credit with it. They run about to borrow money every where, and every body tells them that they have none to lend." —(*Wealth of Nations*, *M'Culloch's edition*, *p.* 191.)

But the writer goes on to say, " 'the law money,' the metallic money, is wanted; it is not procurable, because it does not exist." This is rather a startling proposition; it is, however, qualified as follows: "But the law is peremptory, and will have property represented by this *limited* sort of money; property, therefore, falls in value; in value, as it is called, but, as we contend, in the 'law money' value only; its real value remains the same." Thus it seems that the money exists, but is *limited*; and is so limited that property should not be valued in such money, but in real value. But what is the measure of such real value? Some arbitrary standard which any person may set up as his *sense of value*. In the debates in the House of Commons in 1811 on Mr. Vansittant's ever memorable resolutions, Lord Castlereagh contended that coin, and not bullion, was the measure of value, and that, according *to a seme of value* as measured in all other commodities, bullion excepted, the paper had not been depreciated. This reasoning drew forth from Mr. Canning the following indignant and brilliant burst in reply: —

"'The coin,' says a noble lord who spoke last night, 'is (or was) the standard of that paper.' But this description does not advance us a single step, for the question still remains 'What is the standard of' the coin? What is that common measure to which coin and paper may be equally referred, for the purpose of ascertaining their agreement or disagreement with it, and with each other?'"

"The noble lord (Castlereagh) has indeed devised a singular definition of this measure, in which I should be curious to know whether the honourable gentleman concurs. He compares it to 'a sense of value in reference to currency as compared with commodities.' I hope I do not misquote him. To the best of my recollection these were his very words: 'A sense 'of value'! But whose sense? With whom is it to originate, and how is it to be communicated to others; who is to promulgate, who is to acknowledge, or who is to enforce it? How is it to be defined? and how is it to be regulated? what ingenuity shall calculate, or what authority control its fluctuation? Is the 'sense' of today the same as that of yesterday, and will it be unchanged tomorrow ? It does fill me with astonishment that any man of an accurate and reasoning mind should not perceive that this wild and dangerous principle (if principle it can be called) would throw loose all the transactions of private life, —all contracts and pecuniary bargains, —by leaving them to be measured from day to day, and from hour to hour, by no other rule than that of the fancies and interests of each individual, conflicting with the fancies and interests of his neighbour."

But even with an exclusive paper circulation (unless it should proceed, like the French assignats, by progressive depreciation from excess, to final extinction), if a limit were arrived at of any kind, it would be found, however and whenever applied, to be extremely inconvenient, in cases where engagements on credit were beyond the means of payment, and there would then be as much complaint of a want of paper as there is at present of a want of gold and silver. During the Bank restriction, unscientific and apparently lax as was the principle of limitation applied to the circulation, it yet operated so severely, that in the occasional reactions from overbanking and overtrading, the difficulty of obtaining Bank of England notes was much greater than that of obtaining means of payment of pecuniary engagements in a convertible state of the paper at any time, except in 1825-1826. I mean the period of 1810-1811, when the state of commercial discredit and distress were extreme, and when the difference between the prices of commodities on the usual credit and those for prompt payment in Bank of England notes, was as great as in 1825-1826, if not greater.

There is indeed no conclusion more fully established by the concurrence of universal experience, and sanctioned by the practice of mankind, from the dawn of civilization to the present time, than that gold and silver form the best instrument of exchange, and the best standard or principle of limitation that can be devised for every form of credit.

Divested, however, of the confused phraseology of the paper money school, the probable meaning of those persons whom I have referred to, as contending that there is not enough of the precious metals existing to support the extended commerce of the world, I conceive to he, that the production of gold and silver does not keep pace with the increase of population and of manufacturing industry, nor, consequently, with the increase of transactions requiring the intervention of those metals, and their paper substitutes *at par value*, as a medium or instrument of exchange, and as the commodity which is stipulated in all pecuniary contracts; in other words, that the supply of the metals does not keep pace with the demand, and that they are experiencing an increased value.

As it is principally with reference to the conduct of the suspended American banks that the plea of increased value, from the too limited quantity of the precious metals, has been urged in the apologetic article which I have quoted, I have to offer a few remarks on that plea, as also upon some other of the arguments that are adduced in justification of those banks.

SECTION 8 *Digression on the suspended american banks*

If it were true that the precious metals were experiencing an increased value, it would not, as a distinct ground, form a justification of the suspension of payment by the American banks. They promised to pay in gold or silver (or their equivalent in value), and not in cotton or other commodities. But are there any grounds for inferring an increased value, or purchasing power, of the metals, in the commercial world, within the period that can by possibility be supposed to operate in such a way as to affect the question, whether the American banks, or the debtors generally, are now called upon, for the performance of their obligations, to pay a commodity which possesses greater value than they contemplated when they entered into those obligations to pay, at stipulated periods, a specific quantity of that commodity, or its equivalent?

Of the value of the precious metals, in their general purchasing power, there is no certain criterion. Among the writers of eminence who have entered into the question, some, as Dr. Adam Smith, with the French authors whom he has quoted, and more recently the Marquis Garnier, considered the price of wheat, when spread over the average of a great number of years, to afford the best means of judging; while Mr. Malthus and others relied upon the rate of wages of common day labour, as a better guide. Arthur Young took, not only the prices of corn and of labour, but of some other articles of extensive use, into the comparison. Now, taking the prices of provisions and of the lower metals, and of the raw materials of our principal manufactures, the greater part of them were higher, and money wages were not lower, in 1839 than they were in 1838. And a comparison, limited to that period, is sufficient to embrace the bulk of the pending contracts for payment, proving, consequently, that there is no pretence for the plea of any observable increase of the value of the precious metals.

That a period so limited is insufficient to serve as a criterion, or even as a strong presumption of what may be the tendency to a greater or less value of gold and silver in a more general point of view, may be readily admitted, and that a longer period is necessary for the purpose. If, then, we take a period of ten years, and compare the prices, in 1829, of the articles in the tables appended to the former part of this work, with the quotations of the same articles in the appendix to the present, and with wages, it will be seen that the range of prices has, in the latter period, been decidedly higher, leaving no possible ground for the supposition of an increasing value of the metals. And the same result, in perhaps a more striking degree, would appear, if the value of property in land and houses were compared in those two periods.

In the United States of America, inasmuch as credit and the immediate influence of banking advances were extended in an undue degree to particular objects, those objects bore an inflated price. This was the case with lands, houses, and goods bought on credit; it was likewise the case with cotton in a pre-eminent degree, as being an object to which the abuse of banking was, in a special manner, directed; it was, in a smaller degree, also the case with some other descriptions of produce. But the prices of provisions do not appear to have been under the influence of banking operations, beyond the degree indicated by a difference in the exchange. The price of flour, for instance, at New York, in 1835, when general credit and banking accommodation were in their highest state, was between five and six dollars the barrel; and, after the intermediate rise in 1836 and 1837, caused by the failure of the wheat and corn crops of those two years, the effect of renewed abundance in the crops of 1838 and 1839 has simply brought back the price, in the most restricted state of circulation and of credit, to what it had been previous to the seasons of comparative dearth.

If lands and houses, and produce, and the stocks of imported commodities in their stores, were bought and held on credit, or with promises to pay, beyond the means of the parties to make the payment, and beyond the ordinary rate of demand for such property, it is perfectly natural that prices founded on such purchases could not be maintained when offered for sale to the only persons who were entitled to buy them; namely, those who were disposed and able to pay for them. And it is well known that sales made to satisfy engagements entered into beyond the means of the debtors are commonly sold at a depression as much below the fair value as the credit prices were above the fair value; but that is no reason for not paying the debts, if so required, by realizing the property as far as it will go.

The American suspended banks, and their apologists in this country as well as in the United States, seem to have very peculiar notions of the degree of moral obligation attached to pecuniary engagements. There are two grounds, according to their doctrine, on which the banks are to be considered as not bound to the strict fulfilment of their engagements.

One of these, (the observation, indeed, applies to debtors generally), which, in accordance with the opinions expressed in the preceding extract, refers to the too great restrictiveness of the currency, by confinement to the value of gold and silver, has already been disposed of.

The other ground, according to the doctrine in question, on which the suspension of the southern and western banks in the United States has been attempted to be justified, is, that if they did not continue to discount and make advances, the merchants would fail, and there would be a general prostration, if not destruction, of all trade. This plea is a fit commentary, in the nature of a caricature, upon the system of the Bank of England, in its assumption of a duty to support commercial credit at the risk of its own credit, and of its means of fulfilling its own engagements. The New York and other eastern banks of the United States have, fortunately for the cause of morality in banking, resisted the claims of applicants for discount beyond the extent which could be satisfied consistently with the maintenance of their own engagements. They very properly, and very unlike the Philadelphia banks①, declined to fail in the payment of their

---

① The following is extracted from the American papers: — "*An Address to the Citizens of Pennsylvania from the Philadelphia Banks*, October 23, 1839."

"The banks of Philadelphia were quite as ready to resume as those who were most anxious to begin, for they had greatly reduced their liabilities, and one of their number had no less than 7, 357, 000 dollars in its vaults; but they believed that the country at large had not yet sufficiently recovered from the violent shock to be ready for resumption. They recollected that, under similar circumstances, the Bank of England had continued her suspension for upwards of twenty years; and they avowed their apprehension that a resumption, in the unprepared state of the country, must be followed by a relapse. Overruled in this judgment, and obliged, at the hazard of greater evils, to unite in the resumption, they sincerely co-operated in it; and being satisfied that the measure, in order to be useful or permanent, must be general, they made great efforts, and large advances to the southern and south-western states, who were thus enabled, almost exclusively by the assistance of the Philadelphia banks, to unite in the resumption. But the inefficiency of the measure soon became apparent." [This is surely not to be wondered at, seeing that, by way of putting themselves in a better condition for resuming cash payments, they made large advances to the southern and south-western states.]

The Address then goes on to say, — "Under these circumstances they have had to adopt one of two alternatives, —either to force the community, by sacrifices of its property, to pay its debts in gold and silver, to be shipped forthwith to England, or else to resort to a temporary suspension, until the community, as well as the banks, could have time to recover from the effect of these foreign troubles. They have not hesitated to prefer the latter, as being the most conducive to the true interests of the state."

It cannot fail of being observed, that, independently of the strange reasoning in point of principle on which the suspension of cash payments is justified, the Philadelphia banks gravely remind the citizens of Pennsylvania, that, under similar circumstances, the Bank of England had continued her suspension for upwards of twenty years. This is indeed an instance of similarity most dissimilar in all essential particulars affecting the morality of the proceeding, as regards the banks in question. They agree in the fact of suspension, but in all other respects they differ most widely. In the case of the Bank of England, the adverse exchanges, notwithstanding an unparalleled, sudden, and great foreign expenditure in 1795-1796, were surmounted by an extraordinary contraction of issues, when a run, arising from Internal panic, caused by foreign invasion and a general discredit of paper, induced the government (prematurely, as I think), to interfere, by a restriction on cash payments. But in two years afterwards, without the slightest intervening depreciation of its paper, the Bank officially communicated its ability and readiness to resume payments in specie. And it was distinctly an act of the state, then engaged in a most extensive and expensive war, and for state purposes, that the proposal of the Bank to resume was negatived by the government, and the suspension continued, distinctly upon considerations of state policy, throughout the whole period of the war. I have never been satisfied with the policy of the suspension, and the continuance of it; but to compare that suspension with the suspension of the American banks is a most wonderful stretch of the powers of comparing things dissimilar.

own obligations, according to the clear tenor of them, on the pretence of saving the merchants from failure. The resolution, however, of the eastern banks, so creditable to themselves, and so beneficial in its ultimate consequences to the eventual stability of the trade and the banking of those states, has been attended with a consequence, which the opponents of the Bank of England, and the advocates of competition of banks of issue, would do well to ruminate upon; and that is, that while the effort of contraction requisite to enable them to continue their payments in specie has been in progress, the rate of discount has risen enormously, namely, to two and three, and, in some particular instances, I am assured, to the rate of five per cent, per month upon unexceptionable acceptances.

It did not enter as an essential part into the plan of this work to investigate and criticise the character of American banking, but recent events have forced it in an extraordinary degree upon the attention of the public in this country; and questions arising out of the suspension of the Philadelphia and other banks of the southern and western states of America have recently formed so important a consideration in discussions upon the principles of banking, and upon the connection between paper money, according as it is administered, and prices, that a reference to them in a treatise upon prices and the circulation might naturally be looked for. But it is only a cursory allusion to them that my limits allow; and if in alluding to them I have expressed myself in terms of animadversion upon the principles by which the recent suspension of cash payments by some of those banks has been justified, it is because I consider that the reasonings which have been put forth by the suspending banks, and repeated by their advocates in this country, are such as are calculated, if countenanced by public opinion, to undermine all just grounds of confidence in banking institutions, and greatly to impair the standard of morality in trade.

While this work has been in the press, the Message of the President of the United States, on its meeting in December last, has been received. A considerable portion of the Message is devoted to remarks on the abuses of banking which have produced so serious a derangement of trade and commercial credit, and have interfered so materially with the financial arrangements of the government. The remarks of the President bear so strongly in support of the opinions which I entertain, and which I have ventured to express, on the subject of American banking, reprobating, as he does, on the very grounds which I have stated, the attempts at justification on the part of the United States Bank of Pennsylvania, and of the other suspended banks, that I cannot resist the temptation of the opportunity, still open to me, of here inserting the following extract from it.

The President, after stating objections arising out of occurrences in 1836 and 1837, to allowing the custody of the government funds to be committed to any banking institution, goes on to say,

"Recent events have also continued to develope new objections to such a connection. Seldom is any bank, under the existing system and practice, able to meet, on demand, all its liabilities for deposits and notes in circulation. It maintains specie payments, and transacts a profitable business, only by the confidence of the people in its solvency; and whenever this is destroyed the demands of its depositors and note holders—pressed more rapidly than it can make collections from its debtors—force it to stop payment. This loss of payment, with its consequences, occurred in 1837, and afforded the apology of the banks for their suspension. The public then acquiesced in the validity of the excuse; and, while the state legislatures did not exact from them their forfeited charters, Congress, in accordance with the recommendation of' the executive, allowed them time to pay over the public money they held, although compelled to issue treasury notes to supply the deficiency thus created.

"It now appears that there are other motives than a want of public confidence under which the banks seek to justify themselves in a refusal to meet their obligations. Scarcely were the country and government relieved, in a degree, from the difficulties occasioned by the general suspension of 1837, when a partial one, occurring within thirty months of the former, produced new and serious embarrassments, though it had no palliation in such circumstances as were alleged in justification of that which had previously taken place. There was nothing in the condition of the country to endanger a well-managed banking institution; commerce was deranged by no foreign war; every branch of manufacturing industry was crowned with rich rewards; and the more than usual abundance of our harvests, after supplying our domestic wants, had left our granaries and storehouses filled with a surplus for exportation. It is in the midst of this that an irredeemable and depreciated paper currency is entailed upon the people by a large portion of the banks. They are not driven to it by the exhibition of a loss of public confidence, or of a sudden pressure from their depositors or of note holders, but they excuse themselves by alleging, that the current of business, and exchange with foreign countries, which draws the precious metals from their vaults, would require, in order to meet it, a larger curtailment of their loans to a comparatively small portion of the community than it will be convenient for them to bear, or perhaps safe for the banks to exact. The plea has ceased to be one of necessity. Convenience and policy are now deemed sufficient to warrant these institutions in disregarding their solemn obligations. Such conduct is not merely an injury to individual creditors, but it is a wrong to the whole community, from whose liberality they hold most valuable privileges—whose rights they violate, whose business they derange, and the value of whose property they render unstable and insecure. It must be evident that this new ground for bank suspensions, in reference to which their action is not only disconnected with, but wholly independent of, that of the public, gives a character to their suspensions more alarming than any which they exhibited before, and greatly increases the impropriety of relying on the banks in the transactions of government.

"A large and highly respectable portion of our banking institutions are, it affords me unfeigned pleasure to state, exempted from all blame on account of this second delinquency. They have, to their great credit, not only continued to meet their demands, but have even repudiated the grounds of suspension now resorted to. It is only by such a course that the confidence and goodwill of the community can be preserved, and, in the sequel, the best interests of the institutions themselves promoted.

"New dangers to the banks are also daily disclosed, from the extension of that system of extravagant credit of which they are the pillars. Formerly our foreign commerce was principally founded on an exchange of commodities, including the precious metals, and leaving in its trans-actions but little foreign debt. Such is not now the case. Aided by the facilities afforded by the banks, mere credit has become too commonly the basis of trade. Many of the banks themselves, not content with largely stimulating this system among others, have usurped the business, while they impair the stability, of the mercantile community; they have become borrowers instead of lenders; they establish their agencies abroad; they deal largely in stocks and merchandize; they encourage the issue of state securities until the foreign market is glutted with them; and, unsatisfied with the legitimate use of their own capital, and the exercise of their lawful privileges, they raise by large loans additional means for every variety of speculation. The disasters attendant on this deviation from the former course of business in the country are now shared alike by banks and individuals, to an extent of which there is perhaps no previous example in the annals of our country. So long as a willingness of the foreign lender, and a sufficient export of our productions to meet any necessary partial payments, leave the flow of credit undisturbed, all appears to he prosperous; but as soon as it is checked by any hesitation abroad, or by an inability to make payment there in our productions, the evils of the system are disclosed. The paper currency, which might serve for domestic purposes, is useless to pay the debt due in Europe. Gold and silver are therefore drawn in exchange for their own notes, which are as unavailable to them as they are to the merchants, to meet the foreign demand. The calls of the banks, therefore, in such emergencies of necessity, exceed their demand, and produce a corresponding curtailment of their accommodations and of the currency, at the very moment when the state of trade renders it most inconvenient to be borne. The intensity of this pressure on the community is in proportion to the previous liberality of credit and consequent expansion of the currency; forced sales of property are made at the time when the means of purchasing are most reduced, and the worst calamities to individuals are only at last arrested by an open violation of their obligations by the banks, a refusal to pay specie for their notes, and an imposition upon the community of a fluctuating and depreciated currency.

"These consequences are inherent in the present system. They are not influenced by the banks being large or small; created by national or state governments: they are the results of the irresistible laws of trade and credit. In the recent events, which have so strikingly illustrated the certain effects of these laws, we have seen the bank of the largest capital in the union, established under a national charter, and lately strengthened, as we were authoritatively informed, by exchanging that for a state charter, with new and unusual privileges, —in a condition, too, as it was said, of entire soundness and great prosperity, —not merely unable to resist these effects, but the first to yield to them.

"Nor is it to be overlooked that there exists a chain of necessary dependence among these institutions, which obliges them, to a great extent, to follow the course of others, notwithstanding its injustice to their own immediate creditors, or injury to the particular community in which they are placed. This dependence of a bank, which is in proportion to the extent of its debts for circulation and deposits, is not merely on others in its own vicinity, but on all those which connect it with the centre of trade. Distant banks may fail, without seriously affecting those in our principal commercial cities; but the failure of the latter is felt at the extremities of the union. The suspension at New York in 1837 was everywhere, with very few exceptions, followed, as soon as it was known; that recently at Philadelphia immediately affected the banks of the south and west in a similar manner. The dependence of our whole banking system on the institutions in a few large cities is not found in the laws of their organization, but in those of trade and exchange. The banks at that centre to which currency flows, and where it is required in payments for merchandize, hold the power of controlling those in regions whence it comes, while the latter possess no means of restraining them; so that the value of individual property, and the prosperity of trade, through the whole interior of the country, are made to depend on the good or bad management of the banking institutions in the great seats of trade on the seaboard.

"But this chain of dependence does not stop here. It does not terminate in Philadelphia or New York. It reaches across the ocean, and ends in London, the centre of the credit system. The same laws of trade which gave to the banks in our principal cities power over the whole banking system of the United States, subject the former, in their turn, to the money power in Great Britain. It is not denied that the suspension of the New York banks in 1837, which was followed in quick succession throughout the union, was produced by an application of that power; and it is now alleged, in extenuation of the present condition of so large a portion of our banks, that their embarrassments have arisen from the same cause.

"From this influence they cannot now entirely escape, for it has its origin in the credit currencies of the two countries; it is strengthened by the current of trade and exchange, which centres in London, and is rendered almost irresistible by the large debts contracted there by our merchants, our banks, and our states. It is thus that an introduction of a new bank into the most distant of our villages places the business of that village within the influence of the money power in England. It is thus that every new debt which we contract in that country seriously affects our own currency, and extends over the pursuits of our citizens its powerful influence. We cannot escape from this by making new banks, great or small, state or national. The same chain which binds those now existing to the centre of this system of paper credit must equally fetter every similar institution we create. It is only by the extent to which this system has been pushed of late that we have been made fully aware of its irresistible tendency to subject our own banks and currency to a vast controlling power in a foreign land; and it adds a new argument to those which illustrate their precarious situation. Endangered, in the first place, by their own mismanagement, and again by the conduct of every institution which connects them with the centre of trade in our own country, they are yet subject, beyond all this, to the effect of whatever measures policy, necessity, or caprice, may induce those who control the credit of England to resort to. I mean not to comment upon these measures, present or past, and much less to discourage the prosecution of fair commercial dealing between the two countries, based on reciprocal benefits; but it having now been made manifest that the power of inflicting these and similar injuries is, by the resistless law of a credit currency and credit trade, equally capable of extending their consequences through all the ramifications of our banking system, and by that means indirectly obtaining, particularly when our banks are used as depositories of the public moneys, a dangerous political influence in the United States, I have deemed it my duty to bring the subject to your notice, and ask for it your serious consideration."

Agreeing as I do most fully in the general scope and tenor of the observations of the President on the evils of the banking system, such as it has developed itself in action in the United States, I must be permitted to question the correctness of his views on one point. Alluding to London as the centre of the credit system, and to the dependence of the banks in the United States on the money power in Great Britain, the President adds, —"It is not denied that the suspension of the New York banks in 1837, which was followed in quick succession throughout the union, was produced by an application of that power."

Referring to the remarks which I made on the plea of the suspended American banks, that it was by the "putting on of the screw" by the Bank of England that their recent stoppage of payment in specie was caused, I have to add the following observations on the above passage of the President's Message.

Undoubtedly, if the Bank of England had in 1836 and in 1837 kept its rate of interest at four per cent, and had gone on discounting all the vast mass of circulating American bills which were pressing upon it, the American houses here, and the banks in the United States, might have gone on for some months longer. But considering the excess to which the American system of credit had already proceeded, and the accelerated rate at which it was going on, it would have argued a degree of blindness on the part of the Bank of England beyond even that with which it was justly chargeable, if it had not at length opened its eyes to the consequences, as regarded the safety of its own establishment, of allowing itself to be the passive instrument of the further extension of the system. And it is quite clear that if the Bank of England had been so infatuated as to have neglected taking measures of precaution in 1836, its own solvency would have been endangered. But so far from having exerted any power in stopping the American houses in this country, and the New York banks connected with them, the Bank of England actually nursed them by advances without security for several months, and it was only on seeing no end to the practice of nursing (which by the way was inconsistent with just principles of banking, and was the occasion of the anomalous position in which the Bank of England was placed, of having to send an agent to the United States to collect its debts), that in 1837 it found itself compelled to discontinue its assistance. Now, a discontinuance of assistance, when continued assistance was inconsistent, not only with its ordinary rules, but with a consideration for its own safety, is very different from the inference to which the passage in the President's address leads, namely, that it was a voluntary exertion of power on the part of the Bank of England to stop the American banks. With much more reason might the President of the United States have inferred a dependence of the banks of America upon the money power in France, because a refusal by the French banking house of Hottinguer and Co. to accept the bills drawn upon them by the United States Bank was the proximate cause of the suspension of cash payments by the southern and western states banks.

Under the circumstances in which the government of the United States is placed, and with the experience which it has derived from the results of the system of banking and credit in that country, there can be no question, in my opinion, of the wisdom of the policy which it has announced, of divorcing itself irrevocably from all connection or communication with any of the banks, whether as depositaries of its funds, or agents for the collection and transmission of them.

The probable influence of such a determination on the part of the American government, if supported as it probably will be by Congress, on the future system of banking and credit in the United States, and the consequences, with reference to the state of the circulation in this country, involve considerations of great import, but embracing too wide a field of discussion to be here incidentally entered into.

SECTION 9 *Summary of the preceding review of the state of the circulation, and of some of the alterations proposed in our banking system*

Reverting, from this digression on American banking, to the immediate purpose in hand, it remains only to state the general conclusions that appear to be deducible from the facts and reasonings which have been laid before the reader, with a view to elucidate some of the more important features of our present system of paper circulation, and to suggest such alterations as may be best calculated to obviate the recurrence of evils which have been experienced under the existing mode of management.

The conclusions which seem to be fairly deducible from the preceding review of the state of the circulation during the period under consideration, and of the proposed alterations in our banking system, are, —

1. That the principal evil which can be distinctly and justly ascribed to the system, as it has been administered, is the near approach to exhaustion which the Bank treasure has experienced, with the consequent imminent danger of suspension of cash payments, an event averted only by a very discreditable expedient, namely, that of resorting to aid from the bankers of Paris.

2. That considerable blame attaches to the Bank of England for not having taken earlier and more effectual measures for arresting the drain on its coffers.

3. That no consistent rule or principle is discoverable in actual application to the management of the Bank of England.

4. That the doctrine of the directors, which assumes, as an essential

part of the functions of the Bank, the duty of attending to the trade and aiding and upholding the commercial credit of the country, is unsound and unsafe. Unsound, as it impairs the reliance of individuals on their own prudence; and unsafe, as it may entail an extension of the circulation at the precise time when a view to the exchanges and the state of its coffers would enjoin a contraction.

5. That it has been a great error of the directors to attempt to conduct the management of so large an amount of liabilities upon a reserve of bullion so small as that which has existed in the average of the last seven years; a reserve more especially inadequate, seeing the tendency of the doctrine embraced by the directors, of a duty incumbent on them of attending to the trade of the country, and of aiding and upholding commercial credit.

6. That, on the other hand, the Bank is not justly chargeable with evils such as those which have been imputed to it, of having, by its expansions and contractions of the circulation, caused fluctuations in the prices of commodities, and in the state of credit and the rate of interest.

7. That the prices of commodities are not liable to be influenced in any perceptible degree by variations in the issues of the Bank, in a convertible state of the paper, according to the system by which, since 1825, those issues have been regulated.

8. That variations in the state of credit may and often do arise from circumstances extrinsic to the state of the circulation, and that no regulation of the issues of paper money can operate as an infallible preservative against occasional great fluctuations in the state of credit, and in the rate of interest.

9. That variations in the state of credit and in the rate of interest are

likely to be—

Greatest under a system of competition of banks of issue.

In the next degree, under a system in which the amount of the circulation should vary in the exact manner and degree in which a perfectly metallic currency would vary.

In the most mitigated form and degree, under such a system as that of the Bank of England, attended, however, as that system ought to be, with more of regard to consistent principle than has hitherto been observed in the management, and subject, as a condition sine quâ non, to a provision for the maintenance of a higher average amount of treasure than the directors have hitherto thought fit to retain.

CHAPTER V

OBSERVATIONS ON A RECENT PUBLICATION BY MR. SAMUEL JONES LOYD, "ON THE MANAGEMENT OF THE CIRCULATION, AND ON THE CONDITION AND CONDUCT OF THE BANK OF ENGLAND, AND OF THE COUNTRY ISSUES, DURING THE YEAR 1839"

Since the preceding pages were prepared for the press, a publication of considerable interest on the question of the currency has proceeded from the pen of Mr. Loyd, entitled "Remarks on the Management of the Circulation; and on the Condition and Conduct of the Bank of England, and of the Country Issues, during the Year 1839". As Mr. Loyd unites great experience in the business of banking with scientific views of the general principles of currency, and possesses in an eminent degree the power of luminous exposition, his opinions are calculated to produce a great impression. I cannot, therefore, as I had intended, here conclude the present work, without offering a few observations on a treatise which is of such importance in its bearing on the points relating to the circulation which I had undertaken to discuss; more especially seeing that, while I concur with the writer in most of his general views on the currency, there are some very material points of practical application on which I find myself under the necessity of differing from him.

In every case in which I find that Mr. Loyd's views accord with mine, I feel additional confidence in them from that accordance; and in the instances in which I have not the advantage of his concurrence, I naturally feel some distrust of the foundation for my own conclusions; and I am anxious, in proportion to my confidence from agreement, to feel assured of my grounds when I find my views at variance with him. If, therefore, I enter more fully into the examination of the points on which we differ, it is not because those points are the greater in number or importance, but because assent is most readily and concisely expressed, while dissent from an authority which is justly deemed to be of weight requires a careful investigation and exposition of the grounds of difference.

Of leading points of principle it is impossible that the grounds can be laid down more clearly than is done by Mr. Loyd. Most especially do I agree with him when he observes, that "the principal and most important benefit to be attained by a due regulation of the currency, consists less in the indirect effect which it may have in preventing violent fluctuations in the state of trade and of prices, than in its direct tendency to protect and secure the convertibility of the notes under all possible contingencies. Money, it must be remembered, is not only useful as a medium of exchange, in lieu of barter or credit, but also as a measure of value; and when paper, in itself possessing no intrinsic value, is used as a substitute and representative of the precious metals, the convertibility of that paper becomes essential for preserving its character as a standard of value."

I rejoice also at finding that the results at which I had arrived from observation, confirmatory of all general reasoning on the subject of the usury law, receive the fullest corroboration from the ample experience of Mr. Loyd of the benefits derived from the recent amendment of that law.

It will have been seen, from the account which I have given of the several steps by which, in the descending scale of its treasure, the Bank found itself on the verge of suspension of cash payments, that I fully agree with Mr. Loyd in the opinion, that the directors were wanting in due vigilance in not adopting earlier measures for the counteraction of the drain when the tendency to efflux became manifest, and when there was reason to suspect that the causes of it were extensive and deep seated. And nothing can be more just, or expressed in more considerate terms, than Mr. Loyd's criticism on the inconsistency exhibited between the professed rules and the conduct of the directors; to whom, with him, I am willing, at the same time, to give credit for the best intentions.

Mr. Loyd remarks upon the difficulties attending the regulation of the Bank issues, and attributes a great part of those difficulties to the incongruity involved in the system, and in the functions assumed by that establishment, rather than to any fault of the directors in the administration of that system; and he adds, "The state in which the Bank has stood is the result. The circulation but slightly diminished, and the securities largely increased, whilst the drain upon the bullion has been suffered to acquire such force, and to proceed to such an extent, as to menace the most serious danger to the safety of our monetary system."

Mr. Loyd then points out, as an addition to the difficulties attendant on its incongruous functions, the counteraction to which the Bank of England is liable, in its attempts to control the circulation, by the issues of the country banks.

For these evils attendant on the present system as it is now administered, Mr. Loyd strongly urges, as the only remedy, the plan to which I have before alluded, of a complete separation of the business of issue of paper from the ordinary business of banking, concentrating the business of issue for the whole kingdom under the control of a single responsible body; the circulation of paper money, according to this plan, being supposed to be made to vary exactly as a purely metallic circulation would vary. In support of a plan of this kind, subject only to modification of details not essential to the principle, is an array of high authorities; Mr. Norman, whom I have already quoted, Colonel Torrens, Mr. Samson Ricardo, Mr. M'Culloch, and Mr. Henry Drummond. The principle of such separate business of issue, so regulated, and constituting the only source of the circulation of paper money, is unquestionably the most scientific, the most simple, and the most secure, against a suspension of cash payments, that can be adopted; and the only ground which I have ventured to suggest for hesitation, as to the policy of adopting it, is the question, whether there are not considerations of the greater convenience attending the working of the present less scientific system; considerations which, provided sufficient security can be obtained for the preservation of the constant convertibility of the paper, might be found to preponderate against the expediency of so great a change.

It seems to be assumed, and reasoned upon implicitly, by all the advocates of the proposed change, that the plan of metallic variation would be attended with less fluctuation in the rate of interest, and in the prices of commodities, than the present system of union of deposits and issues. But I have not yet seen, in any of the expositions, ably as they are stated, of the plan of separate issue, an explanation of the precise mode of operation, which should exempt a circulation of that description from the shocks to which the money market, and sometimes the markets for commodities, arc exposed by revulsions of credit. They have adduced no reasons for thinking that we should not be equally liable to variations in the rate of interest in this country, arising from any considerable fluctuations in the state of credit and in the rate of interest abroad; and they have in no instance shown, or attempted to show, that credit might not be unduly extended, —and, in cases readily conceivable, cases such as have occurred, —be equally extended under a correctly metallic variation, as it is liable to be, and as it has been, under the existing system.

It may be taken as a general rule, that whenever credit has been unduly extended there will be a revulsion and contraction proportioned in degree and extent to the previous excess of credit, such revulsion, according to the direction and extent of the previous abuse of credit, being felt in the money market, or in the markets for produce, or in both. Thus, if the undue extension of credit has prevailed only in the market for securities, the rate of interest, that is, the money market, only will be affected; if in the markets for produce, fluctuation of the prices of commodities and commercial failures will ensue; and these will, if occurring to any considerable extent, necessarily affect the money market; whereas fluctuations in the rate of interest do not necessarily affect the markets for produce.

Mr. Loyd refers to the recent instance of the state of the circulation in 1839, as one in which the system of separation would have worked bene-ficially. "If the contraction," he says, "had commenced with the decrease of bullion in the beginning of the year, when the circulation was 18, 201, 000*l.* , and the bullion 9, 336, 000*l.* , and had steadily accompanied it throughout, these evils would in all probability have been avoided. At all events, this would have been the legitimate means for the prevention of them; and failing the adoption of this course, a heavy share of the consequent responsibility must attach to the Bank."

In this I perfectly agree with Mr. Loyd; and I have, as the reader must have seen, instanced the recent circumstances of the trade and the circulation, as those in which a reduction of the issues accompanying a diminution of the stock of bullion would have been advantageous; but still more advantageous would have been the operation of the rule which I have ventured to suggest, namely, that the directors should be guided by a view to retaining a high average amount of bullion, and that they should never consider the Bank as in a perfectly satisfactory position when the treasure was under ten millions. They would, under such a rule, never have thought of volunteering shipments of bullion to the United States, in the spring of 1838, for the purpose of hastening the resumption of cash payments by the American Banks; and long before the close of 1838, they could not have failed to see the propriety of taking moderate precautionary measures for counteracting the tendency to a drain, which had then so clearly manifested itself, instead of designedly enlarging their securities as they did.

Still more beneficially, as compared with a purely metallic variation, would the regulation with a view to a high average amount of bullion have operated in 1835-1836. The treasure having been reduced (from what causes it is not here necessary to inquire) to 6,000,000*l.* in 1835, the directors would not have taken the active measures which they did, by the forced increase of their securities in the autumn of 1835 and the early part of 1836, to stop the tide of the metals which was then flowing in. The stock of bullion would have been higher than it was in the spring of 1836; the circulation would have been the same as it was, being then low enough;

but the rate of interest would have been higher, and the deposits would consequently have been lower, as there would not have been the same inducement to anticipate the instalments on the West India loan; while at the same time there would not have existed the unbounded confidence in continued facility of the money market which led to the unusual extent of credits in the American trade. It must then be quite clear, that with a larger stock of bullion, and a lower amount of deposits and securities, in the spring of 1836, the position of the Bank would have been in every respect better prepared to meet the approaching revulsion of credit in the American trade, in the autumn of that year, than it proved to be, and that the revulsion, when it did occur, would have been in a mitigated degree.

It would be tedious to pursue this point further; and indeed what I have here stated is only a repetition of the reference to this period which I have before made, my excuse for such repetition being, the importance of the illustration which the circumstances of the period referred to afford of the working of the system. I will merely add, that, whether by reference to circumstances such as have occurred, or to supposable cases, it might be shown that fluctuations as great, if not greater, might, and most probably would, occur, in the rate of interest, and in the state of credit, and in the markets for produce, under a correctly metallic variation, as under the more anomalous but more accommodating system, which, by the union of circulation and deposits, allows the action of the foreign exchanges to operate upon the bullion in such a manner as that, if the amount of it be of sufficient magnitude, the money market may be little, if at all, disturbed. Indeed, I have placed the comparison in the light most favourable to the proposed plan of separation, because I am convinced that under such separation the fluctuations would be more frequent, more abrupt, and sometimes of greater extent.

The reasons which Mr. Loyd urges in favour of the proposed separation of departments appear to me to apply still more strongly in favour of the existing system, with the addition only of preserving a larger average amount of bullion. Mr. Loyd says, "She (the Bank) is bound, not only to protect her treasure from actual exhaustion by foreign drain, but also to preserve it at such an amount as shall leave her, at all times, prepared to bear the probable or reasonably possible demands of internal alarm. She must guard, not only against the actual calamity of suspension, but against even the reasonable apprehension of it." Now, this is precisely what I would propose, by the simple precaution of keeping up, in ordinary times, a large amount of treasure, so as to meet any extraordinary exigences with the least possible disturbance of the amount of the circulation, a general uniformity of which is highly conducive to general convenience.

Mr. Loyd adds, "and, at the same time, the measures necessary for this purpose must be rendered as little oppressive to the trade of the country as is consistent with the requisite results." In this passage Mr. Loyd, I am sorry to observe, adopts, in deprecating oppression to the trade, the language of the money market①, which implies, that the regulation of the currency should have a particular view to the trading part of the community; whereas general convenience and security are demonstrably the only legitimate objects of a well-regulated currency. But even admitting a peculiar consideration for trade, I am disposed to dissent from the conclusion, namely, "Hence the importance of making the commencement

① According to that language, measures adopted by the Bank with a view to moderating the efflux of bullion are characterized, according to the degree in which they operate, as *making money tight*, *putting on the screw*, *punishing or oppressing the trade of the country*.

of the action upon the circulation simultaneous with that upon the bullion; it is thus rendered gradual in its operation, and, therefore, comparatively light in its effects."

It does not appear to be a necessary, and hardly, perhaps, a probable, consequence of the proposed separation, that every action upon the bullion by the foreign exchanges should be attended with a simultaneous action upon the amount of the circulation; by which term of circulation I mean the amount of bank notes in the hands of the public. If such, however, were shown to be the probable effect, the inconvenience might, and, I am inclined to think, would be found to be very great, compared with the present system; for, in as far as a certain degree of uniformity in the amount of the circulation, in reference to the general scale of transactions, is to be considered, as I believe it is, a desirable state, in so far would the direct operation of variations in the exchanges, in causing corresponding variations in the amount of the circulating medium, be found to be inconvenient, and sometimes greatly so. When quoting a passage from Mr. Norman's publication, it occurred to me to remark, that I did not see the force of the objection to the union of the banking and issuing departments, merely because it was a mixture of things in their nature distinct; and as little can I concur in the same objection, expressed by Mr. Loyd in still stronger terms, in the following passage: "The two things, the management of a paper currency, and the management of banking deposits, cannot be blended together in one system, and treated as subject to the same laws, and to be governed on the same principle. The attempt to do so is like that of the unskilful chemist who attempts to unite together substances which have no affinity, and will not; combine, and therefore obtains only a confused and useless mixture, when lie looked for a perfect chemical compound."

I had occasion, some pages back, to deny Mr. Hume's position of the complete identity of circulation and deposits; and I must equally call in question Mr. Loyd's view of their *incompatibility for the purpose in view*. The assertion of unsusceptibility of beneficial, or at least harmless, mix-ture, is rather in the nature of an assumption of the point in question. Taking Mr. Loyd's illustration, I should say, the substances, agreeing in some, differ in other properties; and it depends upon the object to be answered, whether, for that particular purpose, a compound of those qualities may not form a very useful mixture. But, perhaps, a better illustration may be derived from mechanics, by likening the movements of the circulation and deposits united in one system, to the contrary revolutions of two wheels working together in machinery so as to produce a desired effect. And such, I am inclined to think, is the more desirable effect of a union of deposits and circulation, always assuming a sufficient average reserve of bullion, than their separate operation.

Mr. Loyd dwells, at considerable length, and with much force, upon the counteraction which the Bank of England has experienced from the country bank circulation. He takes a view directly opposed to that of Mr. Hume, who has endeavoured (very unsuccessfully) to show, that the fluctuations in the circulation of the country banks were less than in that of the Bank of England. But I am not quite clear that Mr. Loyd establishes the case fully against them. After pointing out the fact, that the country issues continued to increase through the whole of the year 1838, and until June 1839, and that there was, in the quarter following, a sudden and large decrease, he observes, "Had the country issues commenced their contraction in April 1838, when the bullion first began to diminish, or in October, when contraction on the part of the Bank of England first commenced, the serious danger to which the monetary system of the country has been exposed might very possibly have been altogether avoided."

I cannot see the force of the grounds on which it could have been expected that the country banks should have commenced a contraction of their issues in April 1838, simply because there had been a small diminution of bullion, which small diminution, however, did not appear till the Gazette return in May 1838. It is well known that the country issuers, with the exception of Mr. Stuckey, and perhaps one or two others, have not, according to their evidence in 1832, professed to be guided by the exchanges, or by any strict attention to the variations in the amount of the Bank treasure. But if such had been their professions and their habits, there was not, most undoubtedly, the remotest signal, from the position of the Bank of England, which should have induced them to take measures for contracting their issues.

By the return of the Bank of England in May 1838 the stock of bullion was still about ten millions, and that was the time when it was stated in the newspapers, and with great approbation by some of them, that the Bank of England, being incumbered with a superfluously large amount of bullion, was sending a considerable sum to the United States of America. Later, too, in the year, that is, by the monthly return in January 1839, the average amount of bullion in the three months preceding was 9, 336, 000*l*. But this amount of bullion, although lower by nearly 800, 000*l*. than the highest return, which had been 10, 126, 000*l*. in April 1838, was in point of fact higher than it had been in January 1838, and higher than at any previous period since January 1834. Surely, therefore, there could be nothing in the returns of bullion so late as January 1839 to induce the country banks to resist the demands, which arose apparently from the greatly extended transactions connected with the increased activity of the corn trade, and the distribution of the large foreign supplies for an enlarged circulation. If, again, they looked at the Bank of England circulation, they would have seen that it had increased between January and September 1838 from 17, 900, 000*l*. to 19, 665, 000*l*. ; and the increase of the country issues was, in that interval, not in a larger proportion.

Mr. Loyd, however, seems to think that the country banks ought to have reduced their circulation, in accordance with the contraction by the Bank in October 1838. But the circulation of the Bank as late as November 1838 was higher than it had been in the first three months of 1838, and higher even than it had been on the average of four years preceding. As far, therefore, as relates to a mere numerical view of the Bank of England issues, there was no particular warning held out by them to the country banks.

There is, moreover, this material consideration, which may go some way in exonerating the country banks from utter disregard, in their movements, of any regulation by the Bank of England. Mr. Loyd, in the passage just quoted, speaks of contraction having first commenced in October 1831. The word *contraction* is liable to some ambiguity, inasmuch as it is sometimes used to signify simply the fact of diminution, while it is more frequently used in a sense including the operative cause of the diminution. Now, from the manner in which it is here used, it might be inferred that the Bank *designedly* diminished its issues in October, as a precautionary measure against the tendency to efflux of its bullion. Such, however, was not only not the case, but the very reverse of the case; inasmuch as the Bank at that time not only did not design, or make any effort, to diminish its issues, but its public acts showed that the diminution was against its intention, because by the notice of increased facilities for advances in November 1838 the directors plainly evinced a desire to extend their securities, that being the only medium through which they could influence their circulation. The country bankers, therefore, if they regulated themselves by the conduct of the Bank of England, seeing that the directors, by their notices in November 1838 and in February 1839, were still willing to maintain their issues at the highest amount which the demand for them at $3\frac{1}{2}$ and 4 per cent, per annum would absorb, might very naturally consider themselves justified in equally availing themselves of the continued demand for their notes. And as far as relates to any intimation from the Bank of impending danger, to serve as a warning to the country issuers, the first public notice of withdrawing the usual facilities for advances and discount was in May 1839. The contraction, therefore, of the country circulation, which took place in the interval between June and September 1839, from 12, 275, 818*l.* to 11, 084, 970*l.* , was as early as could be expected, if it was to be regulated by a reference on the part of the issuers to the conduct of the Bank of England.

When reviewing, as I had before occasion to do, the state of the circulation in 1836, I had the advantage of agreeing with Mr. Loyd in contending that the Bank of England had not succeeded in showing that the whole or the greater part of the derangement at that time was to be attributed to the counteraction which it experienced from the country banks, as far at least as regarded their circulation. And according to the view here taken of their conduct in 1838 and 1839, I am disposed to say of them, in the terms which he used when referring to their conduct in his tract, entitled "*Reflections*, &c. , 1837," "If they have done wrong, it appears to have been from the want of that controlling action on the part of the Bank of England which she might have exerted, and has not."

At the same time, although it is quite clear that the Bank did not make any efforts, as far at least as the public could judge of them, to reduce the circulation, and that therefore there is no ground for charging the country banks with counteracting such endeavours on the part of the Bank, I am strongly of opinion that it would have required more than ordinary efforts (and that at a time when there was no clear indication of a necessity for extraordinary measures) on the part of the Bank to have kept down the country circulation in 1838, seeing how powerful were the causes in operation at that time, leading almost inevitably to an increased issue. And it is highly probable, according to my view of them, that if the country circulation had been wholly conducted through the medium of Bank of England notes, there would, throughout 1838, have been an equal relative increase of them as there was of the country notes. With regard to the decrease of the country circulation after June 1839, there can be little doubt, that, from the cessation of the circumstances which had mainly, if not exclusively, caused the previous increase, there would have been a diminution, independently of any coercive measures for contraction on the part of the Bank, although those measures may have hastened and somewhat increased the reduction.

Mr. Loyd appears to me greatly to over-rate the power of the country banks voluntarily to extend their issues, or, rather, to maintain an extended circulation, except under circumstances justifying that extension.

The opinion which has prevailed generally, on the extent of the country circulation as existing during the restriction, was, and is, I am convinced, exaggerated in a very high degree. Nothing can be more fallacious than the grounds for computation of it given in the Lords Report on Cash Payments in 1819, p. 12. And I must dissent, for that and for other reasons, from Mr. Ward's opinion founded upon it, as quoted by Mr. Loyd, to prove that the action of the Bank of England during the restriction was prevented by the country issues from producing its proper effect upon the exchanges.

While, however, differing from Mr. Loyd as to the degree of counteraction experienced by the Bank of England in the regulation of its issues from the country banks, I fully concur with him in the opinion, that, as regards them, it might be desirable that the business of issue of paper should be separated from that of ordinary banking; but my concurrence in the desirableness of such separation docs not proceed on the ground of incompatibility of the functions, as regards the mere amount of the issues; I do not see how or why the blending of the deposits with the issues should necessarily interfere with a due regulation of the amount of the latter, provided only the convertibility of the paper money into gold, or Bank of England notes, were secured. It is the danger of insolvency of the issuers, more than that of excessive amount of paper money, that is to be apprehended from that part of the circulation.

The phenomena of the great occasional derangement of the country circulation have been referable in a much greater degree to overbanking than to mere over-issues of paper money. By overbanking (which is a phrase of modern introduction) I mean advances, either on insufficient or inconvertible securities, or in too large a proportion to the liabilities. The disproportion of the securities to the liabilities might, perhaps, be set wholly against the deposits; and but for the excess or inconvertibility of the securities, on occasion of unexpected demands by depositors, there might, in the instance of many of the country bankers who failed, have been no unusual demands for payment of their notes.

It is the liability of the issuing country banks to fail, from causes independent of an undue extent of issue, that constitutes one of the greatest objections to the mode in which the country circulation is administered. If a country banker has been imprudent, whether by speculations, by undue expense, or by bad debts, or by keeping too small an available reserve, and consequently fails, the circulation of the district is disturbed by a sudden diminution of the quantity of money below that which the general transactions and the markets at fair bullion prices would require. A considerable inconvenience is thus experienced by an entire neighbourhood, distinct from the losses which the depositors and the holders of the notes sustain. ① And if, from a considerable fall of prices, or some other extensive cause, such, for instance, as the prevalence of a too great previous confidence, the securities held by many of the country banks become greatly depreciated or inconvertible, the derangement of the circulation, in which it is very possible no excess in amount had existed, might be very extensive, and

① Among the parties who suffer by the failure of country bankers the cases of the greatest hardship are those of the holders of the notes. The subscribers, if the case is that of a joint stock bank, arc in point of fact the partners. The depositors, before they intrusted their money with the banker, might or ought to satisfy themselves of his solidity; but the holders of the notes are commonly persons who have taken them upon the general confidence, and are, in a larger proportion of instances, so situated as not to have had the clear option of taking or refusing the notes. The small farmers and tradesmen of a neighbourhood would be seriously injured in their business if they demurred at taking the country notes in payment, when there was no special or ostensible ground for discredit attaching to the banker; accordingly, for practical purposes, they are taken as currently as if they were a legal tender. The case is very different with bills of exchange, inasmuch as the credit of the several signatures upon them enters distinctly as a consideration with the persons receiving them in payment. It is of the very essence of the object of convenience proposed by a circulation of paper money, that it should carry an indubitable certificate of its value on the face of it (barring only the risk of forgery, to which all paper circulation is subject), so as that no doubt or hesitation should arise on its passing from hand to hand in current payment.

seriously injurious.

It is in this point of view chiefly, that is, of undoubted solvency, that the state of banking in Scotland has a decided advantage, for as to occasional undue extension and sudden contraction of credit, as contradistinguished from issues of circulating paper, the Scotch banks are fully as obnoxious to the charge as the banks in the other parts of the united kingdom.

Before taking leave of the subject of banks, I must be allowed to express a hope that the remarks which I have made on what appears to me to be a very general misconception of their legitimate purposes, should not be so misconstrued as to lead to the supposition of my undervaluing or disregarding the important advantages resulting to the agriculture, manufactures, and commerce of the country, from well-regulated and well-conducted banking institutions. The whole purport of my observations has been, to convey the strong impression which I feel, that whenever any bank or banks, professing to have in view to promote the agriculture, or the manufactures, or the trade of their neighbourhood or of the country, make advances to a larger amount, or on more slender or less convertible securities, than may be compatible with the claims of their depositors and the holders of their notes to constant payment on demand, they are chargeable with a departure from the plain path of their duty. There is liability enough to failure without superadding so gratuitous a risk.

I do not mean to say that banks may not be established for purposes of local or public utility, distinct from any immediate consideration of profit to the subscribers, or of convenience and perfect security to the depositors; but then it should be with the distinct understanding and consent of the depositors as well as of the subscribers, that such is intended to be the destination of the funds. Banks, however, professing to have such objects in view, with the knowledge and consent of their depositors, are institutions totally different from those to which questions concerning the state of the circulation apply, and to which alone my remarks have been directed.

In the concluding chapter of Mr. Loyd's work, when treating "On the consequences which depend on a good or bad management of the circulation," the author observes, "Doubts have been raised as to the effect *which any degree of mismanagement of a paper currency*, so long as it is convertible, and the issuers of it continue solvent, can produce, either *in creating, intensifying, or prolonging the evils of commercial oscillations.* Whilst some parlies attribute the fluctuations of trade, and the not unfrequent recurrence of mercantile and commercial difficulty, almost exclusively to mismanagement of the currency, other persons have taken a very different view of the subject. Fluctuations in trade, they contend, are necessarily connected with the very existence of commerce; variations in the relation of supply and demand arise out of natural circumstances, and will produce alternations of prosperity and depression, *whatever be the circulating medium, and in whatever manner regulated.* The case would not be different were the circulation wholly metallic. Speculation, according to their views, originates in causes unconnected with the state of the currency; and although an undue amount of issue may aggravate the evil where it exists, yet prices are but indirectly and distantly connected with variations in the amount of the currency, whilst other causes affect them more immediately and more powerfully."

To this passage is appended a note which contains extracts from the former volumes of this work, and should seem to lead to the inference that

Mr. Loyd refers to me as entertaining the opinions conveyed in the parts of the above quotation which I have marked with italics. If so, I must protest against the supposition that the parts of the foregoing passage so marked afford a correct representation of my views; they differ widely from any thing that I have stated, or intended to state. The opinions which I have delivered on the subject of prices, and fluctuations in the state of trade and of credit, in connection with the currency, have been deduced from views purely historical, and have proceeded entirely on a minute investigation of the circumstances attending the principal variations which actually occurred.

In no instance have I advanced any general proposition, so extreme and unqualified as "that no mismanagement of the currency could create, intensify, or prolong the evils of commercial oscillations." I have merely endeavoured to show that, *managed as the currency has been*, although an undue amount of issue may have aggravated the evil when it existed, yet prices, and the state of trade, *have been*, "so long as the paper has been convertible, and the issuers of it solvent, indirectly only and distantly connected with variations in the amount of the currency, whilst other causes have affected them more immediately and powerfully." It is distinctly stated in the account which I have before given of the great disturbance of the state of markets for commodities in 1825, that, although originating in other causes which would have operated to a great extent under a purely metallic variation, the management of the paper circulation at that time, more especially as being attended with the insolvency of so many of the issuers, and thus deranging commercial credit, was calculated to aggravate the operation of those causes; while, on the other hand, reasons have been adduced for the inference, that the tendency to commercial oscillations between 1827 and 1832 was mitigated by the management which then prevailed, compared with what it would have been under a circulation varying strictly with the variations in the amount of bullion.

I have nowhere maintained, nor intended to convey, the opinion, that it is not in the power of the Bank of England, in any supposable case, to exercise a direct influence upon the prices of commodities. The extent of my meaning is, that it could only do so by a violent operation wholly inconsistent with its professed rules and its ordinary practice. That by extraordinary measures, with that view, it might produce some effect, I am quite ready to admit. If, for instance, the Bank were to determine upon selling so large a portion of its securities, and so limiting its discounts as should, notwithstanding the counteraction of deposits, suddenly reduce the circulation by such an amount as should withdraw from the bankers a considerable portion of the bank notes destined for current payments, the fall in the value of securities would be very great; and if, as is probable, such extreme pressure were attended with commercial discredit, the markets for commodities would be affected, but principally, if not exclusively, those which were connected with the branches of trade to which the discredit attached, and more especially if the articles happened to be at all in excess compared with the ordinary rate of consumption. But even in this extreme case the effect on prices would not be general; there would be some markets for produce not at all affected; such, for instance, as might be composed of articles the holders of which were mostly, if not wholly, independent of credit; while those markets into which a large portion of credit extend might be greatly depressed. At the same time, if these were not over supplied, the effect would be principally felt in a great difference between the money and the credit price.

To the extent, then, of the proposition, that the Bank of England has the power, by a very violent and unusual contraction of the circulation, to produce a partial depression of the prices of commodities, it may be admitted that there is a connection between the Bank of England issues and prices. But it is only in a highly improbable, because an extreme, case, that the Bank can be considered as having the power of producing such a depressing effect, which would of course be only temporary, because under such violence of pressure the exchanges would be so influenced as to cause a rapid influx of bullion, and through that medium there would be a re-issue of money, either in Bank notes or coin.

With regard to the power of the Bank to elevate the markets for produce, the only conceivable mode of producing such an effect would suppose a resort to means still more improbable. It has already been seen that any *forced* operation of the Bank in an increased issue of Bank notes *on securities* would not necessarily or even probably enter into the markets for commodities, nor consequently affect the prices of produce. But if the directors of the Bank of England, taking up the opinion that any commodity or number of commodities were too low in price, such being also the opinion of the holders, were, under the pretence of benefiting commerce, to make direct advances on such commodities, they might (as the United States Bank and other American banks did) cause a temporary undue elevation of prices; the circulation would then prove redundant, the exchanges would fall, and bullion would go out till the level should be restored. But these, although possible and imaginable cases, are not within reasonable probability, nor, therefore, practically applicable to the solution of questions relating to prices, as they have been, or are likely to be, under a regulation of the paper such as has prevailed under the management of the Bank of England.

I have the satisfaction, however, to find, that, whatever may have been Mr. Loyd's misapprehension of my opinions (if the passage which I have quoted had any reference to them), the views which I actually entertain, and have endeavoured to convey, on the connection between the currency and the state of prices and of trade, are in perfect accordance with the opinions which he has expressed on the subject in a still more recent publication.

I allude to the following passage, contained in a letter addressed by Mr. Loyd to J. B. Smith, Esq., President of the Manchester Chamber of Commerce, on occasion of the report of the directors of that body "On the effects of the administration of the Bank of England upon the commercial and manufacturing interests of the country," in which report it is stated, that the alternations of excitement and depression in trade, since 1835, and especially the events of this character which have occurred in 1838 and 1839, are to be attributed entirely to mismanagement of the circulation.

On this charge Mr. Loyd observes, "Fluctuations in the amount of the currency are seldom, if ever, the original and exciting cause of fluc-tuations in prices, and in the state of trade. The buoyant and sanguine character of the human mind; miscalculations as to the relative extent of supply and demand; fluctuations of the seasons; changes of taste and fashion; legislative enactments and political events; excitement or depression in the condition of other countries connected with us by active trading intercourse; an endless variety of casualties, acting upon those sympathies by which masses of men are often urged into a state of excitement or depression; these, all or some of them, are generally the original exciting causes of those variations in the state of trade to which the report refers.

The management of the currency is a subordinate agent; it seldom originates, but it may, and often does, exert a considerable influence in restraining or augmenting the violence of commercial oscillations."

It is impossible to convey, in language more clear and appropriate, the sum and substance of the conclusions which it has been the object of the statements and reasonings in the present and preceding volumes of this work to establish, on the question of the influence of the currency in its convertible state.

The letter of Mr. Loyd, from which I have made the foregoing extract, has called forth a reply from Mr. J. B. Smith, the President of the Manchester Chamber of Commerce. Mr. Smith, proceeding upon the doctrine that the variations in the liabilities of the Bank are identical with variations in the amount of the circulation, and that these, being attended with corresponding variations in the rate of interest, constitute expansions and contractions of the currency, after quoting the passage of Mr. Loyd's letter of which I have given an extract, asks, "What is meant by the management of the currency? Is it the putting out large quantities of paper money at one time, and suddenly taking it in at another, according to the practice of the Bank of England? And can it be meant that such expansions and contractions of the currency 'are seldom, if ever, the exciting causes of fluctuation in prices and in the state of trade?' If so, why complain of the excessive issues of the country banks? It cannot be more dangerous for them to put out large issues of paper money than for the Bank of England to do so. Your letter says, 'a *reduction* of circulation must at all times tend to check the facility of credit, and *to lower* prices.' Must not then an *expansion* of the circulation at all times tend to increase the facility of credit, and to *raise prices*? How then shall we reconcile this with the statement that 'fluctuations in the amount of the currency are seldom, if ever, the original and exciting cause of fluctuations in prices ?'"

I am induced, at the risk of wearying my readers, to notice this passage of Mr. Smith's letter, as it affords me the opportunity of supplying an explanation of one or two points which it escaped me to remark upon in the earlier part of my argument.

Mr. Loyd has, in my opinion, not entirely guarded himself against the appearance, at least, of inconsistency, in laying the stress he has done upon the country bank issues as affecting the value of the currency. But I would more especially remark upon that part of his letter quoted by Mr. Smith, namely, where Mr. Loyd says, "a *reduction* of circulation must at all times tend to check the facility of credit, and to lower prices." Mr. Smith's question here applies, "Must not then an *expansion* of the circulation at all times tend to increase the facility of credit, and to raise prices?" But the question which I should ask of both is, what they mean by facility of credit? If by facility of credit be meant an absence of discredit or distrust, and the power of negociating good securities at the current rate of interest, it is not clear why a reduction of the circulation *must at all* times check such facility. Granting, however, that such must be the effect at all times, we have seen recently that a very decided check to facility of credit did not lower prices. Between, however, a mere check to facility of credit (by which is only meant a rise in the rate of discount), and a state of commercial discredit, the difference is very great; and if Mr. Loyd's remark had been, that a *forcible* reduction of the circulation, such as to cause *a derangement of commercial credit*, was calculated to lower prices, the correctness of the remark might be admitted. It is, however, to the converse of the proposition that I would particularly draw attention. It is asked, whether an expansion of the circulation must not *at all* times tend to increase the facility of credit, and to raise prices. The answer would he, that there can be no increase of facility of credit beyond the most *complete facility*, such as described by Mr. Gurney, in 1833, when any amount of money might be obtained, for commercial purposes, at two and a half to three per cent, on *good security.* And in this sense of facility of credit there is no reason why an expansion of the circulation should increase the facility, or raise prices, any more than it would in 1833.

But if by facility of credit be meant such abuses of banking as allow borrowers to obtain money on *insufficient security*, there can be no doubt that a facility of that kind, if there happen to be any inducement in the state of markets to speculation, will tend to raise prices. It is a facility of credit of this kind, favoured by limited responsibility of the American banks, that has operated on prices of the different objects to which the abuses of banking and credit in the United States have been directed. The propositions thus stated would then merely amount to this; namely, that a forcible reduction of the circulation, entailing derangement of commercial credit, tends to reduce prices; and that the abuses of banking, in making advances on insufficient security, when motives for speculation in commodities exist, tend to raise prices; and I am not aware that I have in any instance called in question the truth of propositions so qualified. The more immediate purpose, however, of my reference to Mr. Smith's letter is, to remark upon his explanation, introduced in a *note* to the passage which I have quoted from his letter, of the manner in which an increase of the Bank of England issues is supposed to operate necessarily in raising prices. The note in question is as follows: —

"Supposing the Bank of England to have a certain amount of paper in circulation against a certain quantity of commodities of all kinds in the market, at a given period; then supposing that the Bank increased its issues by a million, in a loan to the Government, or in any other way, the quantity of commodities remaining the same; it is quite evident that the natural tendency of such an operation would be, to raise the money value of commodities. Either the price of the commodities must rise, or the money must remain without employment. If the money remained for a time without employment, the necessary effect would be, a reduction of the rate of interest, and so a rise in the price of commodities would be produced. This truth is so self-evident, and so consistent with all experience, that it scarcely needs illustration, and it is in perfect harmony with the views expressed by Mr. Loyd, in his pamphlet in 1837: — 'If the currency be in excess, prices of all articles are affected in a corresponding degree; hence the balance of trade is disturbed; the exchanges are consequently affected, and a tendency is produced to export gold.' "①

Mr. Smith says, "Either the prices of commodities must rise, or the money must remain without employment. If the money remained for a time without employment, the necessary effect would be, a reduction of the rate of interest, and *so a rise in the price of commodities would be produced.*" That an additional issue by the Bank of a million or of five millions, on securities, would, caeteris paribus, reduce the market rate of interest, may be granted; but it is *not self-evident*, or *consistent with experience*, that prices of commodities would *therefore necessarily* rise. The persons who obtained such an increased price for their securities as

① "Further Reflections, &c, by Samuel Jones Loyd."

induced them to sell would, doubtless, upon receiving the money, seek some other investment for it. There might not be, nor would it be likely that there should be, any thing in the state of supply and demand in the markets for commodities, to induce persons, not habitually in them, nor so disposed, to speculate in goods; while the probability is, and such has been the course of experience, that, as by the supposition the market rate of interest in this country would, by such an operation of the Bank, be depressed below its ordinary rate relatively to other countries, there would be every inducement to the individuals who thus had their capitals disengaged to seek investment in securities abroad, whether public or private; as there would not, by the operation of the Bank, be necessarily any additional inducement to export commodities, the capitals to be transmitted abroad for such investments would be remitted in bullion; the effect, therefore, of the issue of the million or five millions of bank notes by the Bank might merely be their return upon the Bank for bullion to be exported. This was, in point of fact, the process in 1834, when the Bank increased its securities by between three and four millions, and reduced its treasure by the same amount; while the markets for commodities, although the rate of interest was low, and the facility of credit complete, were in the most quiescent state possible, and the corn markets falling.

Mr. Smith's note gives considerable insight into the foundation of the currency theory. He supposes the Bank of England to have a certain amount of bank notes in circulation, against a certain quantity of commodities of all kinds, at a given period, and then, commodities remaining the same, the price is concluded to vary with the bank notes. This is the familiar notion which prevails to a surprising extent; surprising, because a slight consideration will show how little necessary connexion there is between these two supposed necessarily related quantities.

The rationale of the matter, as appears to me, is this: —Prices are the result of a certain ratio between the quantity of money entering into the markets for commodities, and the quantity of commodities offering for sale on the other; but the money, or that which performs the office of money, that enters into the produce or wholesale markets, consists in a very small, I believe an infinitely small, proportion of bank notes. Nine tenths, or, more probably, ninety-nine hundredths, of the purchases and sales of the wholesale markets, are transacted through the medium of book debts, or simple credit, and cheques on bankers. It is the balances only of these transactions that require the intervention of bank notes; and it depends partly upon the proportion of buyers and sellers, who keep accounts with the same banker, whether any, beyond the smallest possible amount of bank notes, is employed for the final adjustment of the largest wholesale transactions in the markets for commodities. The clearing house in London is a familiar instance of the enormous amount of transactions, many millions, adjusted by a few hundred thousand pounds of bank notes.

A process similar in principle, although perhaps with not quite so small a proportion of bank notes, whether private or Bank of England, takes place, I believe, in most of the principal provincial towns. In the wholesale markets for provisions, among farmers, and millers, and cattle dealers, there may be a larger use of bank notes; and it is this circumstance, I presume, which renders the variations of the country circulation so dependent upon the prices of corn and cattle. But with that exception it will be found, I imagine, that the principal uses of bank notes, beyond the amount which the bankers reserve for possible demands over the counter, are for the payment of rents, dividends, salaries, and wages, and for payments by the smaller class of tradesmen, who do not keep cash with a banker. The smaller notes only, in all probability, circulate along with coin, as the medium of purchases for immediate consumption.

And here we come to the ultimate regulating principle of money prices.

It is the quantity of money constituting the revenues of the different orders of the state, under the head of rents, profits, salaries, and wages, destined for current expenditure, according to the wants and habits of the several classes, that alone forms the limiting principle of the *aggregate of money prices*, —the only prices that can properly come under the designation of *general prices.* As the cost of production is the limiting principle of supply, so the aggregate of money incomes devoted to expenditure for consumption is the limiting principle of demand for commodities.

A view to those simple and constantly operative principles, instead of the doctrine of the effects of expansions and contractions of the quantity of paper money issued by the bank, will serve to throw a steady light upon the circumstances determining the general state of trade and of prices. By the aid of those principles there can be no difficulty in accounting for some of the phenomena of the present period.

The resistance, so unaccountable, according to the currency theory, of the markets for produce, to the reduction of the amount of bank notes, and to the rise in the rate of interest, is easily explained. The trade had been, when the pressure on the money market commenced, in a perfectly sound state; and by a sound state is meant, that the importers and holders were trading strictly with a full proportion of capital, and requiring only so much of credit① at the utmost as would be available under any circumstances of the money market short of total derangement of it. The prices at which the goods were imported or produced, and held, were such as did not admit of their being replaced at a lower cost of production; and the supplies were mostly rather below than above the estimated rate of consumption.

On the other hand, the dull demand, and, in many instances, the reduced prices, and generally the bad trade, so much complained of, for manufactured goods, and the distressed state of the population, may be accounted for by two or three prominent causes, one or more of which would in each case account for the depression. In some articles there had been an excess of manufacturing power applied, in consequence (partly, perhaps, by banking accommodation), of the erection of new mills, in anticipation of continued increasing demand. And while there has been some excess, perhaps, from this cause, in the stock of manufactured goods, there are obvious causes of temporarily diminished consumption. The most striking, the most extensive, and the most distressing, is that which has been noticed in the first chapter of this work, namely, the reduced earnings of the

---

① As book credits and bills of exchange are the medium through which a considerable portion of the purchase of commodities are effected, constituting prices computed in money, as completely as those which are made by the intervention of bank notes or coin, the greater or less degree of credit that enters at different periods into the markets for commodities will naturally operate as a temporary or disturbing cause in those markets. But credit in this sense is not confined to banking advances or discounts, and it has only been with reference to banking, and to paper money issuing from banks, that my remarks on the passage quoted from Mr. Loyd and Mr. Smith, as to the effects on prices of the greater or less facility of credit, were made. If the facility of credit as from producers, whether manufacturers or farmers, or from importers and merchants, to dealers, and from them to shopkeepers, be, as in periods of confidence it is apt to be, carried to an undue extent, prices may be inflated, and a cessation of the excess of confidence, terminating in distrust, will cause a collapse. An extension of the issues of bank notes, and a subsequent contraction, have been commonly the consequences, and not the causes, of occasional undue expansion alternating with collapse of credit.

manufacturing population, and the large proportion of those reduced money earnings which must go to the purchase of food at comparatively high prices. This cause, in its ramifications, will apply also to the power of expenditure of some of the classes immediately above the poorest. The disturbed state of our trade with America, and with China, will of course account, among other causes, for the reduced demand for some of our manufactures, and the consequent diminished employment of the workmen. There is also a cause, of minor importance, however, which affects the power of expenditure of persons in the middling walks of life. I mean the very large amount of capital which is absorbed, and wholly unproductive of immediate income (whether permanently so is another question), in railway and other joint stock concerns, but chiefly the former, in which the sums invested, and for the present yielding no net returns, are computed to amount to many millions. The absence of all income from such an outlay might not, in ordinary times, have a sensible influence on the general scale of expenditure in consumable commodities, and it might be, in a prosperous period, more than compensated by the savings of those same and other classes; but in the present instance it may be mentioned as being possibly among the minor aggravating causes of the present depression.

The subject, however, of the circumstances at present in operation upon the rate of consumption, is too large to admit of being fully entered upon in a discussion to which it is only incidental. I will here, therefore, conclude with the expression of my strong conviction, that the more the question of the connection between the prices of commodities and the state of the circulation, in its convertible state, is gone into, the more surely will be the result in the negative of any direct influence of the issues of bank notes, under the regulation of them which now prevails, as an operative cause of the fluctuation of prices.

At the moment of my being about to close the present work, my friend Mr. Pennington has communicated to me a paper which he had drawn up, in illustration of the mode in which a separation, such as has been proposed, of the banking from the issuing department, would have worked, if it had been in operation at certain periods between January 1834 and July 1839. As it relates to one of the most important points in the discussions now on foot relative to the currency, and as it is one on which Mr. Pennington's peculiarly scientific manner of treating it is calculated to throw considerable light, I am persuaded that I am doing an acceptable service in bringing it under the notice of my readers, and I therefore avail myself of his permission here to insert it.

Paper communicated by Mr. Pennington

"The rule adopted for the guidance of the Bank of England in the management and regulation of its liabilities, as explained by Mr. Horsley Palmer and Mr. Norman, in their evidence before the Parliamentary Committee of 1832, is now supposed to be insufficient for the attainment of the object proposed by it. It is considered that a strict and inflexible application of it to the joint liabilities of notes and deposits would render it frequently ineffectual, and sometimes injurious; that although the deposits at the Bank, and its outstanding notes, are alike payable in specie on demand, yet only the latter affect the rate of interest and the foreign exchange, and that a demand for gold for exportation or for domestic purposes, or an influx of gold, in consequence of a favourable foreign exchange, may act only on the deposits, without lessening or increasing the amount of notes in circulation.

"In order to confine the rule to the promissory notes of the Bank, or, as they are usually termed, its *circulation*, it has been proposed that the business of the Bank shall be separated into two distinct departments, one to be called the circulation department, the other the deposit department; that the circulating department shall hold a fixed and unvarying amount of securities, and that its functions shall be confined solely to the exchange of gold for notes, and of notes for gold; and that the deposit department shall manage the funds intrusted to it on the ordinary principles which are observed by the London bankers, and independently of the promissory note department. "It may be worth while to inquire, what would be the probable operation of such a plan.

"In carrying it into execution, I apprehend, it would be proper, in the first instance, to assign to the deposit department such a proportion of the securities, and of the bullion, in possession of the Bank, as would, together, be equal to the amount of the deposits. Thus, if the Bank held eighteen millions of securities, and nine millions of bullion, against eighteen millions of outstanding notes, and nine millions of deposits, it would probably be deemed expedient to assign to the deposit department six millions of securities, and three millions of bullion, and to retain in the circulating department six millions of bullion, and twelve millions of securities.

"If such a separation were made, it is obvious, that as the exchange of gold for notes, or of notes for gold, between the two branches, would not affect the amount of bank paper in the hands of the public, and as such interchange might take place frequently, and to a great extent, the increase or diminution of outstanding notes would form no certain criterion of the amount of paper circulating out of doors, unless it were, at the same time, known what amount of notes was held by the department of deposit.

"Disregarding, for the present, any objection which it may be supposed would arise from this consideration, let us at once proceed to inquire what effect would be produced by a demand upon the Bank for bullion.

"The action and condition of the deposit department will be more distinctly perceived, if we suppose that, under circumstances above stated, the whole of the three millions of bullion are exchanged, on its first establishment, for three millions of notes. The position of the two departments would then be as follows: —

Circulating Department			Deposit Department		
Outstanding notes	–	£ 21,000,000	Deposite	– –	£ 9,000,000
Securities	– –	£ 12,000,000	Securities	– –	£ 6,000,000
Bullion	– –	9,000,000	Bank notes	–	3,000,000

"This being the position of the two departments, let us suppose that an adverse foreign exchange has created a demand upon the Bank for bullion for exportation. Now, such a demand for bullion may be satisfied, either by a reduction of the notes in the hands of the public, or by a reduction of the deposits at the Bank. If the former, then the separation of the business of the Bank into two departments will have answered the purpose expected from it; if the latter, then, in so far as relates to the increase or diminution of Bank notes in the hands of the public, by the action of the foreign exchange, no satisfactory result will have been produced. In the latter case, no advantage in the regulation of the circulation will have resulted from the separation.

"It may, perhaps, be said, that if the business of banking were separated from that of circulation, and conducted in the manner and upon the principles which are adopted by the private bankers of the metropolis, a diminution of deposits would be immediately followed by the sale or realization of a corresponding amount of securities, and thus the amount of Bank notes, in the external circulation, would be reduced to an extent commensurate with the delivery of bullion.

"But such a sale or realization of securities, in similar circumstances, may be effected under the present system of management. Whether the existing system be continued, or the business of the Bank be separated into two departments, the sale or realization of securities must depend on the views and the discretion of the directors of the Bank. The only difference between the two cases is this; that the counteracting effect occasioned by paying out bank notes to the depositors would be limited to three millions: upon the present system it may be carried to a much greater extent.

"It may be observed, moreover, that if the demand for bullion for exportation should exceed three millions, and if that demand should fall on the deposit department, that department would be reduced to the necessity, cither of forcibly realizing a portion of its securities, or of stopping payment at a time when the circulating department was abundantly provided with specie. It may be desirable to apply the foregoing principles and observations to the actual position of the Bank, at certain periods, within the last four years.

"In January 1834 the liabilities and assets were as follow:

Circulation	–	£ 18, 236, 000	Securities	–	£ 23, 596, 000
Deposits	–	13, 101, 000	Bullion	–	9, 948, 000
Rest	– –	2, 207, 000			£ 33, 544, 000
		£ 33, 544, 000			

"If, at that time, it had been determined to divide the business of the Bank into two departments, it would probably have been deemed expedient to assign 12, 000, 000*l*. of the securities to the circulating department, as a fixed amount which was at no future time to be exceeded. The remaining securities would, of course, go to the banking department. The outstanding notes, amounting to 18, 236, 000*l*., would then have for their basis 12, 000, 000*l*. of securities, and 6, 236, 000*l*. of bullion. But, as the deposit department would probably prefer notes to gold, on account of the greater convenience of the former, the position of the two departments would have been as follows:

"It will be seen, by the foregoing statement, that if the business of the Bank had been separated into two departments in January 1834, and if the rule, which we have supposed to have been at that time established, had, since, been inflexibly adhered to, the paper issues of the circulating department in July last would have been less by 2, 364, 000*l*. than their actual amount at that period, and the cash of the deposit department would have been wholly exhausted. In July 1835 and July 1839 the securities held by the deposit department would have exceeded the aggregate amount of the rest and the deposits. This excess of securities over deposits this department could not have held, unless the circulating department had transgressed the prescribed rule to an extent equal to the amount of that excess.

	CIRCULATING DEPARTMENT			BANKING DEPARTMENT			
	Circulation	Securities	Bullion		Deposits	Securities	Bank Notes
Notes in the hands of the public - -	18,236 3,712			Deposits Rest	13,101 2,207	— 11,596	— 3,712
Notes in the banking department - -	21,948	12,000	9,948		15,308		

The following would have been the position of two branches at the under-mentioned periods:

		Circulation	Securities	Bullion			Deposits	Securities	Bank Notes
1834: Dec. Notes: Public - - - Banking department	18,304 416	18,720	12,000	6,720	Deposits Rest	12,256 2,532	15,778	14,362	416
1835: Jul. Notes: Public - - - Banking department	18,288 nil.	18,283	12,000	6,283	Deposits Rest	11,561 2,644	14,205	14,244	nil.
1836: Jan. Notes: Public - - - Banking department	17,262 1,814	19,076	12,000	7,076	Deposits Rest	19,169 2,599	21,768	19,954	1,814
Aug. Notes: Public - - - Banking department	18,061 264	18,325	12,000	6,325	Deposits Rest	14,796 2,813	17,609	17,345	264
1838: Jan. Notes: Public - - - Banking department	17,900 2,995	20,895	12,000	8,895	Deposits Rest	10,992 2,609	13,601	10,606	2,995
1839: Jan. Notes: Public - - - Banking department	18,201 3,135	21,336	12,000	9,336	Deposits Rest	10,315 2,500	12,815	9,680	3,135
Jul. Notes: Publie - - - Banking department	18,049 nil.	18,049	12,000	3,785	Deposits Rest	7,955 2,686	10,641	12,905	nil.

"In order to prevent the exhaustion of its cash, the banking department would, no doubt, have endeavoured to withdraw bank notes from the hands of the public, by disposing of a large amount of its securities. A rigid adherence to the rule by the directors of the circulating department, and a due regard to its safety by the managers of the banking branch, would have rendered the amount of the securities in possession of the latter, in July last, less by three or four millions than it appears actually to have been or, which comes to the same thing, the amount of bank notes in the hands of the public at that time would have been three or four millions less than it appears to have actually been. The consequence would have been, a very severe pressure on the money market.

"Hitherto, we have supposed the business of the Bank to be separated into two distinct departments, and a formal apportionment of debts and assets to have been made. Now, without such a formal separation and apportionment, precisely the same action upon the currency would result from the strict observance of the following rule; namely, that the Bank shall not, upon any occasion, issue bank notes beyond a certain amount (that amount we have supposed to be 12,000,000*l*.), except upon the deposit of bullion. If this rule had been adopted in January 1839, and afterwards rigidly adhered to, a great reduction of the securities held by the Bank would have been necessary, in order to avoid a suspension of the payment of its deposits. It is probable, indeed, that such a reduction of the securities would have arrested the drain of treasure at an early period of the year. If, however, the drain had continued, notwithstanding the reduction, it would have been necessary, in July last, to have carried the reduction to the extent of three or four millions below the amount which the Bank actually held at that period.

"Whether a formal separation of the Bank into two departments take place, or the rule last mentioned be adopted, it may be expected that the public will be exposed to very great alternations of comparative ease and difficulty in the operations of the money market.

"It may here be proper to observe, that the difference between the rule above mentioned and that explained by Mr. Horsley Palmer and Mr. Norman in their evidence is this; —that, while the former rule would preclude the Bank from issuing notes in the payment of deposits to a greater extent than is equal, in amount, to the difference between the amount of notes at any time outstanding and 12, 000, 000*l*. plus the amount of bullion in possession of the Bank, the latter would allow the Bank to substitute notes for deposits to an unlimited extent. The former rule would be the same in its operation as a division of the Bank into two departments. The sole effect of the latter would be, the increase or diminution of the aggregate amount of the notes and deposits of the Bank with the increase or diminution of its bullion."

"There is one point connected with the proposed division of the Bank into two departments to which I have not adverted, but which it may be material to notice. It has been suggested, that, in order to increase the disposable funds of the banking department, it would be desirable that a certain portion of the capital of the Bank, now lent to the state, should be made available for banking purposes. By this I apprehend it is meant, that a portion of the three per cent, stock in which the original capital of the Bank is invested shall be sold, and the proceeds of the sale invested in other securities, and in commercial loans and discounts, at the pleasure and discretion of the Bank."

"Of this suggestion it may be observed, that it is a proposal to withdraw a certain amount of funds from the use and employment of one class of persons, in order that it may be transferred by the Bank to the use and employment of another class of persons. By this process no new funds would be created in the money market. The change would be merely the transfer of funds already existing from one kind of investment to another. The operation would be the same as that of an individual stockholder who sells his stock in order to employ the money arising from the sale in commercial discounts. The operation of the individual stockholder would, in its consequences, be comparatively of little importance; but if five millions of the original capital of the Bank were sold, as has been proposed, and the proceeds of the sale mixed up with and employed in the same manner as the deposits at the Bank, although no greater reserve of bank notes in the banking department, in consequence of this accession of funds, would be necessary, yet the varying employment of funds of such magnitude, during alternate periods of commercial excitement and depression, might produce a prodigious effect upon the general circulation. At one time the additional fund might be employed in commercial loans and discounts; at another time a great part of it might be withdrawn from the public, and held by the Bank, in bank notes and specie; thus creating an alternate abundance and scarcity of money in the hands of the public, at the pleasure of the Bank."

APPENDIX

Some weeks having elapsed since the account of the state of the Corn Trade in 1838 and 1839, which is given in chapter i. of this volume, was written, I am induced to avail myself of the opportunity of inserting further and more recent information on the subject, contained in the following extract from a circular dated 29th January last, from Messrs. Joseph & Charles Sturge of Birmingham, whose permission I have to make this use of it.

The estimate by Messrs. Sturge of the acreable produce of wheat of the harvest of 1839, as being more deficient than that of 1838, is more unfavourable than that which I had been led to form but as their means of information are more extensive, and come down to a later period, the presumption is that their estimate may be nearer the truth than mine. While, therefore, there now exists a stronger presumption of the scantiness of the last crop of wheat, there are, from the continued extraordinary prevalence of extremely wet weather into this very advanced period of the winter (middle of February) increasing grounds of apprehension for the produce of the next harvest. Under these circumstances the present high duty, arising from the inferiority of the quality and not from the sufficiency of the quantity, of the existing stock in discouraging importation, furnishes a fresh commentary on the mischievous working of the present system.

"*Birmingham*, *January* 29, 1840.

"In presenting our annual circular to our friends, the review of the Corn Trade for the past year, presents some features of unusual interest. A second deficient harvest has rendered indispensable continued large foreign supplies of wheat; and, notwithstanding duty has been paid for home consumption on 4, 532, 651 quarters of wheat and flour in fifteen months, between the 1st of September, 1838, and the 30th of November, 1839, it is supposed that the whole stock of free foreign in the United Kingdom on the 1st inst. did not exceed 550, 000 quarters, now considerably less, and of which about half was in London. Under the present system of Corn Laws, it is impossible that any considerable portion of the value of this import (large as it is) could be exchanged for British manufactures; and the drain of specie for payment, and consequent pressure on the money market, necessarily lessens the demand for labour, at the very time full employment and fair remuneration are most required by the high price of bread: the working classes are therefore compelled to use cheaper though less nutritious food; while, under a system of free trade in corn, the exchange, as with other foreign produce, would generally be in British manufactures, and the artizan would be in a great measure compensated for the increased price of food by a greater demand for labour. The average price of wheat has fluctuated from 61*s*. 10*d*, to 81*s*. 4*d*. , and the duty from 1*s*. to 20*s*. 8*d*. , while the average duty paid on 4, 532, 651 quarters of wheat and flour during the same period, was under 3*s*. 7*d*. per quarter. There is every reason to suppose the quantity of land planted with wheat in the autumn and winter of 1838, was greater than usual, but we believe the harvest of 1839 will prove even more deficient per acre than 1838. The export of this grain from Ireland has gradually decreased since 1832, from 552, 740 quarters, imported that year, to 90, 600 quarters in 1839; and this season will probably amount to little more than the foreign they import, or which is transhipped from this country. The stocks of wheat in all the European shipping ports are light, and with the exception of the flour, which may be drawn from America, we consider it very doubtful if, under the most favourable circumstances for the encouragement of shipments, more than 1, 200, 000 to 1, 500, 000 quarters can be imported before another harvest; and not only the state of the money market, but the fact of the quantity of inferior English and Irish wheat keeping down the averages, and consequently causing the duties to be relatively high, as well as the drooping state of our markets, renders importers very cautious in making distant shipments to this country. Opinions of the future founded on the most accurate data within reach, so often prove erroneous by subsequent unforeseen occurrences, that they should always be advanced with great caution, but we think there is at least considerable probability that prices of wheat will range high till the harvest of 1842; but this will of course much depend on the seasons. If our estimate of the last year's crop, of the stock of foreign wheat on hand, and of the import in the spring, be at all correct, we shall not have much wheat in the country when next harvest arrives; and the present circumstances are very unpromising for a large crop this year, inasmuch as a greater breadth of land than usual sown with wheat in the autumn of 1838 would of course leave less to be thus appropriated in 1839; whilst the long continuance of almost unprecedently wet weather has rendered it impossible as yet to sow a considerable portion of land which was intended for that purpose, and much of what has been planted appears far from healthy: the deficiency, from these causes, can hardly be made up in the spring, and spring-sown wheat is more precarious than what is planted at the usual time. The successive failures of this crop in Ireland will rather discourage its growth there, which, with the increased consumption in that country, renders it very doubtful if any considerable import can be calculated upon from thence. When, also, we take into account that our population is estimated to increase at the rate of half a million annually, it seems very probable that we must have at least two productive crops, before any material reduction in price is likely to take place.

"Barley, as was anticipated, has proved very inferior in quality, and a large portion of it is only fit for grinding purposes."

"Oats are grown but to a limited extent in this part of the country; they have, however, proved on thrashing full an average crop in quantity, but light in quality; and, judging from the large imports from Ireland, we think such must be the case there: yet, though the price and sale are at present much depressed, we expect they will not be so permanently, as the stock of old was completely exhausted; and we believe it will be found, as the season advances, that the demand will keep pace with the supply.

"So small a portion of the last crop of beans has yet appeared at market (some few having only been secured since the commencement of the present month) that we are yet unable to speak definitively as to the yield; scarcely any are in a fit state for consumption without kiln-drying.

"The crop of peas proved quite as deficient as we estimated it at the time of harvest.

Joseph & Charles Sturge."

The following Tables of Quantities and Prices of Corn are extracted from Messrs. Sturge's Circular.

Account of the Foreign Corn, Meal, and Flour, imported into Great Britain and Ireland, in the Years 1827 to 1839

Year	Wheat	Barley	Oats	Flour
	Qrs.	Qrs.	Qrs.	Cwt.
1827	233, 236	208, 117	1, 741, 091	94, 348
1828	715, 242	168, 673	166, 423	151, 038
1829	1, 544, 969	281, 752	541, 858	461, 895
1830	1, 414, 262	131, 715	499, 947	560, 249
1831	1, 857, 278	369, 024	617, 568	1, 627, 742
1832	405, 884	101, 147	31, 862	224, 068
1833	247, 625	85, 221	23, 335	170, 092
1834	131, 566	87, 187	175, 266	149, 554
1835	46, 530	68, 455	117, 673	84, 684
1836	162, 778	81, 631	129, 625	279, 602
1837	452, 369	91, 911	413, 710	346, 325
1838	1, 240, 138	2, 439	50, 981	439, 910
1839	2, 638, 593	581, 086	674, 554	793, 660

Corn, Meal, and Flour imported, entered for Home Consumption, and paid Duty since 1823 inclusive, the first Year it was levied on Corn

Year	Quarters imported	Quarters for Home Consumption	Duty paid		
			£.	s.	d.
1823	53, 866	12, 362	10, 310	4	3
1824	612, 594	677, 195	176, 383	15	6
1825	1, 060, 837	834, 425	304, 919	15	5
1826	2, 252, 271	2, 098, 944	442, 755	14	9
1827	2, 622, 283	2, 998, 866	792, 934	15	8
1828	1, 294, 378	1, 237, 494	196, 834	0	2
1829	2, 694, 432	1, 959, 355	907, 320	5	5
1830	2, 691, 884	2, 649, 348	790, 877	0	0
1831	3, 570, 569	2, 265, 392	547, 809	0	0
1832	668, 422	475, 680	309, 676	0	0
1833	481, 506	112, 408	36, 252	0	0
1834	560, 056	236, 902	99, 416	0	0
1835	321, 206	439, 988	201, 673	0	0
1836	643, 502	408, 217	152, 791	4	0
1837	1, 325, 930	842, 326	580, 200	0	0
1838	1, 534, 730	1, 960, 475	183, 000	0	0
1839	4, 591, 099	4, 657, 146	1, 084, 870[1]	0	0

[1] To 5th December.

The average Duty paid on the 9, 297, 493 quarters of Foreign Wheat imported and entered for home consumption, since the present Corn Law came into operation up to the 5th December, 1839, is under 5*s*. 5*d*. per quarter

Corn and Flour entered for Home Consumption in 1833, 1834, 1835, 1836, 1837, 1838, and 1839

Year	Wheat	Barley	Oats	Flour
	Qrs.	Qrs.	Qrs.	Cwt.
1833	60, 990	1, 207	9, 753	75, 450
1834	45, 872	11, 031	56, 853	65, 726
1835	16, 336	136, 868	175, 907	44, 165
1836	19, 554	110, 021	97, 183	36, 813
1837	232, 793	47, 475	333, 932	40, 187
1838	1, 739, 303	8, 078	11, 057	390, 173
1839	2, 519, 873	590, 149	864, 619	665, 023

Prices of Grain in Foreign Parts, per Quarter, in 1838 and 1839
Mostly taken in December

	Wheat 1838				Wheat 1839			
	s.	*d.*	*s.*	*d.*	*s.*	*d.*	*s.*	*d.*
Dantzic – –	56	0	60	0	44	0	50	0
Do. high mixed –	66	6	70	0	51	0	55	0
Leghorn – –	40	5	64	4	42	0	54	6
Rostock – –	50	0	54	0	47	0	49	0
Trieste – –	48	1	58	5	39	4	44	0
Riga – –	45	2	47	4	44	0	47	0
Hamburg –	57	6	66	0	41	0	54	0
Petersburg –	44	0	47	0	39	0	46	0
Genoa – –	42	6	58	6	43	0	46	0
Archangel –	36	0	38	0	33	0	34	6
Naples – –	38	0	48	3	37	6	44	6
Konigsberg –	55	3	64	1	45	0	54	0
Bordeaux –	56	5	62	9	50	0	58	0
Marseilles –	42	0	53	9	39	6	51	0
Nantes – –	56	0	59	0	47	0	53	0
Lubec – –	53	0	56	0				

Continued

	Wheat 1838				Wheat 1839			
	s.	*d.*	*s.*	*d.*	*s.*	*d.*	*s.*	*d.*
Odessa – –	35	6	42	10	33	0	37	0
Stettin – –	53	0	55	0	48	0	50	0
Sydney – –	56	0	68	0	160	0	170	0
Baltimore –	55	6	63	6				
New York –	62	0	66	0	37	0	41	0
Philadelphia –	54	9	62	0				
Quebec – –	68	9	79	3				
Paris – –	54	0	57	0	57	9	69	0
Kiel – –	53	0	56	0	44	0	49	0
Taganrog –	25	8	38	6	25	0	33	0
Santander –	64	0	68	0	46	0	55	0

Average Price of Grain per Quarter in England and Wales, for Nineteen Years ending 1839

Year	Wheat		Barley		Oats		Beans		Peas	
	s.	*d.*	*s.*	*d.*	*s.*	*d.*	*s.*	*d.*	*s.*	*d.*
1821	56	2	26	0	19	6	30	11	32	9
1822	44	7	21	11	18	2	24	6	26	5
1823	53	5	31	7	22	11	33	1	35	0
1824	64	0	36	5	24	10	40	10	40	8
1825	68	7	40	1	25	8	42	10	45	5
1826	58	9	34	5	26	9	44	3	47	8
1827	56	9	36	6	27	4	47	7	47	7
1828	60	5	32	10	22	6	38	4	40	6
1829	66	3	32	6	22	9	36	8	36	8

Continued

Year	Wheat		Barley		Oats		Beans		Peas	
	s.	*d.*	*s.*	*d.*	*s.*	*d.*	*s.*	*d.*	*s.*	*d.*
1830	64	3	32	7	24	5	36	1	39	2
1831	66	4	38	0	25	4	39	10	41	11
1832	58	8	33	1	20	5	36	5	37	0
1833	52	11	27	6	18	5	35	1	37	0
1834	46	2	29	0	20	11	36	7	33	0
1835	39	4	29	11	22	0	30	0	30	0
1836	48	9	33	2	23	1	38	4	37	3
1837	55	10	30	4	23	1	38	7	37	9
1838	64	4	31	5	22	5	37	4	36	8
1839	70	6	39	1	26	6	41	3	41	1